The Princeton Review®

D0907569

Math Workout for the GED® Test

The Staff of The Princeton Review

PrincetonReview.com

Penguin Random House

The Princeton Review
24 Prime Parkway, Suite 201
Natick, MA 01760
E-mail: editorialsupport@review.com

Published in the United States by Penguin Random House LLC, New York, and in Canada by Random House of Canada, a division of Penguin Random House Ltd., Toronto.

Some of the content in *Math Workout for the GED® Test* has previously appeared in *Cracking the GED® Test,* 2016 Edition, published as a trade paperback by Random House, an imprint and division of Penguin Random House LLC, in 2015.

ISBN: 978-1-101-88211-5
eBook ISBN: 978-1-101-88212-2
ISSN: 2379-2817

Editors: Meave Shelton and Sarah Litt
Production Editor: Harmony Quiroz
Production Artist: Deborah A. Silvestrini

Printed in the United States of America on partially recycled paper.

10 9 8 7 6 5 4 3 2 1

Acknowledgments

Many thanks to the following contributors: Chris Chimera, Clarissa Constantine, Anne Goldberg, Kimberly Beth Hollingsworth, and Sara Kuperstein.

Special thanks to Adam Robinson, who conceived of and perfected the Joe Bloggs approach to standardized tests, and many of the other successful techniques used by The Princeton Review.

Contents

Register Your

1 Go to **PrincetonReview.com/cracking**

2 You'll see a welcome page where you can register your book using the following ISBN: 9781101882115.

3 After placing this free order, you'll either be asked to log in or to answer a few simple questions in order to set up a new Princeton Review account.

4 Finally, click on the "Student Tools" tab located at the top of the screen. It may take an hour or two for your registration to go through, but after that, you're good to go.

NOTE: If you are experiencing book problems (potential content errors), please contact EditorialSupport@review.com with the full title of the book, its ISBN number (located above), and the page number of the error.

Experiencing technical issues? Please e-mail TPRStudentTech@review.com with the following information:

- your full name
- e-mail address used to register the book
- full book title and ISBN
- your computer OS (Mac or PC) and Internet browser (Firefox, Safari, Chrome, etc.)
- description of technical issue

Book Online!

Once you've registered, you can access...

- A bonus supplement on geometry and the GED® test
- A Mathematics Formula Sheet for handy reference
- Custom answer sheets for all of the drills in this book
- Any updates to this edition or the GED® test

GED Ready®: The Official Practice Test

- With your purchase of this book, you are entitled to 20% off the price of the GED Testing Service's official GED® practice test.
- Visit **www.gedmarketplace.com/theprincetonreview** for step-by-step instructions on how to receive this discount.

The Princeton Review®

Part I Introduction

About the GED® Mathematical Reasoning Test
General Strategies

About the GED® Mathematical Reasoning Test

This chapter will provide you with a description of exactly what to expect on the GED® test in general and the Mathematical Reasoning test specifically. It will also explain how to use this book to maximum effect while preparing for the test.

People take the GED® test for many reasons. Some people are homeschooled. Some people leave high school before they graduate. Some people have careers that do not enable them to attend a traditional high school. Whatever their reasoning, all of them have the desire to succeed.

You have the desire to succeed, too. How do we know? Well, for one thing, you bought this book, which means you've decided to take the GED® Mathematical Reasoning test. And taking this test is one step toward making your life work the way you want it to. Passing the GED® test can be an important step in your life because it shows other people *and* yourself that you have the follow-through to decide on a course of action and make it happen. It can be the starting place for admission to college, a promotion, or a pay raise. So, congratulations! You've made an important decision.

This book is here to help you make it happen. Whether you want to supplement your study with further practice or whether you're simply looking to brush up on your skills, the drills in this book cover all of the Mathematical Reasoning topics you can expect to see on test day.

WHAT IS THE GED® TEST?

The GED® test is made up of four subject tests—Reasoning Through Language Arts, Mathematical Reasoning, Social Studies, and Science—that you can take in one day or over a series of days. It's referred to as a high school equivalency test because it awards a credential that most colleges and employers recognize as the equivalent of a high school diploma.

In some ways, passing the GED® test is a lot easier than finishing high school. After all, the test in its entirety takes about seven hours. It takes years—and a *lot* of tests—to finish high school.

Registering for the GED® Test

Call 877-EXAM-GED (877-392-6433) for info on registering and for classes in your area. To reach the individual state programs directly, go online to **www.ged.com** where you can type in your ZIP code to find the nearest testing centers and programs.

How Is the GED® Test Scored?

For each of the four subject tests, you will receive a score between 100 and 200. Because each test has a different number of available points, the GED Testing Service will standardize your raw scores (or the number of questions you answered correctly for each test) through a scoring metric to yield a score between 100 and 200.

The minimum score needed to pass any of the four subject tests on the GED® test is 150. In order to get your completion certificate, you must achieve at least this score on each test. A higher score on one test will not make up for lower score on another. While a passing score is sufficient to obtain your certificate, a score of at least 170 entitles you to a GED® Score with Honors, a distinction that indicates college and career readiness. So, if you are planning to use your GED® test credential to further your career or apply to college, we highly recommend that you attempt to achieve the highest score possible.

Once you receive a passing score on a particular subject test, you do not need to retake that test. If you want to retake the test to receive a higher score, you may do so. If you do not receive your desired score on a particular test, you can retake that test two more times without any waiting period, subject to scheduling availability. After the third attempt, you will have to wait 60 days to test again. This schedule allows for eight testing opportunities in a year, if you need that many to pass a section.

Need Accommodations?
If you require accommodations, simply indicate your intention to apply for them when you register to take the GED® test at www.ged.com. You'll then receive an email with further instructions about what paperwork you need to submit. Accommodation decisions generally take about 30 days and are valid for one year.

If you have questions, email **accommodations@GEDtestingservice.com.**

WHAT'S ON THE MATHEMATICAL REASONING TEST?

The Mathematical Reasoning portion of the GED® test covers high school math. Fortunately, it doesn't cover *all* of the math topics taught in high school—you won't see any calculus or even pre-calculus, for example. Rather, the GED® test writers focus on a few key areas: algebra, geometry, and basic and applied arithmetic. Here's a breakdown of the topics and tested skills for each of these areas:

Basic Arithmetic
- The number line
- Rounding off
- Multiplying positive and negative numbers
- Order of operations
- Commutative and distributive properties
- Fractions
- Decimals
- Percents

Applied Arithmetic
- Setup problems
- Mean, median, mode, range, and weighted mean
- Ratios and proportions
- Rate problems
- Charts and graphs
- Exponents and square roots
- Scientific notation
- Probability
- Counting

Algebra
- Simple equations
- Inequalities
- Translating words into math
- Polynomials
- Simultaneous equations
- Functions

Geometry
- Lines and angles
- Rectangles and squares
- Triangles and pyramids
- Circles, spheres, cylinders, and cones
- Perimeter and area
- Surface area and volume
- Setup geometry
- Graphing points and functions (the coordinate plane)
- Equation of a line and slope

The Mathematical Reasoning test is made up of 46 questions to be answered in 115 minutes and is broken up into two parts:

- In Part I (5 questions), you will *not* be allowed to use a calculator. This first section will test your ability to do basic calculations, and you *must* submit your answers to these five questions before moving on to the rest of the test.
- In Part II (41 questions), you *will* be allowed to use a calculator. In this section, you will be asked to answer questions common in many work scenarios. Many of these will be word problems. About one-half of the questions will be based on diagrams or charts.

About 45 percent of the test focuses on quantitative problem solving, while 55 percent focuses on algebraic problem solving.

A COMPUTER-BASED TEST

Unlike the drills in this book, the actual GED® test is taken on a computer at a testing center. This section will introduce you to the various features you'll need to be familiar with.

Experience the Interface for Yourself
Test out the user interface and practice using the computer functionality by visiting **www.gedtestingservice.com/educators/freepracticetest**, where you will also find a Computer Skills Tutorial.

So how is a computer-based test different from a pencil-and-paper test? To begin with, the questions will be presented one at a time. In some cases the question will be shown on a single screen. In other cases you'll see a split screen, with a passage, chart, or other information on one side and the question on the other. To navigate to the previous or next screen, you'll click the appropriate arrow button at the bottom-right corner. At the top, you'll see the number of the question you're working on, total number of questions, and time remaining for the test. Later in this chapter, we'll show you some sample screenshots of different types of questions.

Other features include user options such as highlighting text, changing the foreground and background colors, and adjusting the text size. For questions that require you to write, you will have access to cut, copy, and paste functions, as well as "undo" and "redo." Where appropriate, an on-screen calculator will be provided, as well as a list of mathematical formulas. You may also bring your own calculator to the test, but it must be a Texas Instruments TI-30XS Multiview Scientific Calculator—more on this in a bit.

The Review Screen

Another important feature of the computer interface is the review screen, which you can use to help keep you on track. This screen indicates which questions you have answered, which you have left blank, and which you have not yet read. It also indicates which questions you have marked for later review. From the review screen you can quickly jump to any questions that have been marked or left unanswered by clicking on the question number.

Here's an example of what your review screen will look like:

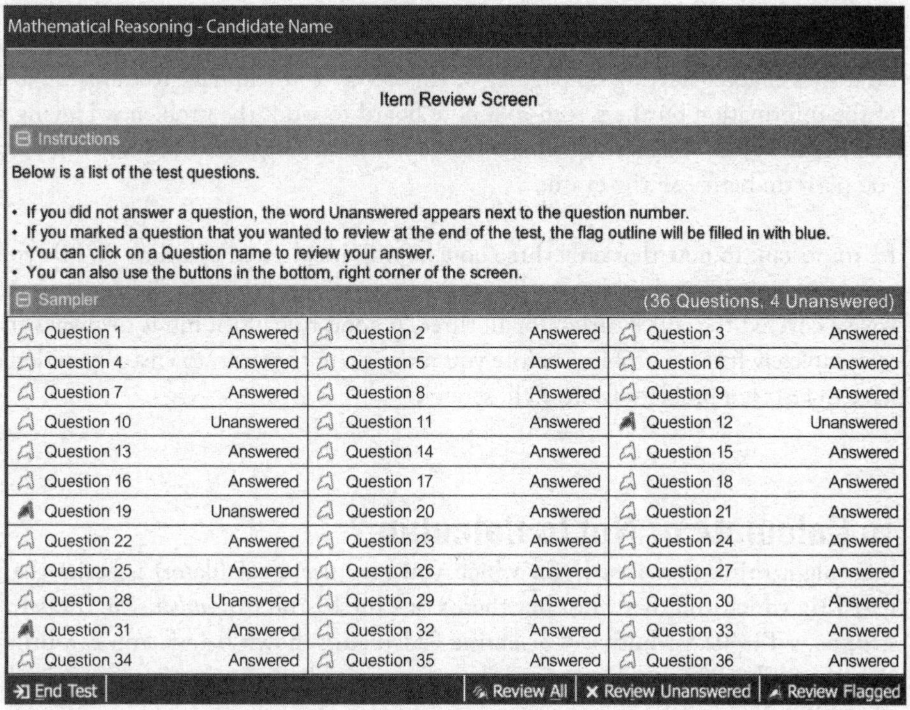

You can check the review screen at any time during the test. We recommend leaving a few minutes at the end of each section of each test to check the review screen to make sure you have answered every question or to look up questions that you marked for later review. For any question you need to answer or revisit, you can click on the question number to go directly to the question.

The Erasable Note Boards

When you take the test, you will not be given scratch paper. Rather, you'll be provided with three erasable note boards, which are laminated pieces of thick cardboard, each the size of a sheet of legal paper (8.5 by 14)—a little bit larger than a standard piece of notebook paper. You will be given one at the beginning of your test, along with a dry-erase marker. If the marker runs out of ink or dries up, you may ask for a new one. Using a note board rather than writing directly on a test booklet takes practice. As you work on the drills in this book, get into the habit of using separate sheets of scratch paper (assuming that you don't have an erasable note board of your own).

We recommend that you lay out a note board strategy as outlined in the General Strategies chapter starting on page 17 of this book. You will have to transfer most of the information on the screen to a note board to work the problems. Having a consistent way of transferring that information in an organized fashion will help you perform better on the exam.

It's important to note that only three note boards are allowed at a time. While you may use the front and back, you may have to erase the work you did earlier once you've covered the entire surface of all three. A good rule of thumb is to always try to completely finish a problem before you move on to the next, to ensure you don't have to restart a problem from, well, scratch.

To Calculate or Not to Calculate?

You might think that Part II (in which you may use a calculator) is easier than Part I (in which you may not), but there's one hitch: You can *only* use a Texas Instruments TI-30XS Multiview Scientific Calculator, shown below. You can bring your own TI-30XS, or you can use the on-screen calculator that is automatically available.

You will be provided an on-screen calculator reference sheet. However, it is vital that you become familiar with this particular model ahead of time. Why spend your valuable test time learning how to use the calculator when that time could be better spent actually solving the questions? We strongly recommend that you buy (or borrow) this specific calculator and practice with it for several weeks before the test. It is available in most office supply stores or online for about $18. You can watch video tutorials of its various functions and features at www.atomiclearning.com/ti30xs, as well as on YouTube. Search for "GED" and "TI-30XS Demonstration Video."

There are two major features of the Texas Instruments TI-30XS that can be pretty confusing. They are the arrow keys and the green "2nd" key.

The arrow keys (located at the top right) can be used to move within a function on the screen or to exit a function and return to the main expression you are calculating. You will use the arrow keys to input fractions, mixed numbers, or numbers in scientific notation.

The Calculator is Color Coded!
The GREEN "2nd" key accesses the function written in GREEN above the other calculator keys.

Pushing the "2nd" key (located at the top left) before another key accesses the function that is written above the key. You will use this to input mixed numbers and to calculate roots and percentages.

Let's take a look at how you would input the mixed number $12\frac{1}{2}$:

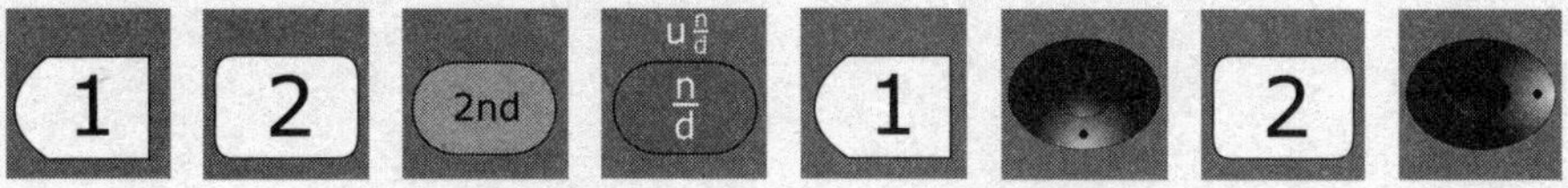

Lots of steps there! You can see why we're telling you to familiarize yourself with this calculator in advance.

Question Formats

In addition to traditional multiple-choice questions, you will encounter several types of questions that may be unfamiliar to you. These enhanced, computer-based question formats require you to use your mouse to perform actions other than clicking the correct bubble.

In this section, we'll familiarize you with the look and feel of these question formats and show you how to enter your answer for each type. We'll also give you an example of each format as it appears in this book.

Note: You can either answer questions by writing directly in this book, or you can use our custom answer sheets which you can download and print out when you register your book at **PrincetonReview.com/cracking**.

Multiple Choice

Multiple-choice questions typically present you with a scenario and ask a question about it. There is one possible answer out of the four choices provided. In order to indicate your answer, use your mouse to click the bubble that corresponds to your answer. Here is an example of what this type of question will look like on your computer screen:

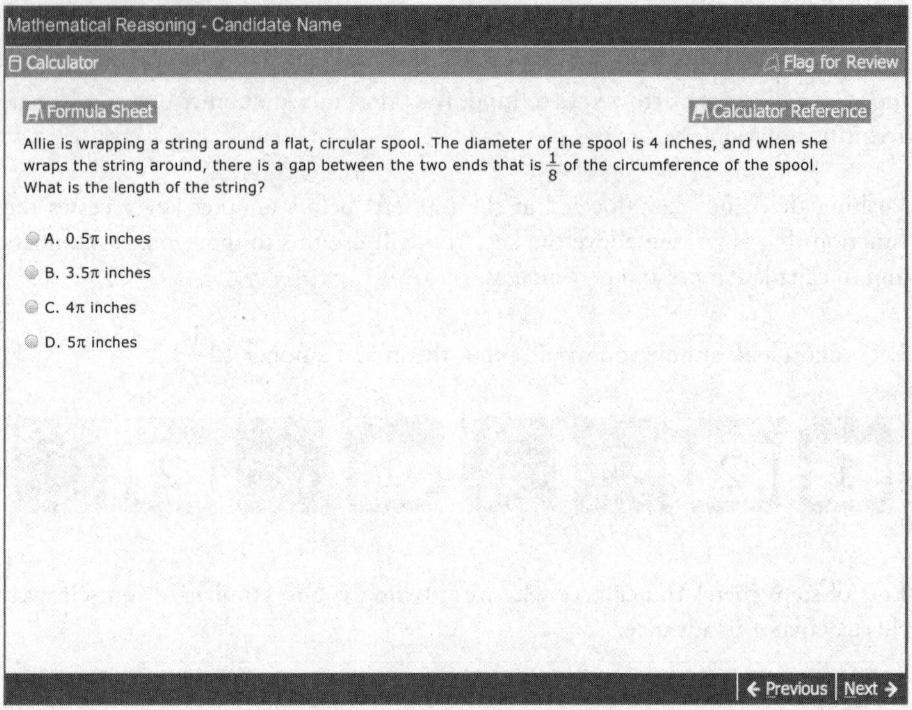

In this book, the multiple-choice format is pretty similar. The only difference is that, rather than clicking the bubble, you can circle the letter with your pencil.

1. Marie drives from her home to the supermarket 10 miles away and then drives back home after shopping. If it takes her two hours for the entire trip, including one hour spent shopping in the supermarket, what was her average speed driving to and from the supermarket?

   A. 5 mph
   B. 10 mph
   C. 15 mph
   D. 20 mph

Drag and Drop

Drag-and-drop questions ask you to choose from several options and, using your mouse, drag each option to the correct location in the question. For some of these questions, not only must you choose the correct options, you must also make sure to place them in the order requested. Here is a sample screenshot:

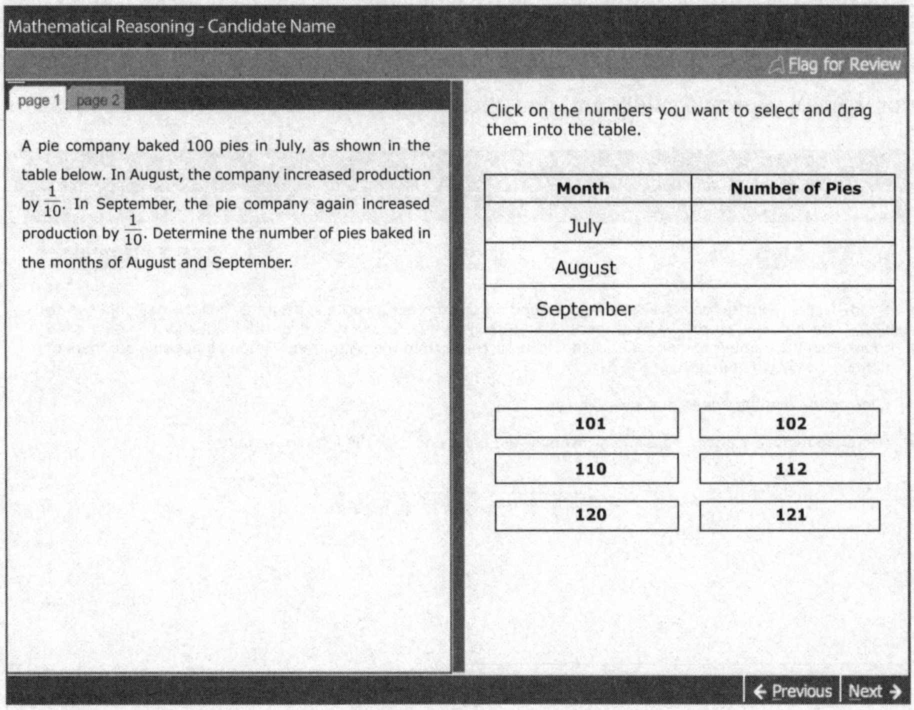

Here is an example of how drag-and-drop questions appear in this book. To answer this question, simply write your selection(s) in the box or boxes provided.

2. If $3x + 6y = 30$ and $2x + 5y = 26$, choose two numbers below that are possible values of x and y.

$x =$		$y =$	

−6	−2
−2	1
6	6

Hot Spot

These questions give you a set of information and pose a question. In order to indicate your answer, use your mouse to click on one or several points in a chart or graph that represent possible answers. While this type of question may seem unusual at first, it's really just a variation on multiple choice. When you have determined the answer, simply mouse over the area for the right answer and click. If you would like to erase a mark, click on it a second time. Make sure to read the question carefully to be sure you know the number of solutions the test is asking for. If it asks for two values and you click on only one, it could hurt your score.

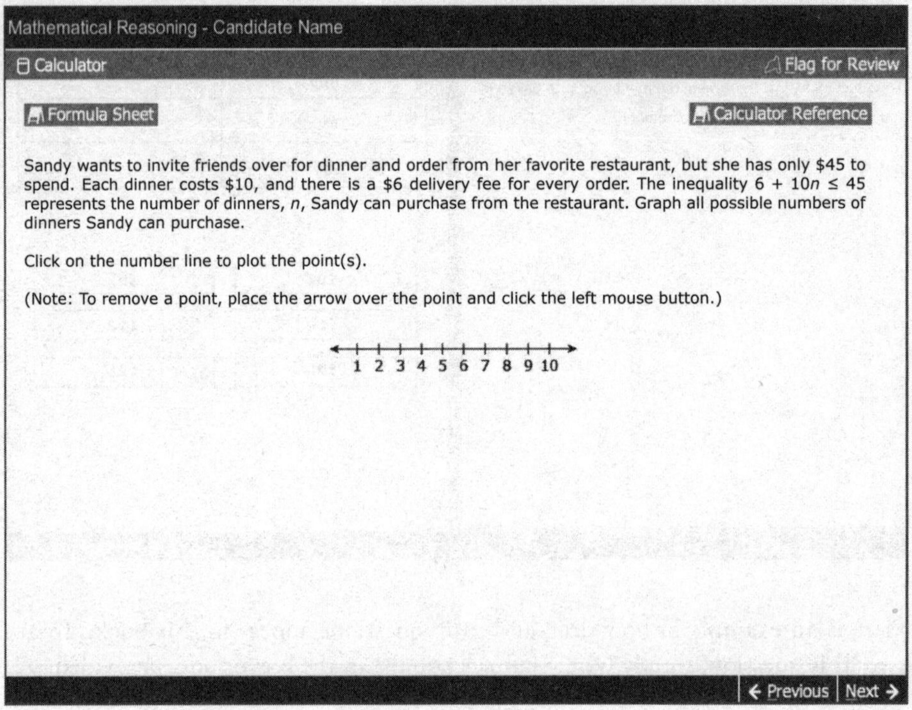

Here's an example of how Hot Spot questions appear in this book. To indicate your answer, mark an X (or multiple X's) with your pencil on the graphic provided.

3. If x is a positive integer and $|3x + 2| \le 8$, plot the highest and lowest values for x on the number line below.

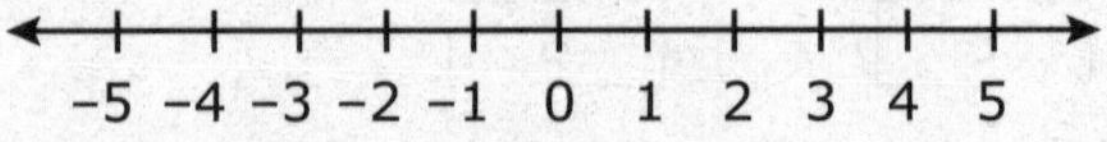

Fill in the Blank

Fill-in-the-blank questions are among the more difficult type of questions. These questions give you a set of information and ask a question. There are no answers provided, and you have to type in your own answer using your keyboard.

Because there are no answers to choose from, these questions are nearly impossible to guess on. Test takers must take care to enter their answer using the correct units and rounded to the correct place. When faced with this type of question, always reread the question to be sure you are following the correct directions in drafting your answer. Here's an example:

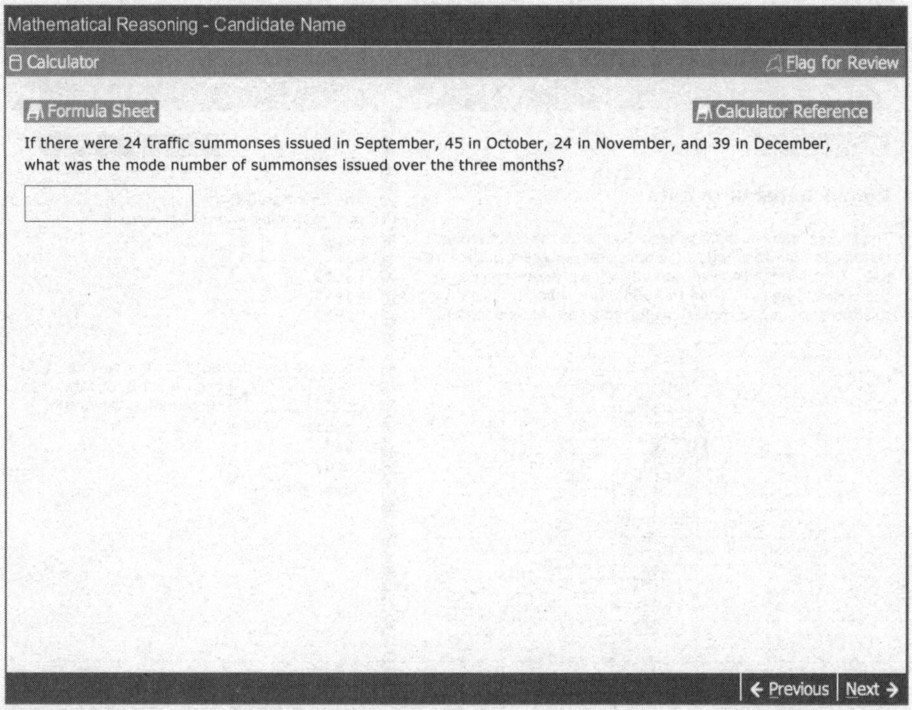
Mathematical Reasoning - Candidate Name
Calculator
Flag for Review
Formula Sheet
Calculator Reference
If there were 24 traffic summonses issued in September, 45 in October, 24 in November, and 39 in December, what was the mode number of summonses issued over the three months?
Previous
Next

In this book, simply write your answer in the box provided.

4. Janelle is deciding how to arrange her files on her bookshelf. If she has 5 files, how many different arrangements of files does she have to choose from?

Drop Down

A drop-down question is most similar to a traditional multiple-choice question. It is often used to place an answer in the context of a sentence. Use your mouse to click the arrow to the right of the box, and several answers appear in an expanded menu. To select an answer, click on your choice.

Because of their similarity to multiple-choice questions, drop-down questions should feel somewhat familiar. However, it is important to remember to open the box and see the options *before* you try the question. Doing so can greatly reduce the amount of time you spend on the question, as it reduces the number of options to consider.

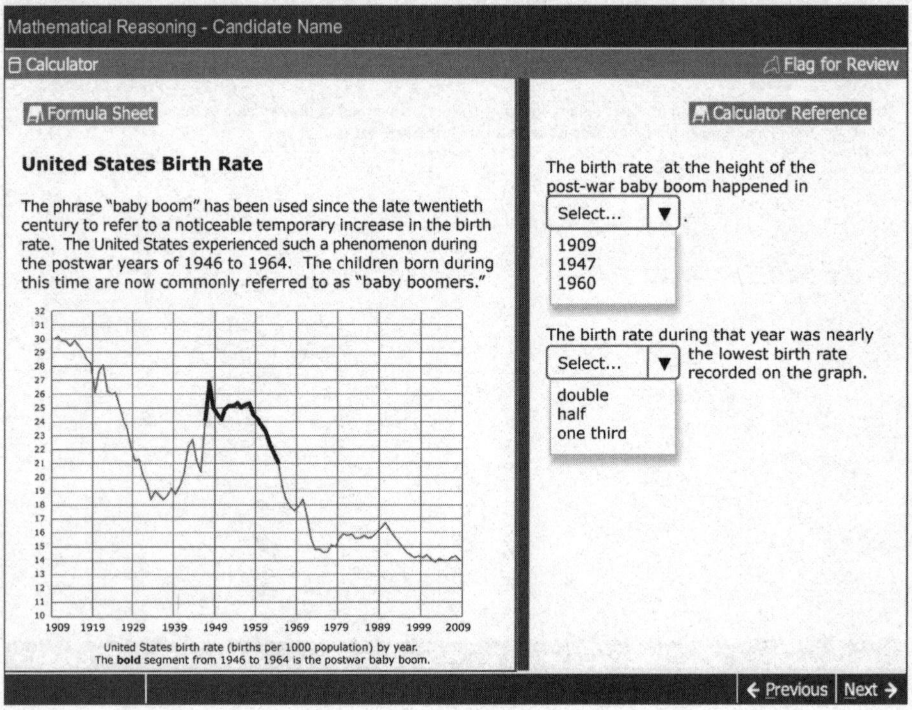

Here is how drop-down questions appear in this book. To answer this question, circle your selection with your pencil.

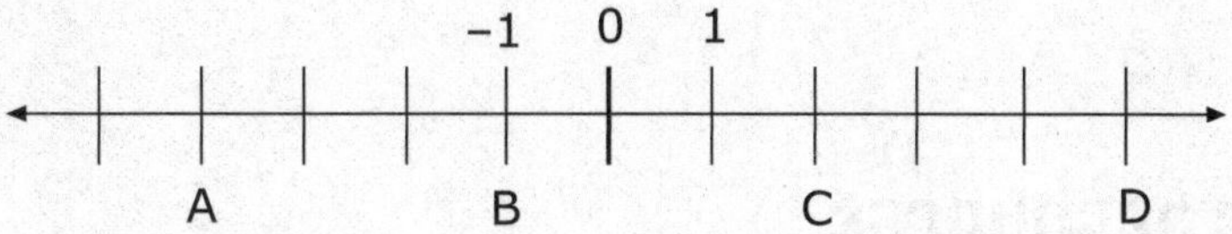

5. On the number line above, point A is

   Select... ▼ point B.

   greater than

   equal to

   less than

HOW TO USE THIS BOOK TO PREPARE

Now that you have a better idea of what to expect on test day, we'll give you some pointers on how to use this book to help you prepare.

The drills in this book cover the topics and tested skills that you'll need to know for the Mathematical Reasoning test. The next chapter will provide you with general strategies to help you out on test day. Some of these strategies are specific to the computer interface; others you can immediately put into practice on the drills. Additionally, at the end of each section, you'll find answer-explanations to guide you through each problem step by step. And at the back of the book, you'll find a Mathematics Formula Sheet that you can tear out and refer to as you're working. You can also download and print out this formula sheet once you register your book at **PrincetonReview.com/cracking**.

What this book does *not* provide is in-depth instruction on the various topics covered on the test. So, if you're unsure whether or not this book is right for you, skim through the four sections—Basic Arithmetic, Applied Arithmetic, Algebra, and Geometry—and take a look at the kinds of problems in each. If you have no idea how to solve most of these problems, we highly recommend buying *Cracking the GED® Test* and beginning with the Mathematical Reasoning review chapters in that book. *Cracking the GED® Test* offers thorough guidance on how to solve every type of question you'll encounter on the test, as well as many helpful tips and tricks.

If, however, you're mostly familiar with what's covered in these drills but are feeling a bit uncertain here and there, this book can help you clarify your study plans. Use the answers and explanations to determine your strengths and weaknesses, and keep track of how many questions you answer incorrectly. This will help you figure out where you need further review and practice.

Cracking the GED® Test is The Princeton Review's comprehensive guide to the GED® test. It includes:

- Complete coverage of all 4 test subjects
- Guided lessons with sample questions
- 2 full-length practice tests
- Review drills for each subject
- 350+ multiple-choice drills online

And of course, if you already own *Cracking the GED® Test* and are simply looking for extra practice, you've come to the right place. *Math Workout for the GED® Test* is a great companion to *Cracking* because it follows the same general order of topics, making it easy to supplement your review.

OTHER RESOURCES

GEDTestingService.com—The official website for the GED® test contains a wealth of free useful information, such as test specifications, sample problems, FAQs, a tutorial on how to use the computer interface, and a short free practice test.

GED Ready®: The Official Practice Test—Once you have worked through this book and feel confident in your ability to take the GED® Mathematical Reasoning test, we recommend that you have a "dress rehearsal" by taking the official practice test. GED Ready® was written by the test creators and gives you the full computer-based experience, making it the best available indicator of how well you'll do on test day. Although GED Ready® is only half the length of the actual GED® test and doesn't require the same level of endurance, it *will* give you accurate feedback on your mastery of the content and required skills; it'll also give you practice with the computer interface and use of scratch paper.

Because you bought this book, you are entitled to a discount of 20 percent off the price of GED Ready®. You can opt to purchase the Mathematical Reasoning test by itself, if you'd like, or you can purchase all four subject tests together. Either way, the discount applies. Moreover, when you take the practice test, your score report will recommend which sections of *Cracking the GED® Test* you should review for further improvement. To access the discount and this feature, visit **www.gedmarketplace.com/theprincetonreview.**

General Strategies

Use the format of the GED® test to your advantage. Learn how to boost your score with key skills designed to maximize your performance.

Taking a standardized test involves more than just knowledge. You need to approach the test with strategy and learned skills. This chapter will introduce you to techniques that are proven to help reduce stress and increase points. We'll also give you tips on common tricks and traps to avoid.

THE HABITS OF EFFECTIVE TEST TAKERS

1. Answer the Easy Questions First

Depending on your specific skill set and your level of comfort with the range of difficulty on the test, some questions will be easier for you than others. It's important to remember that within each section, all of the questions in the Mathematical Reasoning test are worth approximately an equal number of points, which means that getting a difficult question wrong is not going to cost you more than missing an easy question.

When you click to begin the Mathematical Reasoning test, you will probably begin with Question 1, then do Question 2, and then do Question 3, and so on. This is a fine strategy as long as you are prepared to be flexible. Every year, we hear stories from test takers who got stuck on some early problem—let's say it was Question 3. They just couldn't get it. They read it and read it again. They tried solving it one way and then another. But some people have orderly minds, and *darn it*, they aren't going to go on to Question 4 until they get Question 3. After 10 minutes, when they finally give up and go on to number 4, they are thoroughly rattled, jittery, and very angry at themselves for wasting so much time.

The lesson here? Don't be stubborn. There are always going to be problems that, for whatever reason, you just can't get. It might be a mental block, or maybe you never learned a particular type of problem, or maybe the question was simply written so that it is impossible to understand. No matter how easy you think the problem ought to be, don't be mulish. Even if you can't do the very *first* problem, there are 45 others waiting for you, and you will find that many of them are pretty easy.

The Two-Pass System

Of course, it isn't necessary to solve every problem to do very well, and in fact, you will see that by skipping the problems you don't know how to do, you can actually increase your score. Here's how.

On the Mathematical Reasoning test, you *must* finish Part I before proceeding to Part II, and you won't be allowed to return to Part I once you have finished your review. Apart from that, you have the freedom to answer the questions in any order you like. So, we recommend that you take each part in two passes.

First pass: Do the ones you KNOW you can get. On your first pass, you'll begin at the beginning and do every problem that comes easily to you. If you read a question and know just what to do, then it is a first-pass problem. However, if you read a problem and have no idea of how to solve it, click the "Flag for Review" button in the upper right corner and move on. You're not skipping this problem forever; you're merely saving it for later, after you've locked in all the easy points. If you are running out of time, it is best to have already completed all of the "easy" problems so you can spend your remaining minutes guessing on the difficult ones.

Second pass: Go back over your flagged questions. When you finish your first pass, the review screen will show you which questions you flagged along the way. Now you can take a second look. Sometimes, when you read the problem again, you'll immediately see what was unclear to you the first time, and you'll know just what to do. Other times you may not be sure, but you'll be able to eliminate several answer choices by ballparking (more on this technique later).

But what if you have no idea whatsoever? Not a problem! The GED® test doesn't deduct points for incorrect answers—your score is based only on the number of questions you answer correctly. So you have nothing to lose by guessing. In fact, you should *never* leave a question unanswered on the GED® test. Right before you submit the Mathematical Reasoning test, make sure that the status for every question number (even the flagged ones) is "answered."

With efficient use of the flag button and review screen, skipping questions that you consider more difficult is the best use of your time. Remember: Skip early and skip often.

2. Use a Note Board to Stay on Task

As we mentioned, you will be provided not with traditional scratch paper but with three erasable note boards and a dry-erase marker. Although you will not be able to save your work and go back to it later, that doesn't mean you shouldn't think about how to use your note boards strategically.

Keeping your hand moving while you focus on the physical task of writing is an essential way to stay focused on the test itself. If your brain has to communicate with your hand, then it is engaged and active and less likely to be distracted, which can force you to reread a question multiple times.

In addition to keeping your brain focused and on task, writing can help you to stay on target with the techniques presented in this book. Having something to write down, such as a summary of a reading passage or a math formula, may be just the push your brain needs to get it moving in the right direction. Using scratch paper, develop a note board habit for each type of question, and stick to it!

3. Use the Flag Button and Review Screen to Get Unstuck

It is inevitable that at some point during the test you will encounter a question that you don't understand, or one that you *think* you understand...but the answer you want isn't an option. Often, the problem is that you have misread the problem or made a small calculation error. Research shows that once you have misread a problem, you are likely to keep reading it in the same way, no matter how many times you try. Meanwhile the clock is ticking, and you aren't getting any closer to an answer. If you get stuck, the best thing to do is to flag the problem for review, and move on. Distracting your brain by doing other problems is often just what you need in order to come back and read the problem with fresh eyes.

At the end of the section, you will be able to use the review screen to quickly jump to any problems you have marked. Once you come back to them, you will have a better understanding of how much time you have left to deal with your marked problems. Then you can decide whether to sit down and work the problem or to simply put in a guess.

4. Pacing

Many wrong answers are the result of simply going too fast and reading too quickly. However, most test takers feel they have to rush through the "easy" problems because they won't have time on the more difficult ones. Try a few questions untimed, and you will make fewer mistakes. You'll also probably work more quickly than you think. The questions don't get harder when you add a timer, but somehow, test takers tend not to score as highly.

The trick is to take the GED® test at an even pace, recognizing when a question is more difficult and should be marked for later. Work for accuracy, because doing all the problems will not get you a higher score unless you do them correctly.

Slow down and make sure that you are (a) choosing to do the questions you understand first and (b) giving them enough time, attention, and focus to answer them correctly. If you run into a question that feels like a brick wall, flag it and move on to an easier question. The only exception to this rule is in the last few minutes of any section. This is the time to use your review screen and go back to marked questions to ensure that you have guessed on all the questions for which that option was available.

5. Guessing, Process of Elimination, and Ballparking

The GED® test does not penalize you for an incorrect answer. So regardless of whether you know the answer to any given problem, it's always to your advantage to answer every problem. In fact, guessing on problems that you don't know how to solve, or that you don't have time to work through, can actually *add* points to your score. Here's how to maximize your chances of guessing correctly.

Pick a "Guess Letter"

If you had a one-in-four chance to win $10 (and entering didn't cost you anything), you would enter, right? The multiple-choice and drop-down questions on the GED® test are very much like that $10 chance. On any single multiple choice question your chance of correctly guessing is 25 percent, and on drop-down questions that chance can increase depending on the number of answer choices available. If you randomly guess a different answer for each question, those odds probably won't add up to as many points as you had hoped. However, if you choose the same answer for every multiple-choice question on which you randomly guess, you are likely to get one in four of the answers correct. Those are pretty good odds, and simply choosing a consistent "guess letter" for drop down and multiple-choice questions can improve your score.

But what if you could increase your odds even more?

Process of Elimination (POE)

Try the following question:

1. There are 10 students in a class, and their average score on a test is 79 out of 100. If a new student is added to the class, what is the minimum score he would need to achieve in order to bring the class average up to 80 out of 100?

    A. 1
    B. 79
    C. 85
    D. 90

This problem may seem fairly complex to figure out. However, you can understand that if a student's score has to bring *up* the class average, it would have to be *higher* than the class average to begin with. With this information you could eliminate answer choices (A) and (B), and you would have a fifty-fifty chance of guessing the correct number, which is choice (D).

You probably won't be able to narrow down the answer choices to a single one very often, but you may be able to eliminate two answers, which only increases your chance of guessing correctly.

Ballparking

On the Mathematical Reasoning test, you can also use POE to eliminate any out-of-scope answer choices, leaving just the answers that make sense. This is what we call *ballparking*, and it is especially useful for answering those difficult questions that you may not know how to solve.

You may once have encountered a problem on a math test that looked like this:

2. This month, 1,500 new members joined a particular health club. The club's goal for this month was 2,000 new members. What percentage of the club's goal was achieved?

[ ]

Use Common Sense
When you take the GED® test, don't check your common sense at the door. In fact, by taking a step back from a problem, you can often eliminate at least one or two answer choices.

If you weren't sure how to solve this fill-in-the-blank problem during that test, you were pretty much out of luck. It certainly wouldn't have made sense to guess, would it? For example, if you had closed your eyes and picked a number at random ("…uh, 14!"), the chances that you would happen to pick the right answer would have been pretty slim.

But most of the problems on the GED® test are NOT the fill-in-the-blank types. Most questions are in the multiple-choice format. Here's how that question would look on the GED® test:

2. This month, 1,500 new members joined a particular health club. The club's goal for this month was 2,000 new members. What percentage of the club's goal was achieved?

   A. 75%
   B. 82%
   C. 112%
   D. 150%

You may be saying, "Big deal. Same problem." But, in fact, this is not the same problem at all. If you happened to spot this question on the real GED® test and still didn't know how to do it, you would have an enormous advantage because you no longer have to guess completely at random. In the multiple-choice question format, there are only four possibilities, and *one* of them has to be right. Just by guessing among the four answer choices, you have a 25 percent chance of answering the question correctly. We can do even better than that. Fortunately, it turns out that many answers to Mathematical Reasoning questions aren't reasonable at all. In fact, some of them are pretty crazy. Let's just think about that problem above. The health club's goal was 2,000 new memberships, but they actually got only 1,500 new memberships. Did they reach their goal? No way. Putting this in the language of percentages, let's restate the question: Did they reach 100 percent of their goal? The answer is still no.

Obviously, the correct answer to this problem must be *less* than 100 percent. Even if you are unsure about how to calculate the exact percentage, there are several answer choices that are simply way out of the ballpark. Look at choice (D), 150%.

This answer implies that not only did the club meet its goal, it exceeded it as well. Forget choice (D). Look at choice (C), 112%. Again, this is just wrong. The correct answer must be less than 100%. Both of these answers are way out of the ballpark.

We have eliminated two answer choices. This means the correct answer to this question is either choice (A) or choice (B). All of a sudden, your odds of getting this question correct are much better. You now have a fifty-fifty chance of being right. Pick one. If you picked choice (A), you just got the question correct. Even if you picked choice (B) and got the question wrong, there are probably more questions that you can ballpark. Let's say you have two questions that you don't know how to solve, but you can ballpark. You probably get both of them narrowed down to two possible answers (as we just did). Thus, in each question, you are down to a fifty-fifty guess. What would be the results if you were to guess on both of them? The odds say you're going to get one of them wrong (maybe you picked (B) for this question). That's a shame, but after all, there's no guessing penalty, and more to the point, you didn't know how to do the question anyway, so you're no worse off than you were before. However, the odds also say that you're going to get the other one *right*! And that's not bad, considering you had no idea how to do that question either.

Don't know how to "do" a question? Try ballparking and then guess!

Okay, let's say you know exactly how to do a problem. Should you bother to ballpark it first? Definitely. Taking the GED® test does funny things to people. You might be the greatest mathematician in the world ordinarily, but by the time you get to the Mathematical Reasoning test, your brain may be so fried from the other four tests that you just aren't thinking completely straight. Or you may be rushing to finish a question and make a mistake that you would never normally make. You can prevent lots of careless errors by stepping back from a math problem and saying, *Wait a minute. Before I even start multiplying or dividing, which answers don't make sense?*

Once you've gotten rid of the out-of-scope answer choices, then you can start solving the problem. And if your calculations happen to lead you, mistakenly, to one of those out-of-scope answer choices—well, you'll know you just made a mistake, and you'll be able to figure out what went wrong.

You can ballpark on many question types

- Multiple choice
- Drop down
- Drag-and-drop

You'll find that once you start looking at GED® problems in this way, you'll spot many opportunities to ballpark. This is because the test writers construct their incorrect answer choices not to be reasonable but to anticipate common errors that test takers make when they're in a hurry.

Using Graphics to Ballpark

Anywhere from one-third to one-half of the questions on the Mathematical Reasoning test refer to "graphic material": drawings of geometric figures, graphs, and charts. Whenever you see a diagram on the Mathematical Reasoning test, you have the single most efficient way to ballpark that you could possibly imagine: You can just *measure* the diagrams. We know it's bizarre, but it's true.

Here's a typical drag-and-drop geometry problem:

Question 3 refers to the following diagram.

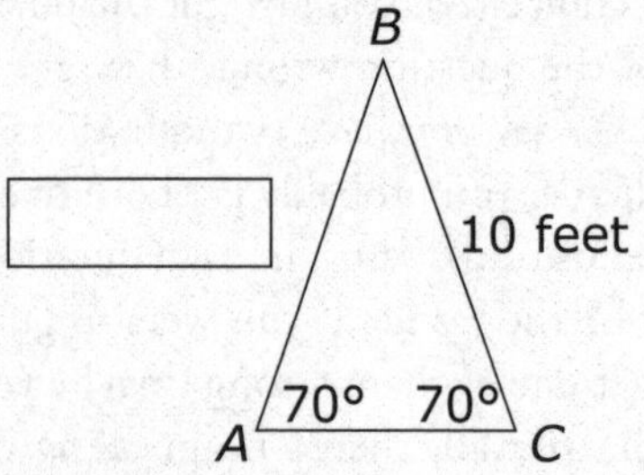

3. If angle A and angle C both equal 70°, then what is the length of side AB? Click on the number you want to select and drag it into the box.

3 feet	7 feet	9 feet
10 feet	12 feet	15 feet

The question is, how long is side *AB*? Let's find out. Simply take any straight edge you can find, and carefully measure side *BC*, which the diagram says is 10 feet long. Mark the length of side *BC* along the edge of one of the erasable note boards that is provided to you for the duration of the test. Now all you have to do is compare that length to side *AB*. If it's a lot bigger, you can get rid of any choices less than 10. If it's a lot smaller, you can get rid of any choices greater than 10.

If you measured our diagram correctly, you probably noticed that side *AB* appears to be exactly the same size as side *BC*. So is the correct answer 10 feet? Well, in fact it is. However, because the GED® drawings are only drawn *roughly* to scale, you wouldn't know for sure that the answer is exactly 10 feet unless you knew the geometric reasoning behind the problem. Going by the diagram alone, you could only have gotten the answer down to either 9 feet or 10 feet. Between these two, it would have been too close to call. However, you could be pretty certain that the answer was *not* 3 feet, 7 feet, 12 feet, or 15 feet.

TRICKS AND TRAPS

Earlier we mentioned that the GED® test writers construct questions to anticipate common errors. In this section, we'll show you how to avoid two more ways in which they try to trip you up.

Partial Answers

The test writers know that a stressed test taker tends not to read the question carefully enough, or solves only some of what the question asks. These mistakes can lead you to wrongly choose a *partial answer* (even though you may be on the right track). Let's look at another multiple-choice problem.

4. Eric buys a coat from a mail-order catalog. The coat costs $140, plus an $8 shipping charge and a $2 handling fee. If there is a 10% sales tax on the entire amount, what would be the total cost of buying the coat?

   A. $135
   B. $150
   C. $160
   D. $165

Like many problems on the Mathematical Reasoning test, this requires several steps. What is the first thing you would do if you were actually buying this coat? We add up the costs we have so far.

the coat $140

shipping $8

handling + $2

$150

We are already up to $150, and we haven't even added in the tax yet. Do you see any answer choices we can cross out? If you said choices (A) and (B), you are right on the money. The correct answer must be *greater* than $150, which means there are only two possibilities left: choices (C) and (D). Look at that—we just created another fifty-fifty chance of guessing the correct answer.

Why did the test writers choose two answers that didn't make sense? Because they wanted to include some answers that many test takers are likely to pick by mistake. For example, let's say that you were doing this problem, and you got to the point we have already reached: You added up the numbers and got $150. If you were in a hurry (and who isn't during the GED® test?), you might look at the answer choices, see choice (B), $150, figure that you must be done, and click the bubble for choice (B) on the screen. However, this number is only a *partial* answer to the question.

Slow Down for "Traps"
GED® test writers love to leave "trap" answers for you—such as an answer that subtracts two numbers instead of adding them. Watch out for these traps by working the problem carefully, which may mean you need to SLOW DOWN. It is better to take your time and answer one question correctly than to hurriedly answer two questions incorrectly.

To find the correct answer to this question—choice (D), $165—you must do three separate calculations. First, add up the cost of the coat and the postage and handling. Check. Second, calculate the tax. To compute this, you find 10 percent of $150, which turns out to be $15. Third, add the tax to the previous total. If a test taker chose choice (B), $150, it was not because he made a mistake in his calculations. The answer to step one of this problem is $150. And if a test taker chose choice (A), $135, it was likely due to subtracting the tax instead of adding it.

On the GED® test, you will frequently find partial answers lurking in wait for you. To avoid getting taken in by one of these, you have to read the problem very carefully the first time and then read it again just as carefully right before you select your answer. Because the test writers employ partial answers so often on the Mathematical Reasoning test, you can actually use the partial answers as clues to help you find the final answer. For example, working on a two-step problem, you may find that the answer to the first step of the problem is also one of the answer choices. This is a good sign. It means you are on the right track. If the answer to your first step is *close* to one of the answer choices, but just a little off, you might try redoing the calculation to see if you made a mistake.

Spot the Red Herring

On every Mathematical Reasoning test, there will be several problems that give you more information than you actually need. We call this extra information the "red herring." Here's an example of a fill-in-the-blank question:

5. This year, $\frac{3}{4}$ of the employees at Acme made contributions to a voluntary retirement fund. Last year, only $\frac{2}{3}$ of the employees contributed. If there are now 2,100 employees, how many contributed to the voluntary retirement fund this year?

[ ]

The most important part of any GED® math problem is the last line, which is where the test writers tell you what they really want. In this case, they want the number of employees who contributed to their retirement fund *this* year. In this problem, the only year you care about is *this* year. To answer the question, you have to find out from the problem what fraction of the total employees contributed this year, and then multiply that fraction by the total number of employees.

Sounds Fishy to Me
A "red herring" is an expression in which a clue or piece or information is intended to be misleading or distracting from the actual question. Distractor answers are common on standardized tests like the GED® test.

Look at the problem and ask yourself, "Is there any information that is not about this year?" Well, as a matter of fact, there is. The second sentence, "Last year, only $\frac{2}{3}$ of the employees contributed," has nothing to do with what the question asks. The GED® test writers threw that sentence in to see if it would trick you. It was a red herring.

To answer this question, we need to take $\frac{3}{4}$ of 2,100. The correct answer is 1,575.

A FINAL WORD

No one question is that important to your score. Don't spend any time beating yourself up for not knowing how to do the problem, as everyone is likely to find at least some questions they don't know how to do. Keeping track of how many questions you think you got correct, or getting upset because you think you aren't doing well, can only impact your score negatively.

Sometimes the questions on this test may seem complex and unusual, especially if you have been away from school for a long period of time. It is important to recognize the strengths that you bring to this test; they can help you to achieve the score you are looking for. Use the drills in this book to help identify these strengths, and remember, the GED® test is only that—a test. It doesn't measure your worth as a human being. It measures how effectively you have acquired a few skills and how you make use of that knowledge in a timed, stressful situation. Use the test's own limitations to your advantage, and with a little hard work, you can earn your GED® test credential.

If you follow the strategies outlined in this chapter, are diligent in your work, and assess your progress throughout your preparation, by the time you sit for the GED® test, you should find it familiar and manageable, and you should be able to take it with confidence.

Happy studies and best wishes for a successful future!

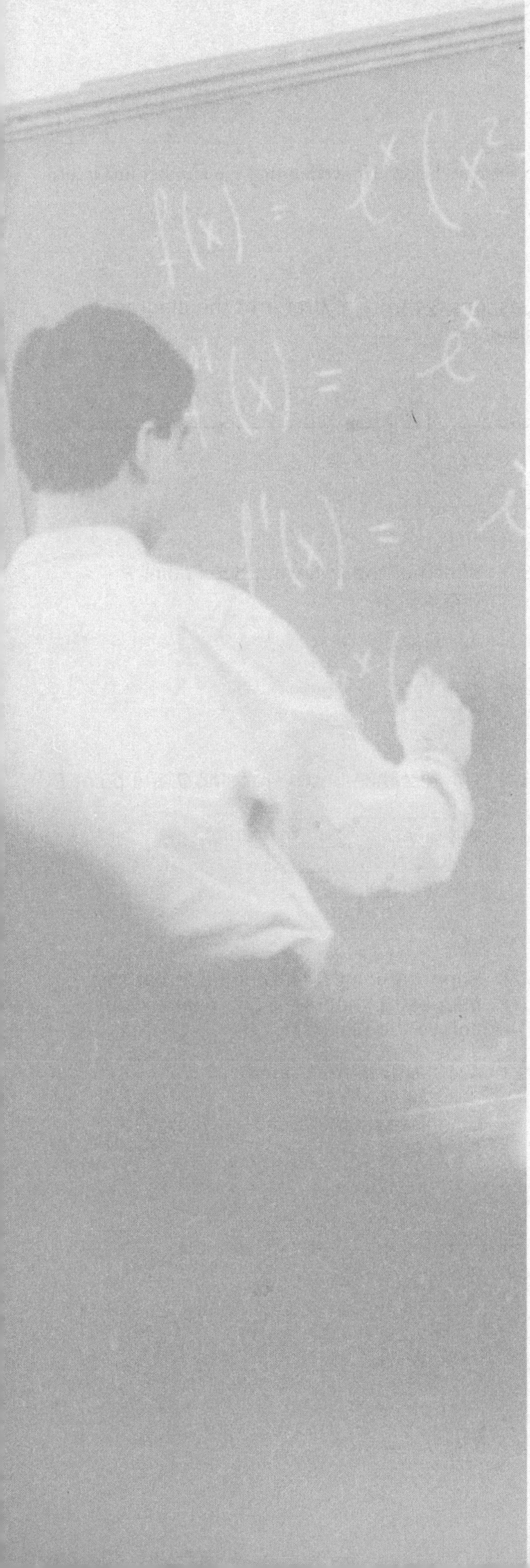

Part II
Basic Arithmetic

Number Line Drill

You will likely find some questions on the test that look similar to the ones below. Understanding the number line is also key to addition and subtraction with positive and negative numbers.

DO NOT USE A CALCULATOR FOR THIS DRILL.

Questions 1 through 4 refer to the diagram below.

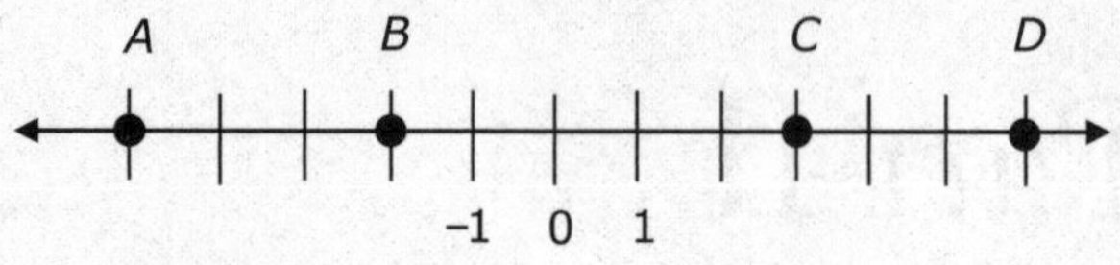

1. Which point represents the number −4? Mark the location of −4 with an X.

2. Which two points are 5 units apart?

   A. *A* and *B*
   B. *B* and *C*
   C. *A* and *C*
   D. *B* and *D*

3. On the number line above, what number does point *D* represent?

4. On the number line above, what is the distance between points *C* and *D*?

   A. 1
   B. 2
   C. 3
   D. 4

Questions 5 through 7 refer to the diagram below.

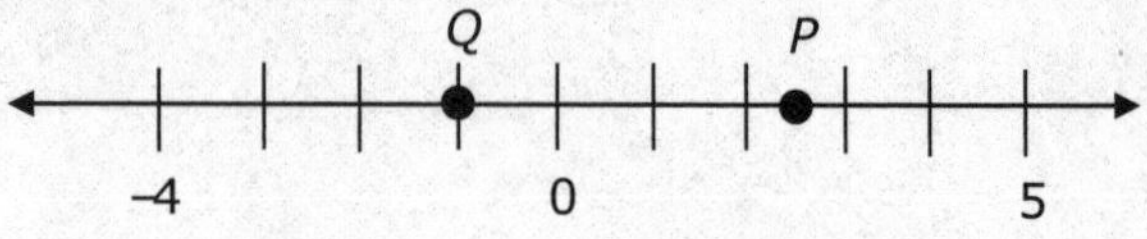

5. Which of the following does point *P* represent?

   A. 1.5
   B. 2
   C. 2.5
   D. 3

6. The distance between point *Q* and point *P*

   is [Select... ▼] 3 units.
   - less than
   - equal to
   - greater than

7. Suppose point *R* is to be added at the midpoint of segment *QP*. Where would point *R* be placed?

   A. Between −1 and 0
   B. At 0
   C. Between 0 and 1
   D. At 1

<u>Questions 8 and 9</u> refer to the diagram below.

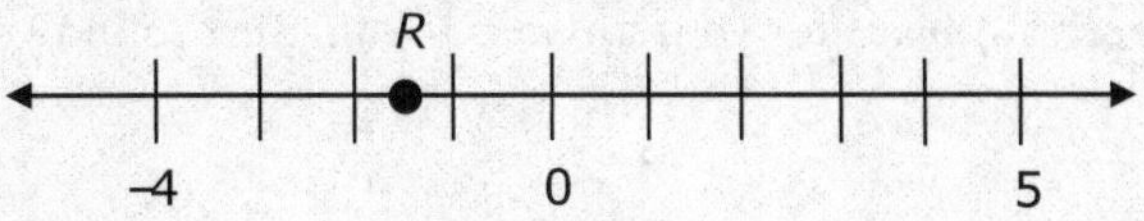

8. What is the distance from 0 to point *R*?

   A. −1.5
   B. −1
   C. 1
   D. 1.5

9. Mark with an X the point exactly between −1 and 3.

<u>Questions 10 and 11</u> refer to the diagram below.

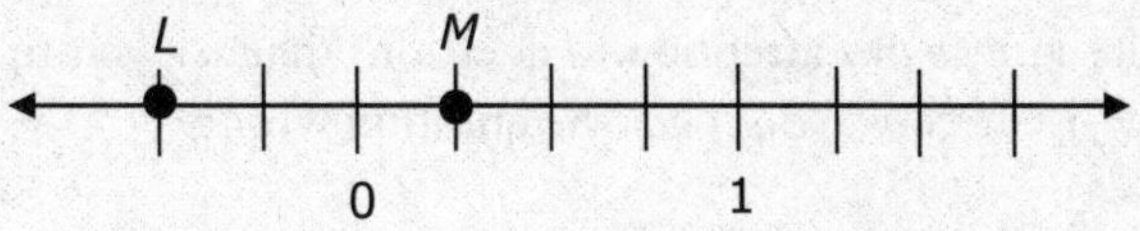

10. Which of the following is the value of point *M*?

   A. $\frac{1}{5}$
   B. $\frac{1}{4}$
   C. $\frac{1}{3}$
   D. $\frac{1}{2}$

11. Point *L* is at ☐. Write the number in the box.

-1	$-\frac{3}{4}$	$-\frac{1}{2}$
$-\frac{1}{4}$	$\frac{1}{4}$	$\frac{1}{2}$

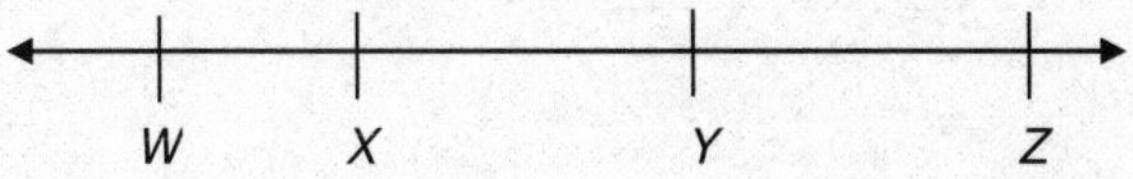

12. In the number line above, the distance from *W* to *Z* is 20. If $2WX = XY = YZ$, what is the length of *WX*?

   A. 4
   B. 5
   C. 8
   D. 10

Rounding Off Drill

Make sure to pay attention to questions that ask you to round to a certain place for your answer. If you don't round your answer correctly, you'll get the question wrong.

1. What is 246.942 rounded to the nearest tenth?

   [ ]

DO NOT USE A CALCULATOR FOR QUESTION 2.

2. Mariana runs 2.6 miles on Monday, 3.3 miles on Tuesday, 2 miles on Wednesday, and 1.9 miles on Thursday. Rounded to the nearest mile, how many miles does Mariana run in the four-day period?

   A. 8
   B. 9
   C. 10
   D. 11

3. 24.65 rounded to the nearest tenth is [Select... ▼], 24.66 rounded to the nearest tenth.

   - greater than
   - equal to
   - less than

4. Match the correct number to each written description. Write the numbers you want in the boxes.

   2,368.47 rounded to the nearest thousand [ ]

   2,368.47 rounded to the nearest tenth [ ]

2,368.4	2,368.5	2,368
2,370	2,400	
2,000	3,000	

5. An office administrator needs to purchase 150 cupcakes for a party. If cupcakes are sold only in boxes of 12, how many boxes of cupcakes must the office administrator purchase?

   A. 12
   B. 12.5
   C. 13
   D. 14

6. Which of the following has the greatest value?

   A. 234.6
   B. 234.6 rounded to the nearest whole
   C. 234.6 rounded to the nearest ten
   D. 234.6 rounded to the nearest hundred

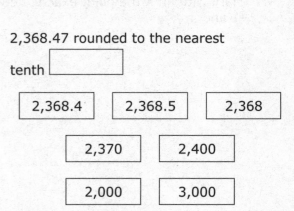

Addition and Subtraction Drill

Always imagine the number line for addition and subtraction. Addition moves to the right, and subtraction moves to the left. You can also use the calculator when it is allowed—just remember to put parentheses around all negative numbers.

DO NOT USE A CALCULATOR FOR QUESTIONS 1–5.

1. $22 + (-5) =$

   A. −27
   B. −17
   C. 17
   D. 27

2. $-15 + 7 =$

   A. −22
   B. −8
   C. 8
   D. 22

3. $-10 + (-12) =$

   [ ]

4. 12 + (−6) is [Select... ▼] 12 − 6.
   - greater than
   - equal to
   - less than

5. $22 - (-5) =$

   A. −27
   B. −17
   C. 17
   D. 27

6. Write the number that correctly completes the equation.

   $-8 +$ [ ] $= -15$

−8	−7	7	8

7. $-9 - (-2) =$

   A. −11
   B. −7
   C. 7
   D. 11

8. Marcus overdrafts his bank account, resulting in a balance of −$5.45. Then he deposits $30.00. What is his new balance?

   A. −$35.45
   B. −$24.55
   C. $24.55
   D. $35.45

9. On a game show, contestants earn 200 points for every correct answer and lose 200 points for every incorrect answer. If a contestant has 400 points and then answers three questions incorrectly, what will be the contestant's resulting score?

[ ]

10. In a math class, students are asked to pick numbers on a number line. Keshia picks the number −36, and Alex picks a number that is 23 less than Keshia's number. What is Alex's number?

A. −59
B. −13
C. 13
D. 59

Multiplication and Division Drill

Many multiplication and division problems are easiest to solve with the calculator, when it is allowed. Just remember to put parentheses around negative numbers.

1. $9 \times -6 =$

   A. −54
   B. −45
   C. 45
   D. 54

2. $-20 \times -15 =$

   [ ]

DO NOT USE A CALCULATOR FOR QUESTION 3.

3. $-8{,}967 \times 1{,}248$ is [Select... ▼ | less than | equal to | greater than] $-43{,}214 \times -1{,}063$.

4. $354 \div -12 =$

   A. −30
   B. −29.5
   C. 29.5
   D. 30

5. Write the number that correctly completes the equation.

   [ ] $\div 8 = -8$

−64	−54	−8	0
8	54	64	

DO NOT USE A CALCULATOR FOR QUESTION 6.

6. The temperature in a certain city decreases by 5 degrees Fahrenheit each hour for 3 hours. What is the total change in temperature, in degrees Fahrenheit, after the 3 hours?

   A. −15
   B. −5
   C. 5
   D. 15

Order of Operations Drill

Even when the calculator is allowed, these types of problems should usually be done by hand. It's difficult to enter them into the calculator and make sure the order of operations is done correctly. The calculator is a good tool for single steps of more complicated problems, though. Be careful with negatives!

DO NOT USE A CALCULATOR FOR QUESTIONS 1–2.

1. $4 \times 5 + 3 =$

   A. 12
   B. 18
   C. 23
   D. 32

2. $12 + 3 \times 10 =$

   A. 25
   B. 42
   C. 150
   D. 360

3. $9 \times (4 + (-2)) =$

   [ ]

4. $23 - (5 \times 2 + 1) =$

   A. 8
   B. 12
   C. 14
   D. 37

5. $2^3 \times (8 - (-2)) =$

   A. 36
   B. 48
   C. 60
   D. 80

6. $(3 + 4) \times 6 \div (-2) =$

   [ ]

7. $(20 - (2 \times 3))^2 =$

   A. −16
   B. 14
   C. 196
   D. 2,916

DO NOT USE A CALCULATOR FOR QUESTION 8.

8. $6 + (-9) - (-2) + 5 =$

   [ ]

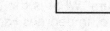

9. $2 \times (12 - 6)^{(3-2)} + 10 =$

DO NOT USE A CALCULATOR FOR QUESTION 10.

10. $\frac{(6 + 6)^2}{2^3} =$

A. 3
B. 5.25
C. 18
D. 24

11. $45 + 2 \times 6 \div 3 + 28 - 21 + 1^{18} =$

A. 57
B. 74
C. 102
D. 119

12. $\left(\frac{5 \times (4 + 2)}{(20 \div 2) \div 2}\right)^2 - 6^1 =$

Commutative and Distributive Properties Drill

DO NOT USE A CALCULATOR FOR THIS DRILL.

1. Choose the expression that correctly completes the equation.

$x(y+z) = \square$

$xy + z$	$x + y + z$	$xy + xz$
$y + xz$	xyz	$z + xy$

2. Which of the following is NOT equivalent to $a - b - c$?

A. $c - b - a$
B. $-b + a - c$
C. $-c - b + a$
D. $a - c - b$

3. $\frac{1}{3}(5) + \frac{1}{3}(7) = \square$

4. $20 + (x + 5) =$

A. $20x + 100$
B. $20x + 5$
C. $x + 25$
D. $20 + 5x$

5. If $10x + 10y = 80$, what is the value of $x + y$?

A. 4
B. 8
C. 10
D. Not enough information is given.

6. Choose the expression that correctly completes the equation.

$4x \div (x + 1) = \square$

$(x + 1) \div 4$	$4x \div x + 1$	5
$(x + 1) \div 4x)$	$x + 1 \div 4x$	
$\frac{4x}{x + 1}$	$4 + 4x$	

7. Which of the following is equal to $2x(x + 2) - 5(4x - 3)$?

A. $2x^2 - 16x + 15$
B. $2x^2 -16x - 15$
C. $2x^2 -20x + 19$
D. $-14x + 15$

8. $5(2 + 4) + 6(2 + 4) + 2(2 + 4) =$

9. If $10x^2 + 5x - 15 = 30$, what is the value of $2x^2 + x - 3$?

10. Which of the following equations is false?

A. $a \times b \times c = b \times c \times a$
B. $a - b - c = b - c - a$
C. $a + b + c = b + c + a$
D. None of the above

11. $\frac{3}{4}(x + 3) + \frac{3}{4}(3x + 5) =$

A. $\frac{3}{4}x + 8$

B. $\frac{9}{4}x + 15$

C. $\frac{9}{16}x + 8$

D. $3x + 6$

12. Which of the following is NOT equal to $10x^2 + 4x - 7$?

A. $4x + 10x^2 - 7$
B. $7 - 10x^2 + 4x$
C. $4x - 7 + 10x^2$
D. $10x^2 - 7 + 4x$

Simplifying Fractions Drill

You aren't likely to see a question that's only about simplifying fractions, but it is an important skill when working with fractions. Put the following fractions in simplest form.

DO NOT USE A CALCULATOR FOR THIS DRILL.

1. $\frac{10}{15}$

2. $\frac{4}{8}$

3. $\frac{10}{120}$

4. $\frac{7}{17}$

5. $\frac{200}{900}$

6. $\frac{8}{10}$

7. $\frac{144}{150}$

8. $\frac{64}{80}$

9. $\frac{12}{9}$

10. $\frac{30}{6}$

11. $\frac{21}{8}$

12. $\frac{19}{38}$

Adding and Subtracting Fractions Drill

Solve the following problems, making sure the answer is in simplest form. Keep in mind that it is always possible to change fractions to decimals with the calculator if you find decimals easier to work with. But for non-calculator problems, adding and subtracting fractions is an important skill.

DO NOT USE A CALCULATOR FOR THIS DRILL.

1. $\frac{1}{5} + \frac{2}{5} =$

2. $\frac{9}{10} - \frac{1}{10} =$

3. $\frac{1}{2} + \frac{1}{4} =$

4. $\frac{3}{4} - \frac{1}{2} =$

5. $\frac{4}{5} - \frac{2}{3} =$

6. $\frac{5}{6} + 7 =$

7. $\frac{1}{2} + \frac{3}{4} =$

8. $\frac{2}{3} - \frac{3}{4} =$

9. $\frac{1}{4} + \frac{2}{11} =$

10. $\frac{7}{8} - \frac{2}{3} =$

11. $\frac{5}{6} + \frac{1}{2} + \frac{1}{4} =$

12. $\frac{9}{10} - \frac{3}{4} - \frac{1}{8} =$

Multiplying and Dividing Fractions Drill

Solve the following problems, making sure the answer is in simplest form. Keep in mind that it is always possible to change fractions to decimals with the calculator if you find decimals easier to work with. But for non-calculator problems, multiplying and dividing fractions is an important skill.

DO NOT USE A CALCULATOR FOR THIS DRILL.

1. $\frac{1}{2} \times \frac{3}{4} =$

2. $\frac{4}{5} \times \frac{1}{3} =$

3. $\frac{3}{10} \div \frac{1}{2} =$

4. $\frac{5}{6} \div \frac{3}{4} =$

5. $\frac{9}{10} \times \frac{5}{7} =$

6. $\frac{2}{3} \div \frac{2}{3} =$

7. $\frac{5}{9} \times 5 =$

8. $10 \div \frac{3}{5} =$

Converting Fractions Drill

For the following problems, change the improper fractions to mixed numbers and change the mixed numbers to improper fractions. Make sure the answer is in simplest form. It is important to be able to do fraction conversions for the non-calculator questions, but they can also be done on the GED calculator using the [U n/d] key.

DO NOT USE A CALCULATOR FOR THIS DRILL.

1. $\frac{11}{4}$

5. $\frac{21}{2}$

2. $3\frac{2}{3}$

6. $8\frac{3}{4}$

3. $\frac{10}{6}$

7. $\frac{100}{5}$

4. $2\frac{9}{10}$

8. $1\frac{1}{4}$

Fraction Word Problems Drill

DO NOT USE A CALCULATOR FOR QUESTION 1.

1. On Monday, $\frac{3}{10}$ of a cake is eaten. On Tuesday, another $\frac{1}{10}$ of the cake is eaten. After this, how much of the cake is left?

   A. $\frac{3}{10}$
   B. $\frac{2}{5}$
   C. $\frac{3}{5}$
   D. $\frac{7}{10}$

2. Of the 100 members of a club, $\frac{1}{4}$ of them have no siblings. How many club members do have siblings?

   [ ]

3. A staircase that is 30 feet long is made up of a certain number of steps that are each $\frac{3}{4}$ foot long. How many steps are in the staircase?

   A. 23
   B. 30
   C. 34
   D. 40

DO NOT USE A CALCULATOR FOR QUESTIONS 4–5.

4. A recipe calls for $5\frac{1}{3}$ grams of sprinkles, and each gram of sprinkles contains 33 sprinkles. How many sprinkles are needed for the whole recipe?

   A. 105
   B. 165
   C. 176
   D. 561

5. Julia has completed $\frac{2}{3}$ of her homework. Eric has completed $\frac{16}{21}$ of his homework. Julia has completed [Select... ▼] of her homework compared to Eric.

   - much less
   - a little less
   - an equal amount
   - a little more
   - much more

6. Antonia bought $\frac{7}{8}$ of a pound of chocolates and ate $\frac{1}{3}$ of a pound. What fraction of a pound is left?

A. $\frac{7}{24}$

B. $\frac{13}{24}$

C. $\frac{6}{5}$

D. $\frac{21}{8}$

7. A track is $\frac{3}{8}$ of a mile long. If a person running on the track runs a total of 12 miles on the track, how many laps around the track did the runner make?

[ ]

8. Janae has a wooden board that is $6\frac{2}{3}$ feet long. She cuts off $2\frac{1}{2}$ feet of the wood. How much, in feet, is left?

A. $3\frac{5}{6}$

B. 4

C. $4\frac{1}{6}$

D. $9\frac{1}{6}$

DO NOT USE A CALCULATOR FOR QUESTION 9.

9. Put the following fractions in order from least to greatest.

$\frac{7}{2}$	$\frac{2}{3}$	$\frac{8}{5}$	$\frac{3}{2}$

10. In a bag of marbles, $\frac{2}{3}$ of the marbles are purple. Of the purple marbles, $\frac{1}{4}$ are sparkly. What fraction of all the marbles in the bag are sparkly purple?

A. $\frac{1}{6}$

B. $\frac{1}{4}$

C. $\frac{2}{7}$

D. $\frac{8}{3}$

11. $\frac{5}{6}$ of the 48 books in a collection are non-fiction. Of the non-fiction books, $\frac{2}{5}$ are science books. How many non-fiction books are not science books?

[ ]

12. A developer wants to turn $6\frac{1}{4}$ acres of land into space for 10 houses, with an equal amount of land for each house. How much land, in acres, will each house have?

A. $\frac{5}{8}$

B. $1\frac{21}{40}$

C. $16\frac{1}{4}$

D. $62\frac{1}{2}$

Adding and Subtracting Decimals Drill

Solve the following problems. Remember to line up the decimal points correctly. When it is allowed, the calculator is the best way to solve these problems, but make sure to know how to do them by hand for the non-calculator questions.

DO NOT USE A CALCULATOR FOR THIS DRILL.

1. $3.4 + 2.9$

2. $6 - 1.43$

3. $12 + 3.7$

4. $10.5 - 3$

5. What number is 2.4 more than 16.87?

   A. 14.47
   B. 17.11
   C. 19.27
   D. 40.87

6. Which number correctly completes the equation below?

   $26.3 - \square = 15.62$

1.068	9.68	10.68
11.68	24.738	106.8

Multiplying and Dividing Decimals Drill

Solve the following problems. When it is allowed, the calculator is the best way to solve these problems, but make sure to know how to do them by hand for the non-calculator questions.

1. 3.6×6.5

2. $18.54 \div 2$

3. 12×0.9

4. $17.64 \div 2.8$

5. A video game costs $56.95 and 5 friends share the cost equally. How much must each person pay?

6. A certain car can run for 26.4 miles for every gallon of gas. The car is filled with 7.4 gallons of gas. How many miles can it travel?

7. The temperature in Anchorage is 0.9 degrees Fahrenheit. The temperature in Miami is 80.8 times the temperature in Anchorage. What is the temperature in Miami, in degrees Fahrenheit?

   A. 72.72
   B. 79.9
   C. 80.8
   D. 89.8

8. A catering company makes 150 sandwiches for an event. The company expects each person to eat 1.5 sandwiches. At this rate, how many people can be served with the sandwiches the company has made?

   A. 10
   B. 100
   C. 148.5
   D. 225

Percents Drill

Most percent problems are easiest to solve using the calculator, but be familiar with changing percents to fractions in order to solve by hand. Mental math can also be useful for some percent problems.

DO NOT USE A CALCULATOR FOR QUESTIONS 1–3.

1. 10% of 80

2. 10% of 395

3. 30% of 40

4. 45% of 80

5. 96% of 205

DO NOT USE A CALCULATOR FOR QUESTION 6.

6. 60 is 50% of what number?

7. 24 is 10% of what number?

8. 80 is 20% of what number?

9. 90 is 45% of what number?

10. 36 is 75% of what number?

DO NOT USE A CALCULATOR FOR QUESTION 11.

11. 10 is what percent of 20?

12. 55 is what percent of 550?

13. 30 is what percent of 150?

14. 25 is what percent of 80?

15. 100 is what percent of 125?

Percent Word Problems Drill

DO NOT USE A CALCULATOR FOR QUESTION 1.

1. At a certain store, shirts are on sale for 10% off. How much would a customer save on a $15.00 shirt?

   A. $1.00
   B. $1.50
   C. $2.00
   D. $10.00

2. On a test with 80 questions, a student got 75% of the questions correct. How many questions did the student get correct?

   ☐

DO NOT USE A CALCULATOR FOR QUESTION 3.

3. In a bag of 300 candies, 45% of the candies are blue. How many blue candies are in the bag?

   A. 7
   B. 45
   C. 135
   D. 667

4. At a certain restaurant, a sandwich costs $5.50 plus 8% tax. What is the cost of the sandwich including tax?

   A. $0.44
   B. $5.06
   C. $5.94
   D. $9.90

DO NOT USE A CALCULATOR FOR QUESTION 5.

5. On a test, a student gets 40 questions correct, which is 80%. How many questions are on the test?

   ☐

6. A shopper saves $5 on an item using a 10% off coupon. What was the original price of the item?

   A. $5
   B. $10
   C. $50
   D. $100

7. Choose the number that correctly completes the sentence below.

25 is 20% of [ ].

5	20	25	50
100	125	250	

8. 35% of the residents of a town work part-time. If 5,250 residents work part-time, how many residents are there total?

A. 150
B. 1,838
C. 10,000
D. 15,000

DO NOT USE A CALCULATOR FOR QUESTION 9.

9. In a two-hour business meeting, 30 minutes are spent discussing a certain project. What percent of the meeting is spent discussing this project?

A. 25%
B. 30%
C. 50%
D. 120%

10. 2 books on a shelf of 16 books are fiction. What percent of the books on the shelf are non-fiction? Disregard the percent sign when entering your answer.

[ ]

11. A mechanic has a checklist of 25 steps for a vehicle examination. If the mechanic has completed 8 steps, what percent of the steps have not yet been completed?

A. 25%
B. 32%
C. 48%
D. 68%

12. 27 of the 36 students in a class pass the course. What percent of students do not pass?

A. 25%
B. 27%
C. 36%
D. 75%

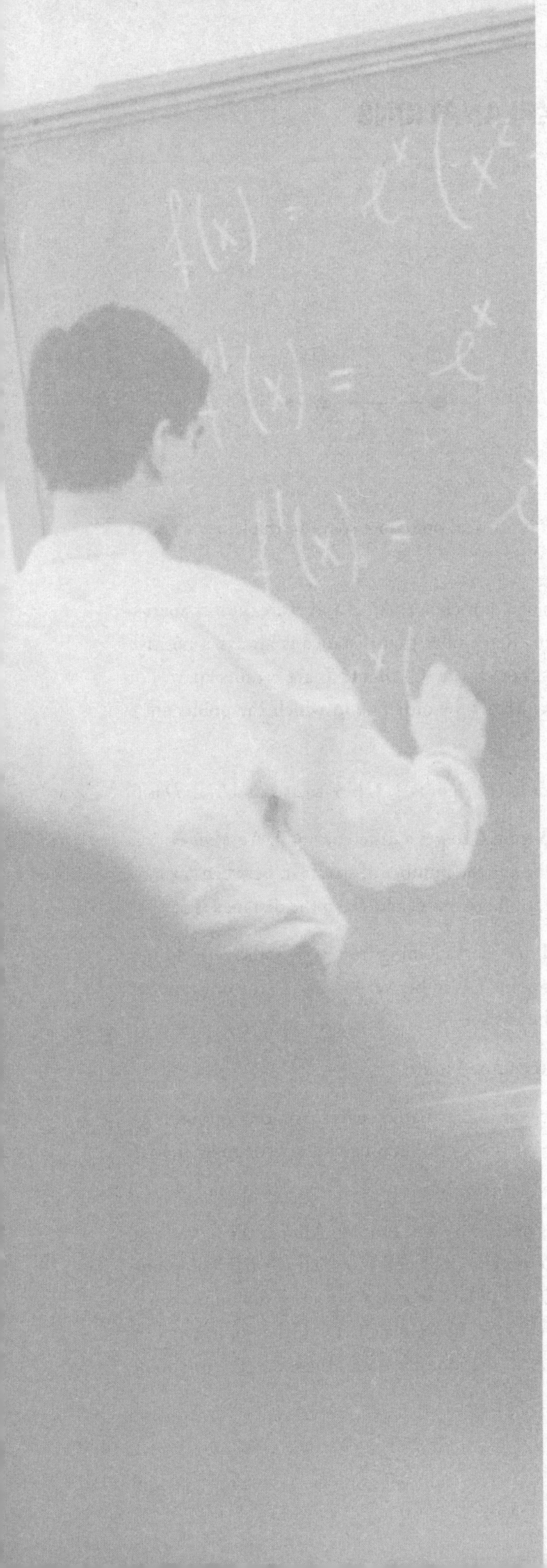

Basic Arithmetic: Answers and Explanations

BASIC ARITHMETIC: ANSWERS AND EXPLANATIONS

Number Line Drill

1.

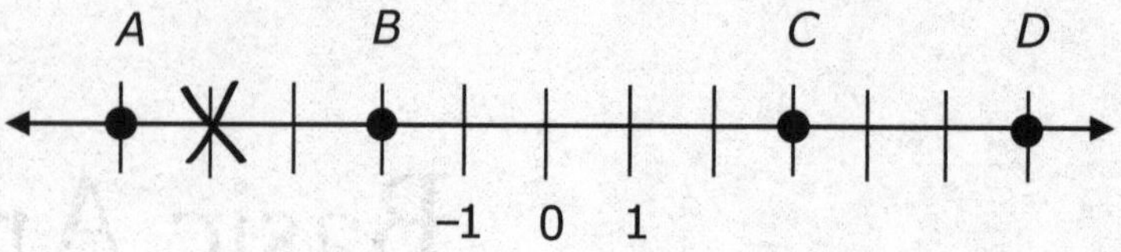

Count to the left from –1. *B* is –2, to the left of *B* is –3, and one more space to the left is –4. *A* is –5.

2. **B** Process of elimination is the best way to solve this one. For choice (A), *A* and *B* are 3 units apart—find this by counting the spaces in between them. Remember that distance is always a positive value, even when the points are negative numbers. For choice (C), *A* and *C* are 8 units apart. For choice (D), *B* and *D* are also 8 units apart. Choice (B) is the only one in which the points are 5 units apart.

3. **6** Count up from the point labeled as 1. The next spot to the right is 2, *C* is 3, then 4 and 5, so *D* is 6.

4. **C** Counting up from 1, *C* is 3 and *D* is 6. Subtract 3 from 6 to get a difference of 3. Another option is to count by looking at the figure. Remember to count the number of spaces in between the two points, not the number of lines. There are three spaces between *C* and *D*, so the distance is 3.

5. **C** Use the numbers given to determine the unlabeled tick marks. Going from 0 to 5, there are 4 lines in between, so they are 1, 2, 3, and 4. Notice that point *P* is in between 2 and 3. The only answer choice between 2 and 3 is (C), 2.5, so it must be the answer.

6. The distance between point *Q* and point *P* is **greater than** 3 units.

   Count the spaces between *Q* and *P*. There is a little bit more than 3 spaces. Another option is to count up from *Q*, which is at –1. 3 spaces up from –1 is –1 + 3 = 2. Since *P* is a little more than 2, the distance is greater than 3 units.

7. **C** The best way to solve this problem is to use process of elimination. From looking at the figure, putting a point between 0 and 1 would not be in the middle of *Q* and *P*, which is what "midpoint" means, so (A) cannot be correct. If the point is at 0, it will be 1 unit away from *Q* and more than 2 units away from *P*, so since that's not the middle, (B) can't be right. For (D), if the point is at 1, it will be 2 units from *Q* but less than 2 units from *P*, so that doesn't work. Therefore, the midpoint

must be between 0 and 1, answer choice (C). To solve mathematically, find the distance from Q to P. By counting the spaces, it is a distance of 3.5. Since the midpoint is the same distance from each point, divide 3.5 by 2 to get 1.75. The midpoint must be 1.75 units away from each point. Going 1.75 units to the right of Q, the point must be between 0 and 1.

8. **D** First find where point R is. It is to the left of 0, so it is a negative number. Since there are three lines between 0 and –4, those lines are, from right to left, –1, –2, and –3. So, the line just to the left of 0 is –1 and the next one is –2. Since point R is right between those two lines, it must be at –1.5. Now, be careful. Although that is the point, a distance is always positive. Therefore, the distance from 0 to R is 1.5.

9.

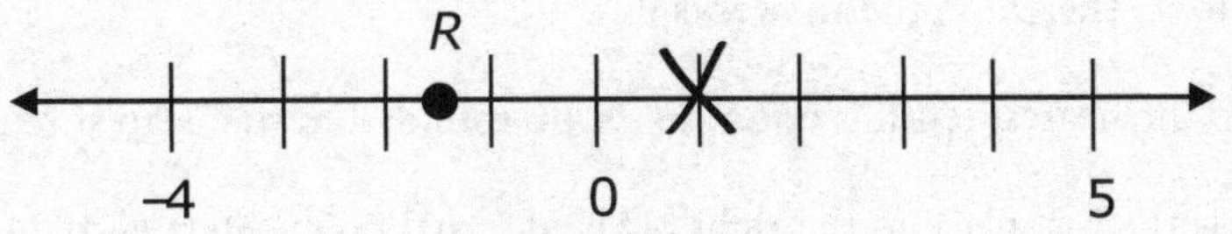

First find the distance from –1 to 3. Since –1 to 0 is 1 unit and 0 to 3 is another 3 units, they are a total of 4 units apart. Therefore, the number in the middle is 2 units away from each of them. 2 units to the left of 3 or 2 units to the right of –1 is 1.

10. **B** First determine what each line represents on the figure. The number line shows the points 0 and 1 with lines in between. Look for the line representing $\frac{1}{2}$, which is exactly in the middle of 0 and 1. Notice that point M is between 0 and $\frac{1}{2}$. The number that is exactly between 0 and $\frac{1}{2}$ is $\frac{1}{4}$, so that means point M is $\frac{1}{4}$. Another way to think about it is that there are 4 spaces between 0 and 1 in this number line, so it is counting by one-fourths. Since point M is one space away from 0, it is at $\frac{1}{4}$.

11. $\mathbf{-\frac{1}{2}}$ As determined in question 10, the lines each count $\frac{1}{4}$. Point L is two lines to the left of 0, which means it is $-\frac{2}{4}$. $-\frac{2}{4}$ simplifies to be $-\frac{1}{2}$ by dividing the top and bottom of the fraction by 2.

12. **A** The easiest way to solve this one is to use the answer choices. Try choice (A). If WX is 4 units, according to the equation, twice that number gives the lengths of XY and YZ. Therefore, XY and YZ are each 8. This leads to a total of $4 + 8 + 8 = 20$. Since the problem says the total distance WZ is 20, this is the correct answer. Trying the other answer choices would make the total distance greater than 20, so they can't be correct. Another option is to set up an equation, using x (or any variable) for the unknown distance WX: $x + 2x + 2x = 20$, since the other two pieces are each twice as much as x. Then combine like terms: $5x = 20$ and divide both sides by 5: $x = 4$, so WX is 4.

Rounding Off Drill

1. **246.9** The tenths place is the first decimal place to the right of the 0. To round to that place, look at the place to the right. That number is 4. 4 rounds down to 0, so the 9 in the tenths place stays the same and everything after becomes 0. With decimals it is not necessary to write 0s at the end, but it is okay if you do. The number has the same value either way.

2. **C** Since the calculator is not allowed, make sure to put the 2 in the correct place since it is the only one that does not have a decimal point. Whole numbers don't show the decimal point, but it should go directly after the number: 2 can be written as 2.0 since there are no extra tenths. The total of the four numbers is 9.8. Since it needs to be rounded to the nearest whole, look at the number in the tenths place, 8. Since 8 is greater than 4, it rounds up, so 9.8 rounds up to 10 rather than rounding down to 9. Therefore, the answer is (C).

3. 24.65 rounded to the nearest tenth is **equal to** 24.66 rounded to the nearest tenth.

   The tenths place is the first place to the right of the decimal point. Start with 24.65 rounded to the nearest tenth. Look at the hundredths place, which is the next one to the right. 5 rounds up, so the 6 in the tenths place changes to a 7 and the number becomes 24.7. Now round 24.66 to the nearest tenth. The 6 in the hundredths place rounds up, so again the tenths place increases from 6 to 7, making the number 24.7. Therefore, these numbers are equal when they are rounded to the tenths place.

4. **2,000** and **2,368.5**

   For the first part, note which is the thousands place. It is the place to the left of the comma where the 2 is. Now look to the right of that place to see the number 3. Since 3 is less than 5, it rounds down, so the 2 stays the same and everything to the right turns to a 0. This makes 2,368.47 round to 2,000 when rounded to the nearest thousand. For the second part, find the tenths place—it is the place just to the right of the decimal point where the 4 is. Look to the right to see the number 7. 7 rounds up, so the 4 changes to a 5 and everything to the right becomes a 0, making it 2,368.50. Zeroes at the end of decimals don't matter, so another way of writing this is 2,368.5.

5. **C** Divide 150 by 12 since the cupcakes come in boxes of 12. 150 ÷ 12 = 12.5. However, since the cupcakes are only sold in boxes of 12, it's not possible to buy .5 of a box. In this case, it is necessary to round up because 12 boxes will not be enough—that would only be 144 cupcakes. It is okay to have extra cupcakes, but not to have too few cupcakes. Therefore, 12.5 rounds up to 13 and 13 boxes will need to be purchased.

6. **B** The best way to solve this is to use process of elimination. Check (B). To round to the nearest whole, find the number in the ones place: 4. The 6 to the right of it rounds up, so the 4 changes to a 5. Choice (B), then, is 235, which is greater than (A), so eliminate (A). Now check (C): 3 is in the tens place and the 4 to the right rounds down, so 3 stays the same and the answer is 230. This is less than (B), so eliminate it. For (D), 2 is in the hundreds place and the 3 to the right rounds down, so 2 stays the same and it rounds to 200. Again this is less than (B), so eliminate it and choose (B).

Addition and Subtraction Drill

1. **C** Adding a negative number is the same as just subtracting. Therefore, the problem could be written as 22 – 5, and the answer is 17.

2. **B** Think about where –15 is on the number line. Now, since 7 is being added, move 7 spaces to the right, since addition always goes to the right on the number line. 7 spaces to the right of –15 is –8.

3. **–22** Adding a negative number is the same as subtracting, so this problem can be written as –10 – 12. Think about where –10 is on the number line. Since this is subtraction, it moves to the left because subtraction always goes to the left on the number line. Moving 12 spaces to the left from –10 results in –22.

4. 12 + (–6) is **equal to** 12 – 6.

   Adding a negative number is the same as subtracting, so 12 + (–6) is the same as 12 – 6. Therefore, these two expressions are equal.

5. **D** Two negative signs become a positive sign, so a simpler way of writing this expression is 22 + 5, which equals 27.

6. **–7** Use process of elimination here. –8 + –8 is another way of writing –8 – 8. Moving 8 spaces to the left from –8 results in –16, which is not correct. –8 + –7 = –8 – 7, and moving to the left 7 spaces from –8 equals –15, so this is the correct answer. –8 + 7 moves to the right 7 spaces from –8 for an answer of –1. –8 + 8 = 0.

7. **B** Subtracting a negative number is the same as adding because two negative signs cancel out and become positive. Rewrite the expression as –9 + 2. Now move to the right two spaces from –9 to get –7.

8. **C** Start with the number –5.45. Since Marcus is depositing money, the number 30 is being added to –5.45. The problem is –5.45 + 30. Moving right on the number line 30 spaces will result in a positive answer, so eliminate (A) and (B). (C) can be chosen through process of elimination because the answer can't be more than 30, since the starting number is less than 0. Using the calculator is also a good way to solve.

9. **–200** The starting number is 400. If the contestant gets 3 questions wrong and each wrong answer is –200 points, this is a total of –600 points. Therefore, the problem is 400 – 600. Use the calculator or think about it like 4 – 6, which is moving 6 spaces to the left from 4 and results in –2. Therefore, 400 – 600 = –200.

10. **A** The starting number is –36. Since Alex's number is less than that number, this is a subtraction problem: –36 – 23. Subtraction moves left on the number line, so the answer must be (A) as it is the only option that is to the left of (less than) –36.

Multiplication and Division Drill

1. **A** Remember that a negative times a positive always equals a negative. Next, do 9×6 with mental math or on the calculator to get 54, which makes the answer –54.

2. **300** Two negatives cancel out to make a positive, so the answer will just be the positive answer to 20×15, which is 300.

3. $-8{,}967 \times 1{,}248$ is **less than** $-43{,}214 \times -1{,}063$.

   Don't try to calculate the answers—it would take forever since the calculator is not allowed. Remember that a negative times a positive equals a negative, so the first expression will have a negative answer. A negative times a negative always equals a positive, so the second expression will have a positive answer. Since a positive number is always greater than a negative number, the first expression is less than the second.

4. **B** Remember that a positive divided by a negative, or a negative divided by a positive, results in a negative answer, so (C) and (D) must be wrong. Since $354 \div 12 = 29.5$, the answer is –29.5.

5. **–64** Use the answer choices to do process of elimination. $-64 \div 8 = -8$ because $64 \div 8 = 8$ and one negative sign will make the answer negative. This means that any value that is not negative couldn't be the right answer. $-54 \div 8 = -6.75$, and $-8 \div 8 = -1$.

6. **A** The word "each" means that this is a multiplication problem. 5 degrees per hour × 3 hours = a total decrease of 15 degrees. Since this is a decrease, the *change* would be described as –15 degrees.

Order of Operations Drill

1. **C** For order of operations, multiplication and division come before addition and subtraction. Start by multiplying $4 \times 5 = 20$. Then add 3: $20 + 3 = 23$.

2. **B** Remember that multiplication and division come before addition and subtraction. Start by multiplying $3 \times 10 = 30$. Now rewrite the problem as $12 + 30 = 42$.

3. **18** Start with the parentheses. $4 + (-2)$ is the same as $4 - 2$, which equals 2. Now rewrite the problem as $9 \times 2 = 18$.

4. **B** Start with the parentheses. Within the parentheses, multiplication comes before addition, so first multiply $5 \times 2 = 10$, then add 1: $10 + 1 = 11$. Now rewrite the equation as $23 - 11 = 12$.

5. **D** Start with the parentheses. Subtracting a negative is the same as adding because two negatives equal a positive. Thus, the parentheses can be rewritten as $8 + 2$, which equals 10. Now rewrite the problem as $2^3 \times 10$. The next step is to do exponents. $2^3 = 2 \times 2 \times 2 = 8$. The problem is now $8 \times 10 = 80$.

6. **–21** Start with the parentheses. $3 + 4 = 7$. Now rewrite the problem as $7 \times 6 \div (-2)$. Multiplication and division go from left to right, so solve for 7×6 and rewrite as $42 \div (-2)$. $42 \div 2 = 21$, but since there is a negative sign, the answer is –21.

7. **C** Start with the innermost parentheses. $2 \times 3 = 6$, so rewrite the expression as $(20 - 6)^2$. Now solve for the parentheses: $20 - 6 = 14$. Now the problem is $14^2 = 196$.

8. **4** Since the only operations in this problem are addition and subtraction, work from left to right. $6 + (-9)$ is the same as $6 - 9$, which equals –3. Now rewrite the problem as $-3 - (-2) + 5$. Subtracting a negative is the same as adding, so rewrite as $-3 + 2 + 5$. $-3 + 2 = -1$ and $-1 + 5 = 4$.

9. **22** Start with the parentheses. $12 - 6$ is 6 and $3 - 2 = 1$. Rewrite the problem as $2 \times 6^1 + 10$. The next step is exponents. $6^1 = 6$ because any number to the first power is the number. Now the problem is $2 \times 6 + 10$. Multiplication comes next, so $2 \times 6 = 12$. Now $12 + 10 = 22$.

10. **C** Start with the parentheses. $6 + 6 = 12$. Now exponents: $12^2 = 12 \times 12 = 144$ and $2^3 = 2 \times 2 \times 2 = 8$. Now the problem is $\frac{144}{8}$. The fraction bar means division, so divide 144 by 8 to get 18.

11. **A** Start with exponents. 1 to any power is 1, so $1^{18} = 1$. Now multiply and divide from left to right before adding or subtracting. $2 \times 6 = 12$ and then $12 \div 3 = 4$. Rewrite the problem as $45 + 4 + 28 - 21 + 1$. Now add and subtract from left to right: $49 + 28 - 21 + 1$, then $77 - 21 + 1$, then $56 + 1$, and finally 57.

12. **30** Start with the innermost parentheses. $4 + 2 = 6$ and $20 \div 2 = 10$. Rewrite the problem as $\left(\frac{5 \times 6}{10 \div 2}\right)^2 - 6^1$. Next do the top and bottom of the fraction in parentheses. $5 \times 6 = 30$ and $10 \div 2 = 5$. Now rewrite as $\left(\frac{30}{5}\right)^2 - 6^1$. Then solve the fraction in parentheses: $30 \div 5 = 6$. Rewrite as $6^2 - 6^1$. Don't skip any steps here. Exponents can't be added or subtracted, so they need to be solved individually here. $6^2 = 6 \times 6 = 36$ and $6^1 = 6$. Now the problem is $36 - 6 = 30$.

Commutative and Distributive Properties Drill

1. ***xy + xz***

To change this expression, use the distributive property. Since the x is right on the outside of the parentheses, it is being multiplied by each term in the parentheses. $x \times y = xy$ and and $x \times z$ is xz, so this is equal to $xy + xz$. Another strategy is to pick numbers for x, y, and z and see what happens. Say $x = 2$, $y = 3$, and $z = 4$. Then the problem is $2(3+4) = 2(7) = 14$. Then check each answer choice to see whether it equals 14. $xy + z = 2 \times 3 + 4 = 6 + 4 = 10$. This can't be right because it's not 14. $x + y + z = 2 + 3 + 4 = 9$, which also doesn't work. $xy + xz = 2 \times 3 + 2 \times 4 = 6 + 8 = 14$. This works, and it's the correct answer. $y + xz = 3 + 2 \times 4 = 3 + 8 = 11$, so that doesn't work. $xyz = 2 \times 3 \times 4 = 6 \times 4 = 24$, so it doesn't work. $z + xy = 4 + (2 \times 3) = 4 \times 6 = 10$, so it doesn't work.

2. **A** Subtraction, unlike multiplication and division, is not commutative. This means that, for instance, while 5 + 3 and 3 + 5 equal the same value, 5 – 3 and 3 – 5 do not equal the same value. (A) rearranges the answer choices in this way, which will not be equal. Based on the original problem, *a* must have a + in front of it, *b* must have a – in front of it, and *c* must also have a – in front of it. Choices (B), (C), and (D) do this correctly, but (A) does not. Another option is to pick numbers for *a*, *b*, and *c*. Say $a = 8$, $b = 2$, and $c = 3$. Then $a - b - c = 8 - 2 - 3 = 6 - 3 = 3$. Check the answer choices to see what equals 3. For (A), 3 – 2 – 8 equals a negative number, so it doesn't equal 3. The other answer choices do, so (A) is the one that doesn't work.

3. **4** One option is to multiply both numbers by $\frac{1}{3}$ as indicated in the problem $\frac{1}{3} \times \frac{5}{1}$ can just be written as $\frac{5}{3}$. $\frac{1}{3} \times \frac{7}{1} = \frac{7}{3}$. Then $\frac{5}{3} + \frac{7}{3} = \frac{12}{3} = 4$. Another option is to realize that this involves the distributive property. Since both things are being multiplied by $\frac{1}{3}$, it is possible to add $5 + 7 = 12$ and then multiply that by $\frac{1}{3}$ to get 4.

4. **C** Think of this problem as having an invisible 1 to the left of the parentheses, multiplying each thing in the parentheses by positive 1. Distribute this to get $20 + 1x + 5$ or just $20 + x + 5$. Now combine like terms to get $25 + x$ or $x + 25$.

5. **B** This is the reverse of the distributive property. Both *x* and *y* are being multiplied by 10, so it is possible to factor out the 10 from both. This means writing it like $10(x + y) = 80$. Now, since two things are being multiplied together, divide both sides by 10 to be left with $x + y = 8$. This is what the question asks for, so it is the answer. Notice that it isn't clear exactly what *x* and *y* are—they just have to add up to 8. Another strategy is to guess numbers for *x* and *y*. If *x* is 4, $40 + 10y = 80$, subtract 40 to get $10y = 40$, divide by 10 to get $y = 4$. So *x* could be 4 and *y* could also be 4, for a total of 8. Try $x = 2$. $20 + 10y = 80$, $10y = 60$, $y = 6$. In this case $x = 2$ and $y = 6$. Again they add up to 8, so it is clear that (B) is the answer.

6. $\mathbf{\frac{4x}{x+1}}$

This is tricky. Unlike multiplication, it isn't possible to divide by the first part of the term and then divide by the second part of the term. $\frac{4x}{x+1}$ is simply changing the division sign to a fraction bar, which is the same thing. This can't be simplified further—denominators can't be split up. Also remember that division isn't commutative (doesn't give the same result when you switch the numbers), so an answer like $(x + 1) \div 4x$ won't be equal. Another option to help prove the right answer is to choose a number for *x* and see what happens. If $x = 2$, $4(2) \div (2 + 1) = 8 \div 3$ or $\frac{8}{3}$. Check the options to see what equals $\frac{8}{3}$. $(x + 1) \div 4$ will be $(2 + 1) \div 4 = \frac{3}{4}$, which isn't $\frac{8}{3}$, so it doesn't work. $4x \div x + 1$ is $4(2) \div 2 + 1 = 8 \div 2 + 1 = 4 + 1 = 5$. This isn't $\frac{8}{3}$, so it doesn't work. 5 isn't $\frac{8}{3}$, so that doesn't work. $(x + 1) \div 4x$ is $(2 + 1) \div 4(2) = 3 \div 8$ or $\frac{3}{8}$, so that doesn't work. $x + 1 \div 4x$ is $2 + 1 \div 4(2) = 2 + 1 \div 8 = 2 + \frac{1}{8}$ or $2\frac{1}{8}$. This doesn't work. $\frac{4x}{x+1} = \frac{4(2)}{2+1} = \frac{8}{3}$, so that does work. $4 + 4x = 4 + 4(2) = 4 + 8 = 12$, so it doesn't work.

7. **A** Start by distributing the $2x$ to each item in $(x + 2)$. $2x \times x = 2x^2$ and $2x \times 2 = 4x$. Now distribute the -5 to the $(4x - 3)$: $-5 \times 4x = -20x$ and $-5 \times -3 = 15$. Now put it all together: $2x^2 + 4x - 20x + 15$. Combine like terms, which are the $4x$ and the $-20x$. $4x - 20x = -16x$. The expression is equal to $2x^2 - 16x + 15$. A second option is to pick a number for x, such as $x = 2$. Solve $2x(x + 2) - 5(4x - 3)$ when $x = 2$: $2(2)(2 + 2) - 5(4 \times 2 - 3) = 4(4) - 5(8 - 3) = 16 - 5(5) = 16 - 25 = -9$. Now check the answer choices to see which one equals -9 when $x = 2$. The only one that does is (A).

8. **78** One option is to solve for each term individually, but the faster way is to realize that each term includes a number being multiplied by the same thing, $(4 + 2)$. Add the outside numbers to get $5 + 6 + 2 = 13$. Thus, the problem can be written as $13(4 + 2)$. Now solve for the parentheses: $4 + 2 = 6$, and $13(6) = 78$.

9. **6** Don't try to solve the equation for x. Pay attention to what the question is asking for and notice that 5 is a common factor of every term. Thus, factor out a 5 from each term to get $5(2x^2 + x - 3) = 30$. Notice that the expression in the parentheses is what the question asks for. Simply divide both sides by 5 to be left with $2x^2 + x - 3 = 6$.

10. **B** This problem is testing knowledge of the commutative property. Remember that addition and multiplication expressions are the same when the numbers are moved around: $5 + 2 = 2 + 5$ and $6 \times 3 = 3 \times 6$. However, subtraction and division are not commutative. $5 - 2$ is not the same as $2 - 5$. Thus, (B) is false and is the correct answer.

11. **D** It is possible to distribute the ¾ to each term, but why deal with fractions more than is necessary? Since both items are being multiplied by $\frac{3}{4}$, add the terms in the parentheses. $x + 3 + (3x + 5) = 4x + 8$. The problem can be rewritten as $\frac{3}{4}(4x + 8)$. Now distribute the $\frac{3}{4}$: $\frac{3}{4} \times \frac{4}{1} = \frac{12}{4} = 3$, so $\frac{3}{4} \times 4x = 3x$. $\frac{3}{4} \times \frac{8}{1} = \frac{24}{4} = 6$. The expression, therefore, is equal to $3x + 6$.

12. **B** This question doesn't require any calculations, just an understanding of the commutative property. The terms can be rearranged as long as the ones that are positive remain positive and the ones that are negative remain negative. Answer choice (B) makes the 7 positive and the $10x^2$ negative, so it can't be equal, which means it is the right answer.

Simplifying Fractions Drill

1. $\frac{2}{3}$ The only common factor of 10 and 15 is 5. $10 \div 5 = 2$ and $15 \div 5 = 3$.

2. $\frac{1}{2}$ The greatest common factor (GCF) of 4 and 8 is 4. $4 \div 4 = 1$ and $8 \div 4 = 2$.

3. $\frac{1}{12}$ The GCF of 10 and 120 is 10. Any number that ends with a 0 has 10 as a factor. $10 \div 10 = 1$ and $120 \div 10 = 12$.

4. $\frac{7}{17}$ This fraction is already in simplest form. The factors of 7 are 1 and 7, and the factors of 17 are 1 and 17. Since these numbers have no common factor besides 1, the fraction cannot be simplified.

5. $\frac{2}{9}$ Since both numbers end in two zeros, they each have 100 as a factor. $200 \div 100 = 2$ and $900 \div 100 = 9$.

6. $\frac{4}{5}$ The only common factor of 8 and 10 is 2. $8 \div 2 = 4$ and $10 \div 2 = 5$.

7. $\frac{24}{25}$ No need to write out all the factors of such large numbers. Since 144 and 150 are both even, start by dividing top and bottom by 2 to get $\frac{72}{75}$. Now realize that 72 and 75 are both divisible by 3. An easy way to determine whether a value is divisible by 3 or 9 is to add up the digits and if that sum is divisible by $\frac{3}{9}$, so is the original number. $72 \div 3 = 24$ and $75 \div 3 = 25$. 24 and 25 have no common factors, so this is simplest form. Alternatively, start with the GCF of 144 and 150, which is 6.

8. $\frac{4}{5}$ You probably already knew that 8 is a factor of both 64 and 80, so start by dividing top and bottom by 8 to get $\frac{8}{10}$. 8 and 10 both have 2 as a factor since they are both even, so divide both by 2 to get $\frac{4}{5}$. Alternatively, start with the GCF of 16.

9. $\frac{4}{3}$ The only common factor of 12 and 9 is 3. $12 \div 3 = 4$ and $9 \div 3 = 3$.

10. 5 The GCF of 30 and 6 is 6. $30 \div 6 = 5$ and $6 \div 6 = 1$. $\frac{5}{1}$ is correct, but the simplest way is just to write 5.

11. $\frac{21}{8}$ The factors of 21 are 1, 3, 7, and 21. The factors of 8 are 1, 2, 4, and 8. Since these two numbers have no common factors besides 1, the fraction is already in simplest form.

12. $\frac{1}{2}$ The only factors of 19 are 1 and 19. 19 goes into 38 twice, so this simplifies to $\frac{1}{2}$.

Adding and Subtracting Fractions Drill

1. $\mathbf{\frac{3}{5}}$ Since the two fractions already have a common denominator, simply add the numerators.

2. $\mathbf{\frac{4}{5}}$ Since the two fractions already have a common denominator, simply subtract the numerators to get $\frac{8}{10}$. Since both of these are even, divide top and bottom by 2 to get the simplified answer of $\frac{4}{5}$.

3. $\mathbf{\frac{3}{4}}$ The least common multiple (LCM) of 2 and 4 is 4. $\frac{1}{2}=\frac{2}{4}$, so add $\frac{2}{4}+\frac{1}{4}=\frac{3}{4}$.

4. $\mathbf{\frac{1}{4}}$ The LCM of 2 and 4 is 4. $\frac{1}{2}=\frac{2}{4}$, so subtract $\frac{3}{4}-\frac{2}{4}=\frac{1}{4}$.

5. $\mathbf{\frac{2}{15}}$ The LCM of 5 and 3 is 15. $\frac{4}{5}=\frac{12}{15}$ and $\frac{2}{3}=\frac{10}{15}$. $\frac{12}{15}-\frac{10}{15}=\frac{2}{15}$. These have no common factors so it is in simplest form as is.

6. $\mathbf{\frac{47}{6}}$ **or** $\mathbf{7\frac{5}{6}}$

   Remember that a whole number can be written as a fraction by putting it over 1. So, $7=\frac{7}{1}$. Now change $\frac{7}{1}$ so that 6 is in the denominator by multiplying top and bottom by 6 to get $\frac{42}{6}$. Next, add $\frac{5}{6}+\frac{42}{6}=\frac{47}{6}$. This can also be written as a mixed number, $7\frac{5}{6}$, by dividing the numerator by the denominator.

7. $\mathbf{\frac{5}{4}}$ **or** $\mathbf{1\frac{1}{4}}$

   The LCM of 2 and 4 is 4. $\frac{1}{2}=\frac{2}{4}$. $\frac{2}{4}+\frac{3}{4}=\frac{5}{4}$. This can also be written as a mixed number, $1\frac{1}{4}$.

8. $\mathbf{-\frac{1}{12}}$ The LCM of 3 and 4 is 12. $\frac{2}{3}=\frac{8}{12}$ and $\frac{3}{4}=\frac{9}{12}$. $\frac{8}{12}-\frac{9}{12}=-\frac{1}{12}$.

9. $\mathbf{\frac{19}{44}}$ The LCM of 4 and 11 is 44. The easiest way to find this is simply to multiply 4 and 11. $\frac{1}{4}=\frac{11}{44}$ and $\frac{2}{11}=\frac{8}{44}$. $\frac{11}{44}+\frac{8}{44}=\frac{19}{44}$. These numbers have no common factors, so the fraction is in simplest form.

10. $\mathbf{\frac{5}{24}}$ The LCM of 8 and 3 is 24. $\frac{7}{8}=\frac{21}{24}$ and $\frac{2}{3}=\frac{16}{24}$. $\frac{21}{24}-\frac{16}{24}=\frac{5}{24}$.

11. $\mathbf{\frac{19}{12}}$ **or** $\mathbf{1\frac{7}{12}}$

    The LCM of 6, 2, and 4 is 12. It is okay to use a bigger number like 24, but just remember to reduce at the end. $\frac{5}{6}=\frac{10}{12}$, $\frac{1}{2}=\frac{6}{12}$, and $\frac{1}{4}=\frac{3}{12}$. $\frac{10}{12}+\frac{6}{12}+\frac{3}{12}=\frac{19}{12}$ or $1\frac{7}{12}$.

12. $\mathbf{\frac{1}{40}}$ The LCM of 10, 4, and 8 is 40. It is okay to use a bigger number like 80 or 320, but just remember to reduce at the end. $\frac{9}{10} = \frac{36}{40}$, $\frac{3}{4} = \frac{30}{40}$, and $\frac{1}{8} = \frac{5}{40}$. $\frac{36}{40} - \frac{30}{40} = \frac{6}{40}$. $\frac{6}{40} - \frac{5}{40} = \frac{1}{40}$.

Multiplying and Dividing Fractions Drill

1. $\mathbf{\frac{3}{8}}$ To multiply fractions, multiply straight across the top and straight across the bottom. 1 × 3 = 3 and 2 × 4 = 8, so the answer is $\frac{3}{8}$, which is in simplest form.

2. $\mathbf{\frac{4}{15}}$ Multiply across the top and bottom: 4 × 1 = 4 and 5 × 3 = 15, so the answer is $\frac{4}{15}$.

3. $\mathbf{\frac{3}{5}}$ To divide fractions, multiply the first fraction by the reciprocal of the second. What this means is to change the second fraction to its reciprocal, which means flip the fraction over, and then multiply. Therefore, the problem should be rewritten as $\frac{3}{10} \times \frac{2}{1}$. Now multiply across the top and bottom to get $\frac{6}{10}$. Since these are both even, divide top and bottom by 2 to get the simplified answer of $\frac{3}{5}$.

4. $\mathbf{\frac{10}{9}}$ **or** $\mathbf{1\frac{1}{9}}$

   Find the reciprocal of $\frac{3}{4}$, which is $\frac{4}{3}$. Now multiply: $\frac{5}{6} \times \frac{4}{3} = \frac{20}{18}$. Both of these are even, so divide top and bottom by 2 to simplify: $\frac{10}{9}$. This can also be written as a mixed number, $1\frac{1}{9}$.

5. $\mathbf{\frac{9}{14}}$ Multiply across the top and bottom to get $\frac{45}{70}$. Both of these are multiples of 5, so divide top and bottom by 5 to get $\frac{9}{14}$.

6. **1** Find the reciprocal of $\frac{2}{3}$, which is $\frac{3}{2}$. Now multiply $\frac{2}{3} \times \frac{3}{2} = \frac{6}{6}$, which simplifies to 1. Or, remember that any number divided by itself is always equal to 1.

7. $\mathbf{\frac{25}{9}}$ **or** $\mathbf{2\frac{7}{9}}$

   Remember that a whole number can be written as a fraction by putting it over 1. Write the problem as $\frac{5}{9} \times \frac{5}{1}$. Now multiply across the top and bottom to get $\frac{25}{9}$. 25 and 9 have no common factors, so this is in simplest form. It can also be written as a mixed number: $2\frac{7}{9}$.

8. $\frac{50}{3}$ or $16\frac{2}{3}$

Rewrite 10 as $\frac{10}{1}$. Next, find the reciprocal of $\frac{3}{5}$, which is $\frac{5}{3}$. Now rewrite the problem as $\frac{10}{1} \times \frac{5}{3} = \frac{50}{3}$. This can't be simplified, but it can be written as a mixed number: $16\frac{2}{3}$.

Converting Fractions Drill

1. **$2\frac{3}{4}$** The fraction bar represents division. Divide 11 by 4. 4 goes into 11 two times, so the whole number is 2. 2 × 4 = 8 and 11 – 8 = 3, so the remaining amount is 3 out of 4. Thus, the mixed number is $2\frac{3}{4}$.

2. **$\frac{11}{3}$** Change 3 wholes to thirds. One whole has $\frac{3}{3}$, so three wholes have $\frac{9}{3}$. Now add $\frac{9}{3} + \frac{2}{3} = \frac{11}{3}$.

3. **$1\frac{2}{3}$** Divide 10 by 6. It goes in 1 time with 4 left over, so the mixed number is $1\frac{4}{6}$. $\frac{4}{6}$ simplifies to $\frac{2}{3}$ when dividing both the top and bottom by 2.

4. **$\frac{29}{10}$** First find how many tenths are in 2 wholes. One whole has $\frac{10}{10}$, so two wholes have $\frac{20}{10}$. Now add $\frac{20}{10} + \frac{9}{10} = \frac{29}{10}$.

5. **$10\frac{1}{2}$** Divide 21 by 2. It goes in 10 times with 1 left over, so the mixed number is $10\frac{1}{2}$.

6. **$\frac{35}{4}$** First find how many fourths are in 8 wholes. One whole has $\frac{4}{4}$, so eight wholes have $\frac{32}{4}$. Now add $\frac{32}{4} + \frac{3}{4} = \frac{35}{4}$.

7. **20** Divide 100 by 5. It goes in exactly 20 times with no remainder, so it can be written as just 20.

8. **$\frac{5}{4}$** One whole has $\frac{4}{4}$, so add $\frac{4}{4} + \frac{1}{4}$ to equal $\frac{5}{4}$.

Fraction Word Problems Drill

1. **C** A whole cake is $\frac{10}{10}$. If $\frac{3}{10}$ is eaten, there is $\frac{7}{10}$ left. Next subtract another $\frac{1}{10}$ that has been eaten to get $\frac{6}{10}$. That isn't in the answer choices, so it needs to be simplified. Divide the top and bottom by 2 to get $\frac{3}{5}$.

2. **75** Start with $\frac{1}{4}$ of 100. Another way to think of this is $\frac{1}{4} \times \frac{100}{1} = \frac{100}{4} = 25$. Now be careful—this is how many students *don't* have siblings, but the question asks how many *do*. The rest of the students must have siblings, so this is 100 – 25 = 75.

3. **D** The total is 30 feet, and it's being split up into steps that are each $\frac{3}{4}$. Thus, to find how many $\frac{3}{4}$s there are in 30, divide 30 by $\frac{3}{4}$. This is the same as multiplying 30 by $\frac{4}{3}$: $\frac{30}{1} \times \frac{4}{3} = \frac{120}{3} = 40$.

4. **C** *Each* of the $5\frac{1}{3}$ grams contains 33 sprinkles, so the problem is $5\frac{1}{3} \times 33$. The best way to solve this is to change $5\frac{1}{3}$ to an improper fraction. 5 wholes = $\frac{15}{3}$, then add $\frac{1}{3}$ to equal $\frac{16}{3}$. Now multiply $\frac{16}{3} \times \frac{33}{1} = \frac{528}{3} = 176$.

5. Julia has completed a **little less** of her homework compared to Eric. In order to compare fractions, they must have the same denominator. The least common multiple of 3 and 21 is 21. Change $\frac{2}{3}$ to be out of 21 by multiplying top and bottom by 7: $\frac{14}{21}$. Now compare $\frac{14}{21}$ and $\frac{16}{21}$. $\frac{14}{21}$ is a little less than $\frac{16}{21}$. Another way to compare fractions is to change them to decimals with the calculator, when the calculator is allowed.

6. **B** The starting number is $\frac{7}{8}$. Since chocolates are being eaten, this is a subtraction problem: $\frac{7}{8} - \frac{1}{3}$. To subtract fractions, they must have the same denominator. The least common multiple of 8 and 3 is 24. $\frac{7}{8} = \frac{21}{24}$ (multiply top and bottom by 3). $\frac{1}{3} = \frac{8}{24}$ (multiply top and bottom by 8). Now subtract $\frac{21}{24} - \frac{8}{24} = \frac{13}{24}$.

7. **32** The total is 12 miles, and each lap is $\frac{3}{8}$ of a mile. Find how many times $\frac{3}{8}$ goes into 12, which means this is a division problem: $12 \div \frac{3}{8} = \frac{12}{1} \times \frac{8}{3} = \frac{96}{3} = 32$.

8. **C** The starting number is $6\frac{2}{3}$. The number is decreasing because some of the board is being cut off. This makes it a subtraction problem. Choice (D) can be eliminated right away because it is bigger than $6\frac{2}{3}$. The problem is $6\frac{2}{3} - 2\frac{1}{2}$. The best strategy is to first change both to improper fractions. 6 wholes = $\frac{18}{3}$, $\frac{18}{3} + \frac{2}{3} = \frac{20}{3}$. 2 wholes = $\frac{4}{2}$, $\frac{4}{2} + \frac{1}{2} = \frac{5}{2}$. Now the problem is $\frac{20}{3} - \frac{5}{2}$. In order to subtract, the fractions need to have a common denominator. The least common multiple of 2 and 3 is 6. $\frac{20}{3} = \frac{40}{6}$ (multiply top and bottom by 2) and $\frac{5}{2} = \frac{15}{6}$ (multiply top and bottom by 3). Now subtract $\frac{40}{6} - \frac{15}{6} = \frac{25}{6}$. Notice the answer choices are mixed numbers, so convert

this back to a mixed number by dividing 25 by 6. It goes in 4 times with a remainder of 1 out of 6. Thus, it is equal to $4\frac{1}{6}$.

9. $\mathbf{\frac{2}{3}, \frac{3}{2}, \frac{8}{5}, \frac{7}{2}}$

Start by changing the improper fractions to mixed numbers. $\frac{7}{2} = 3\frac{1}{2}$. $\frac{2}{3}$ is less than 1. $\frac{8}{5} = 1\frac{3}{5}$. $\frac{3}{2} = 1\frac{1}{2}$. $\frac{2}{3}$ must be the smallest number because it's less than 1. $\frac{7}{2}$ is the biggest because $3\frac{1}{2}$ is bigger than either of the other two, which are both between 1 and 2. Now compare $\frac{3}{5}$ to $\frac{1}{2}$. Using a common denominator of 10, $\frac{3}{5} = \frac{6}{10}$ and $\frac{1}{2} = \frac{5}{10}$. Therefore, $1\frac{3}{5}$ is greater than $1\frac{1}{2}$, so $\frac{3}{2}$ must come before $\frac{8}{5}$.

10. **A** The part of the whole that is purple is $\frac{2}{3}$. $\frac{1}{4}$ is a part of that, so this is a multiplication problem: $\frac{2}{3} \times \frac{1}{4} = \frac{2}{12}$. Simplify by dividing top and bottom by 2 to get $\frac{1}{6}$.

11. **24** The starting number is 48. $\frac{5}{6}$ of the 48 books are non-fiction, so multiply $\frac{5}{6} \times \frac{48}{1} = \frac{240}{6} = 40$. 40 books are non-fiction. Now, the problem states that of these 40, $\frac{2}{5}$ are science books. $\frac{2}{5} \times \frac{40}{1} = \frac{80}{5} = 16$. But, be careful. The problem asks how many of the 40 non-fiction books are NOT science books. Subtract 40 – 16 to get 24 non-fiction books that are not science books.

12. **A** The starting number is $6\frac{1}{4}$ and it's being cut up into 10 equal pieces, so this is a division problem: $6\frac{1}{4} \div 10$. First, $6\frac{1}{4}$ needs to be changed to an improper fraction. 6 wholes = $\frac{24}{4}$. $\frac{24}{4} + \frac{1}{4} = \frac{25}{4}$. Now the problem is $\frac{25}{4} \div \frac{10}{1} = \frac{25}{4} \times \frac{1}{10} = \frac{25}{40}$. Now divide top and bottom by 5 to get $\frac{5}{8}$. Another strategy is to think about the fact that it is about 6 divided by 10. The result is going to be less than 1 since 6 is less than 10, so the answer must be less than 1. Only (A) is less than 1.

Adding and Subtracting Decimals Drill

1. **6.3** Line up the decimal points and add normally. 9 + 4 = 13, carry the 1, and 1 + 3 + 2 = 6. Remember the decimal point stays in the same place in the answer.

2. **4.57** Start by rewriting the 6 with the same number of decimal places as the 1.43. 6 can be written as 6.00. Now line up the decimal points and subtract 6.00 – 1.43. Start by borrowing from the 6 to make the 0 to the right into a 10, then borrow from that 10 and make it a 9, turning the last 0 into a 10. See the figure below.

$$\begin{array}{r} \scriptstyle 9 \\ \scriptstyle 5\ \cancel{10}\ 10 \\ \cancel{6}.\cancel{0}\cancel{0} \\ -\ 1.43 \\ \hline 4.57 \end{array}$$

3. **15.7** Change 12 to 12.0 so it matches the number of digits in 3.7. Now line up the decimal points and add 12.0 + 3.7 to get 15.7

4. **7.5** Change 3 to 3.0 to see where the decimal point is. Now line up the decimal points and subtract 10.5 – 3.0. Borrow from the 1 and change it to a 0, making the 0 to its right into a 10. See the figure below.

$$\begin{array}{r} \scriptstyle 0\ 10 \\ \cancel{1}\cancel{0}.5 \\ -\ 3.0 \\ \hline 7.5 \end{array}$$

5. **C** Since this is multiple choice, use the answer choices to help. The question uses the phrase *more than*, so it is an addition problem, and the answer is going to be *more than* 16.87. Eliminate (A). Now consider that the problem asks to add a little more than 2 to 16.87. This means the answer must be greater than 18, so eliminate (B), but it won't be as big as 40, so eliminate (D). Only (C) is left. Alternatively, solve 16.87 + 2.40 by lining up the decimal points.

6. **10.68** Start by doing process of elimination in the answer choices. Estimate the numbers in the problem as 26 – _____ = 16. The answer should be close to 10, so eliminate 1.068, 24.738, and 106.8. Now check each answer choice. Do 26.30 – 9.68. The result is 16.62, which is not 15.62, so eliminate it. Try 26.30 – 10.68. In this case, the answer is 15.62, so this is the correct answer. Alternatively, subtract 26.30 – 15.62 to get 10.68.

Multiplying and Dividing Decimals Drill

1. **23.4** Set up the problem as though it didn't have decimals. Then multiply normally to get 2340. Remember that the second row of multiplication always has to have a 0 first. Since there are two digits to the right of the decimal points in the problem, move to the left two spaces to get the answer of 23.4. See the figure below.

$$\begin{array}{r} 3.6 \\ \times\ 6.5 \\ \hline 180 \\ +\,2160 \\ \hline 23.40 \end{array}$$

2. **9.27** Set up the problem like a regular long division problem. The decimal goes in the same place in the answer as it is in the number under the long division sign. Then divide normally. See the figure below.

$$\begin{array}{r} 9.27 \\ 2\,\overline{)\,18.54} \\ -18 \\ \hline 05 \\ -\ \ 4 \\ \hline 14 \\ -14 \\ \hline 0 \end{array}$$

3. **10.8** Set up the problem as though it didn't have decimals. Don't worry about lining up the decimals or adding any extra zeroes. In fact, it's easier if you get rid of the extra 0 before the decimal point in 0.9. Multiply normally to get 108. There is one digit to the right of the decimal point in this problem, so move the decimal point to the left one space to get the answer of 10.8. See the figure below.

$$\begin{array}{r} 12 \\ \times\ .9 \\ \hline 10.8 \end{array}$$

4. **6.3** Set up the problem as long division. Now, since this problem divides by a decimal, move the decimal place in 2.8 to the right one to get 28. Do the same in 17.64 to get 176.4. Now it is easier to divide since the divisor, or the number outside the division sign, is a whole number. Remember that the decimal point in the answer will be in the same place it is in the dividend, or number under the long division sign. See the figure below.

$$\begin{array}{r} {}^{4} \\ 28 \\ \times\ 6 \\ \hline 168 \\ {}^{2} \\ 28 \\ \times\ 3 \\ \hline 84 \end{array} \qquad \begin{array}{r} 6.3 \\ 28.\overline{)176.4} \\ -168\downarrow \\ \hline 84 \\ -84 \\ \hline 0 \end{array}$$

5. **$11.39**

Since the friends are *sharing* the cost, this is a division problem: 56.95 ÷ 5. Set up the problem with long division and put the decimal point in the right spot for the answer. See the figure below.

$$\begin{array}{r} 11.39 \\ 5\overline{)56.95} \\ -5\downarrow \\ \hline 06 \\ -5\downarrow \\ \hline 19 \\ -15\downarrow \\ \hline 45 \\ -45 \\ \hline 0 \end{array}$$

6. **195.36**

This is a multiplication problem because there are 7.4 gallons and *each one* can make the car run for 26.4 miles. Multiply 26.4 × 7.4. Set up the problem like normal multiplication, ignoring the decimals. Don't forget to put the 0 in the second row. Since there are two numbers to the right of the decimal point, move the decimal two spaces to the left in the answer. See the figure below.

$$\begin{array}{r} {}^{4\ 2} \\ 26.4 \\ \times\ 7.4 \\ \hline 1056 \\ +18480 \\ \hline 195.36 \end{array}$$

7. **A** This is a multiplication problem, since it says *times the temperature.* The problem is 80.8 × .9. Set it up like a normal multiplication problem and multiply. Since there are two digits after the decimal point, move the decimal point two digits to the left in the answer. See the figure below.

$$\begin{array}{r} ^{7} \\ 80.8 \\ \times \quad .9 \\ \hline 72.72 \end{array}$$

8. **B** One option is to use the answer choices to avoid having to do division. If 10 people are served 1.5 sandwiches each, this is 10 × 1.5 = 15 sandwiches. This is too small, since there are 150 sandwiches, so eliminate (A). Now try (B). If 100 people are served 1.5 sandwiches each, this is 100 × 1.5 = 150 sandwiches. Since this is exactly how many sandwiches there are, this is the correct answer and (C) and (D) are too big. Another option is to divide 150 ÷ 1.5. To do this, move the decimal point over one space in 1.5 to make it 15, so that it is no longer a decimal. Do the same to 150, which makes it 1500 (a zero fills in the extra decimal spot). Now solve 1500 ÷ 15 with long division. See the figure below.

$$\begin{array}{r} 100 \\ 15.\overline{)1500.} \\ -15 \\ \hline 00 \\ -00 \\ \hline 00 \\ -00 \\ \hline 0 \end{array}$$

Percents Drill

1. **8** 10% means $\frac{10}{100}$ because percent means out of 100. Do $\frac{10}{100} \times \frac{80}{1}$ as a normal multiplying fractions problem. This results in $\frac{800}{100}$, which simplifies to just 8. Alternatively, solve using mental math. To find 10% of a number, move the decimal place one space to the left. For 80, this results in 8.0 or just 8.

2. **39.5** 10% means $\frac{10}{100}$, so do $\frac{10}{100} \times \frac{395}{1}$ to get $\frac{3950}{100}$. To divide by 100, move the decimal place two spaces to the left, resulting in 39.5. Alternatively, to find 10% of a number using mental math, move the decimal one space to the left. For 395, this results in 39.5.

3. **12** 30% means $\frac{30}{100}$, so do $\frac{30}{100} \times \frac{40}{1}$. This results in $\frac{1200}{100}$, which simplifies to 12. Alternatively, solve using mental math. Find 10% of 40 by moving the decimal one space to the left—the result is 4.0. To find 30%, multiply that by 3 because 30 is 3 times 10. Thus, $4 \times 3 = 12$.

4. **36** 45% means $\frac{45}{100}$. To solve by hand, do $\frac{45}{100} \times \frac{80}{1}$. Multiply across to get $\frac{3600}{100}$ and simplify to get 36. Alternatively, solve using the calculator by doing $\frac{45}{100}$ and then multiply by 80.

5. **196.8** It is possible to do this by hand, but you aren't likely to see such a difficult percent problem in the non-calculator section. The best way to solve is to use the calculator to do $\frac{96}{100}$ and then multiply by 205.

6. **120** Since this problem uses a simple percent, 50%, it's easiest to solve using mental math. 50% is the same as $\frac{1}{2}$. Ask: 60 is one-half of what number? The answer is 120. To solve mathematically, translate the words to math. 'Is' means =, % means $\frac{}{100}$, 'of' means ×, and 'what number' or 'a certain number' means 'x.' Thus, this problem can be written as $60 = \frac{50}{100} \times x$. Now simplify $\frac{50}{100}$ to $\frac{1}{2}$. $60 = \frac{1}{2}x$. Now divide 60 by $\frac{1}{2}$, which is the same as multiplying by $\frac{2}{1}$ (the reciprocal). This results in 120.

7. **240** Write this problem using math: $24 = \frac{10}{100}x$. Simplify $\frac{10}{100}$ to $\frac{1}{10}$ by dividing top and bottom by 10. Now the problem is $24 = \frac{1}{10}x$. Divide 24 by $\frac{1}{10}$, so multiply 24 by $\frac{10}{1}$ to get 240.

8. **400** Write this problem using math: $80 = \frac{20}{100}x$. Simplify $\frac{20}{100}$. Since both numbers end in a 0, top and bottom can be divided by 10 to get $\frac{2}{10}$. Now both are even, so divide top and bottom by 2 to get $\frac{1}{5}$. Now the problem is $80 = \frac{1}{5}x$. Divide 80 by $\frac{1}{5}$, which means multiply it by $\frac{5}{1}$. The result is 400.

9. **200** Write this problem using math: $90 = \frac{45}{100}x$. Now simplify $\frac{45}{100}$ by dividing top and bottom by 5 to get $\frac{9}{20}$. Now the problem is $90 = \frac{9}{20}x$. Divide 90 by $\frac{9}{20}$, meaning multiply it by $\frac{20}{9}$. The result is $\frac{1800}{9}$, which simplifies to 200.

10. **48** Write this problem using math: $36 = \frac{75}{100}x$. 75 and 100 are both divisible by 25, so simplify this fraction to $\frac{3}{4}$. Now the problem is $36 = \frac{3}{4}x$. Now divide 36 by $\frac{3}{4}$, which means multiply it by $\frac{4}{3}$. The result is $\frac{144}{3}$, which simplifies to 48.

11. **50%** Write this problem using math: $10 = \frac{x}{100} \times 20$. Since the 20 is being multiplied, this can be written as $10 = \frac{20x}{100}$. Now multiply both sides by 100 to get $1{,}000 = 20x$. Divide both sides by 20 to get $x = 50$.

12. **10%** Write this problem using math: $55 = \frac{x}{100} \times 550$. This can be rewritten as $55 = \frac{550x}{100}$. Now multiply both sides by 100 to get $5500 = 550x$. Divide both sides by 550 to get $x = 10$.

13. **20%** Write this problem using math: $30 = \frac{x}{100} \times 150$. Now rewrite as $30 = \frac{150x}{100}$. Next, multiply both sides by 100 to get $3{,}000 = 150x$. Divide both sides by 150 to get $x = 20$.

14. **31.25%**

Write this problem using math: $25 = \frac{x}{100} \times 80$. Now rewrite as $25 = \frac{80x}{100}$. Multiply both sides by 100 to get $2500 = 80x$. Divide both sides by 80 to get $x = 31.25$.

15. **80%** Write this problem using math: $100 = \frac{x}{100} \times 125$. Now rewrite as $100 = \frac{125x}{100}$. Multiply both sides by 100 to get $10{,}000 = 125x$. Divide by 125 to get x = 80.

Percents Word Problems Drill

1. **B** The customer is saving 10% of $15. To find 10% of 15, the quickest way is to use mental math to move the decimal place one space to the left, since this is 10%. This results in 1.5, or $1.50. Another way is to write $\frac{10}{100} \times 15$ because % means $\frac{}{100}$ and "of" means ×. Now simplify $\frac{10}{100}$ to $\frac{1}{10}$ by dividing top and bottom by 10. Now the problem is $\frac{1}{10} \times \frac{15}{1}$, which results in $\frac{15}{10}$. 15 divided by 10 equals 1.5 or $1.50 in this problem.

2. **60** The question is essentially asking for 75% of 80. Use the calculator to do .75 × 80, or solve by hand. 75% is the same as $\frac{75}{100}$, which can be simplified as $\frac{3}{4}$ by dividing the top and bottom by 25. Now the problem is $\frac{3}{4} \times \frac{80}{1}$. Multiplying across the top and bottom results in $\frac{240}{4}$, which equals 60.

3. **C** The problem is essentially asking for 45% of 300. One way to solve is to think about the fact that "percent" means "per hundred." This means that for every 100, 45 are blue. If there are 3 hundreds, there will be 3 × 45 blues, which equals 135. Another way to solve is to write an equation. 45% equals $\frac{45}{100}$. To make the problem a little easier, divide the top and bottom by 5 to simplify the fraction: $\frac{9}{20}$. Now do $\frac{9}{20} \times \frac{300}{1}$. The result is $\frac{2700}{20}$, which equals 135. One final way is to do process of elimination. Since 50% is half, 45% is a little less than half. Half of 300 is 150, so 135 is the only answer choice that is a little less than half.

4. **C** Since this is a multiple choice question, the easiest strategy is to go straight to the answer choices. The tax is being added on to the original amount, so the final price will be more than \$5.50. This eliminates (A) and (B). Now thinking about (C) and (D), 8% is only a little more, but (D) is almost twice as much. Choice (C) is the logical answer since it's only a little more than the original price. To actually solve, take 8% of 5.5 by using the calculator: $\frac{8}{100}$ (or 0.08) × 5.5 = .44. Now remember to add this to the original 5.5. \$5.50 + \$0.44 = \$5.94.

5. **50** The problem states that 80% of the questions on the test is equal to 40 questions. This can be written as math: $\frac{80}{100}x = 40$, with x standing for the missing total. Now simplify $\frac{80}{100}$. Both are divisible by 20, so the result is $\frac{4}{5}$. Now $\frac{4}{5}x = 40$. Divide both sides by $\frac{4}{5}$, which means multiply by $\frac{5}{4}$. $\frac{40}{1} \times \frac{5}{4} = \frac{200}{4} = 50$. One other, less mathematical way is to guess and check. If there are 100 questions on the test, $\frac{40}{100} = 40\%$. This doesn't work because it should be 80%. A smaller number, closer to 40, is needed for the total. Guess and check until you find that $\frac{40}{50} = 80\%$.

6. **C** The problem is indicating that 5 is 10% of some number. Since 10% is only a small part, the number must be quite a bit larger than 5. This eliminates (A) and (B). To solve, write this as math: $5 = \frac{10}{100}x$. Now simplify $\frac{10}{100}$ to $\frac{1}{10}$ by dividing top and bottom by 10. Now the problem is $5 = \frac{1}{10}x$. Now divide both sides by $\frac{1}{10}$, which means multiply by $\frac{10}{1}$. $\frac{5}{1} \times \frac{10}{1} = \frac{50}{1} = 50$. One other option is to use the answer choices. Having eliminated (A) and (B) for being too small, if

the cost is \$50, 10% of 50 is 5, so this works. If the cost is \$100, 10% of 100 is 10, so this answer choice doesn't work.

7. **125** The easiest way to do this is to use the answer choices to help. It's a good idea to start in the middle. 20% of 50 is 10 ($\frac{20}{100} \times 50$), so that's too small. Anything less than 50 is also too small. Now try 100. 20% of 100 is 20 ($\frac{20}{100} \times 100$), so that's closer, but still too small. 20% of 125 is 25 ($\frac{20}{100} \times 125$), so that is the correct answer. Another option is to solve by writing the problem as math: $25 = \frac{20}{100}x$. Then simplify $\frac{20}{100}$ to $\frac{1}{5}$ by dividing top and bottom by 20. $25 = \frac{1}{5}x$, so then divide both sides by $\frac{1}{5}$, which means to multiply by 5: $\frac{25}{1} \times \frac{5}{1} = \frac{125}{1}$, or 125.

8. **D** The problem states that 35% of the total number of residents is equal to 5,250 people. This means the total number must be greater than 5,250 because 5,250 is only a part of the whole. This eliminates (A) and (B). To solve, write this problem using math: $\frac{35}{100}x = 5{,}250$. Now simplify $\frac{35}{100}$ by dividing top and bottom by 5 to get $\frac{7}{20}$. $\frac{7}{20}x = 5{,}250$. Now divide both sides by $\frac{7}{20}$, meaning multiply by $\frac{20}{7}$. $5{,}250 \times \frac{20}{7} = 15{,}000$.

9. **A** First convert the hours to minutes. 2 hours × 60 minutes in each hour = 120 minutes. $\frac{30}{120}$ minutes are spent discussing the project. Divide top and bottom by 10 to get $\frac{3}{12}$, then divide both by 3 to simplify to $\frac{1}{4}$. Now this needs to be converted to a percent. Since percents are out of 100, do $\frac{1}{4} \times \frac{100}{1}$, which equals $\frac{100}{4}$ or 25%.

10. **87.5** Be careful with the question here. It asks what percent are *non-fiction*. If 2 books are fiction, the rest, which is 14, are non-fiction. Therefore, the non-fiction books are $\frac{14}{16}$. Multiply this by 100 with the calculator to make it a percent. The result is 87.5.

11. **D** Be careful with the question here. It asks what percent of the steps have *not* been completed. If 8 out of 25 have been completed, the remaining number, 17, have not been completed. This is $\frac{17}{25}$. Use the calculator to multiply this fraction by 100 to change it to a percent, which results in 68%.

12. **A** Be careful with the question here. It asks what percent do *not* pass. If 27 students pass, the remaining 9 do not pass. This is $\frac{9}{36}$ (or $\frac{1}{4}$), so multiply the fraction by 100 to change it to a percent. The result is 25%.

Part III
Applied Arithmetic

Setup Problems Drill

1. Megan is saving to buy a new TV. She saves $20 out of each weekly paycheck and has already accumulated $140. If the price of the TV is $560, how many more weeks must she save before she can make the purchase?

   A. $\frac{(560 - 140)}{20}$

   B. $560 - \frac{140}{20}$

   C. $\frac{560}{20} + 140$

   D. $\frac{(560 + 140)}{20}$

2. One year ago, Joe deposited $1,000 in a savings account that earns 2% simple interest annually. How much interest has he earned?

   A. 1,000 × 2
   B. 1,000 × .2
   C. 1,000 × .02
   D. 1,000 × 1.02

3. A dog groomer bathes up to ten dogs per day. If she charges $50 per bath and works every day for two weeks, bathing the maximum number of dogs possible, how much money will she earn?

   A. 10 × 50
   B. 10 × 50 × 2
   C. 10 × 50 × 7
   D. 10 × 50 × 14

4. Bob is planning a picnic for his family of 16 people. His total budget is $900. In addition to food, he wants to rent a bounce house for the kids who will be attending. If the cost of the bounce house is $390, which inequality represents how much he can spend, per person, for food and beverages?

   900 [ ] 390 [ ] 16*x*

   $\geq$ + $\leq$ − $>$ $<$

5. There are *s* lampposts between A Street and G Street. Between G Street and V Street there are 15 more lampposts than 4 times the number of lampposts between A Street and G Street. Which expression represents the number of lampposts between G Street and V Street?

   A. $s + 15$
   B. $3s + 15$
   C. $4s + 15$
   D. $3s + 15$

6. Scott earns $22 per hour for up to 40 hours in any one-week period. For any hours he works in excess of 40 hours in a one-week period, he earns 50% more per hour. Which expression represents the amount of money he earns if he works 46 hours in a one-week period?

A. 22×46
B. $40 \times 22 + 22 \times 1.5 \times 6$
C. $6 \times 22 + 40 \times 1.5 \times 22$
D. $2 \times 46 \times 1.5$

7. Seven years ago, the price of a certain MP3 player was 60% more than the price of the same MP3 player today. If the MP3 player costs $45 today, how much did it cost seven years ago?

A. $45 \times \frac{60}{100}$

B. $45 + 45 \times \frac{60}{100}$

C. $45 - 45 \times \frac{60}{100}$

D. $45 \times 45 \times \frac{60}{100}$

8. A pair of sneakers that originally sold for $200 was discounted by 15%. How much is the pair of sneakers, after the discount?

A. $200 - 15$

B. $200 - \frac{15}{100}$

C. $200 - 200 \times \frac{15}{100}$

D. $200 \times \frac{15}{100}$

9. A homeowner rented a moving truck from 10AM to 5PM on Saturday. If he paid a total of $173.00, what was the hourly rate to rent the truck?

Select... ▼
173/8
173/7
173/6
173/5

10. Ella deposited all of her birthday money into a CD account that pays 5% interest annually. If she deposited $300 to open the account, and one year later withdrew $100, how much is the CD worth after her withdrawal?

A. $(300 - 100) \times \frac{5}{100}$

B. $\left(300 + 300 \times \frac{5}{100}\right) - 100$

C. $\left[\left(300 \times \frac{5}{100}\right) - 100\right] \times \frac{5}{100}$

D. $\left(300 \times \frac{5}{100}\right) - \left(100 \times \frac{5}{100}\right)$

11. In order to get an A in English class, Antonio needs to earn 90% of the 1400 total possible points throughout the semester. As he studies for his final, which is worth 300 points, he checks his grades and sees that he has accumulated a total of 940 points, so far. How many points must he earn on the final in order to receive an A in the class?

A. $(1400 - 300) \times \frac{90}{100}$

B. $\left(1400 \times \frac{90}{100}\right) - 940$

C. $\left(1400 \times \frac{90}{100}\right) - 300$

D. $(1400 - 940) \times \frac{90}{100}$

12. A group of 10 friends agreed to split the proceeds of a winning lottery ticket. The total prize was $500,000, and they had to pay tax of 18%. Which expression represents the amount that each friend received, after taxes?

A. $500{,}000 - 500{,}000 \times \frac{18}{100}$

B. $500{,}000 \times \frac{18}{100}$

C. $\frac{500{,}000 - 500{,}000 \times \frac{18}{100}}{10}$

D. $\frac{500{,}000}{10} - 500{,}000 \times \frac{18}{100}$

Mean, Median, and Mode Drill

1. On his first four physics exams, Brady earned scores of 86, 90, 84, and 95, respectively. How many points must he earn on his next exam in order to increase his average on all five exams to 91?

   A. 89
   B. 71
   C. 94
   D. 100

2. When photographing a wedding, Dorene usually takes between 800 and 1000 pictures throughout the day. So far this year, Dorene has photographed 17 weddings and has taken a total of 15,844 pictures. What is the average number of pictures she has taken at each wedding this year?

   A. 1732
   B. 932
   C. 832
   D. 882

3. The 85 members of a local chorus spend an average of 12 hours per week rehearsing. How many total hours per week do the members rehearse?

4. Mark an X above the value that represents the median of the list of numbers below.

   32, 6, 11, 12, 0, 16, 14, 7, 28

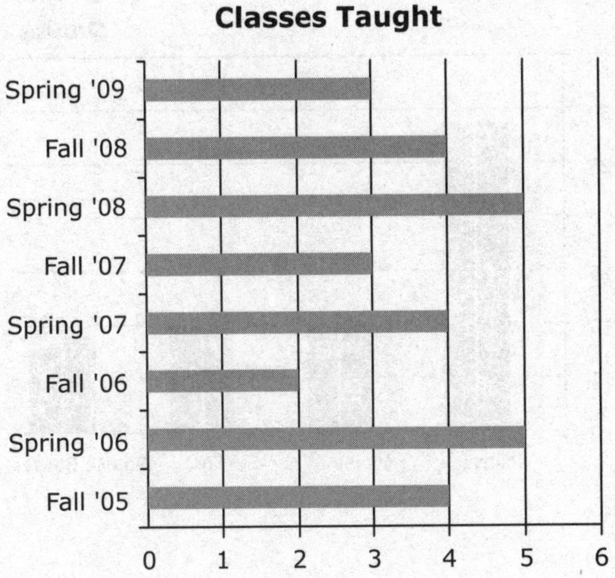

5. The graph above represents the number of classes taught by Professor Sandstrom during recent semesters. What is the mode of the number of classes he taught?

   A. 2
   B. 3
   C. 4
   D. 5

6. In an automotive class, participation is worth 15% of the final grade, quizzes are worth 25% of the final grade, tests are worth 35% of the final grade, and the final is worth 25% of the final grade. If Sara has had perfect attendance, has an average quiz score of 95%, a test average of 87%, and earned a 94% on her final, what is her weighted final average for the course?

Questions 7 and 8 refer to the chart below.

The chart below shows information about the number of string musicians in symphony orchestras around the world.

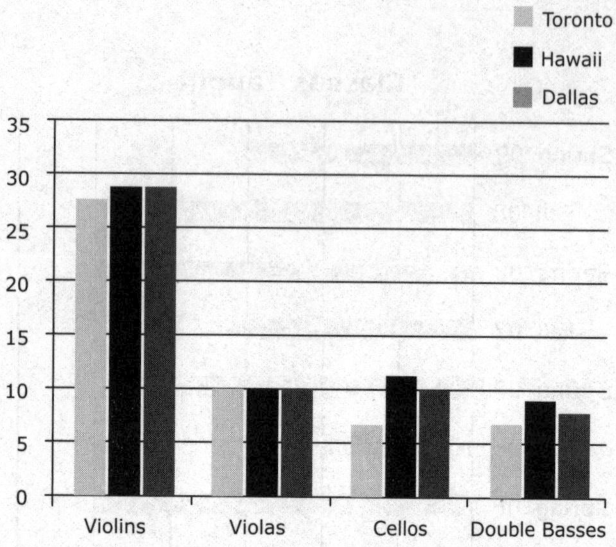

7. What is the approximate mean number of string musicians in all three symphonies?

A. 86
B. 56
C. 29
D. 14

8. What is the difference between the mode of the number of violas and the median number of cellos?

A. 10
B. 8
C. 5
D. 0

9. In one weekend, a police officer wrote 38 citations that had an average cost of $237. What was the total value of all the citations the officer wrote?

A. $6
B. $275
C. $4,503
D. $9,006

10. The graph below shows the number of hours Jonathan worked each day last week. What is the median number of hours he worked on a single day last week?

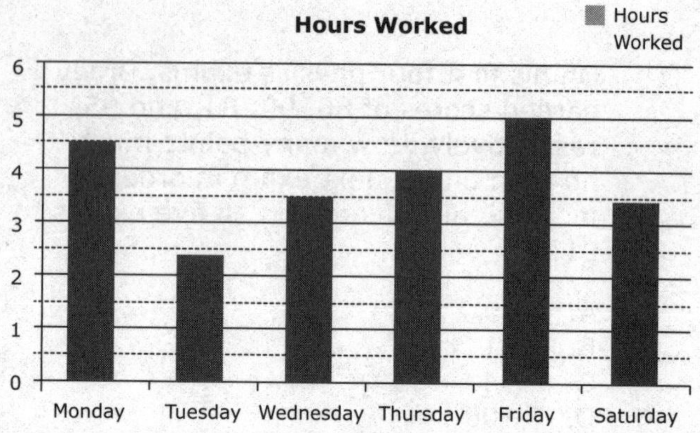

11. The 15 employees at a law firm earn an average annual income of $40,000. If 3 of these employees earn an average annual income of $80,000 and 5 of them earn an average annual income of $20,000, what is the average income of the remaining employees, rounded to the nearest dollar?

$

12. Kaarina drove from her home in Los Angeles to Palm Desert, a distance of 125 miles. On the way to her destination, she maintained an average speed of 55 miles per hour. On her return trip, she maintained an average of speed of 72 miles per hour. What was the average speed for the entirety of her trip, in miles per hour?

A. 55
B. 62.5
C. 63.5
D. 65

Questions 13 and 14 refer to the table below.

A gymnastics team recently competed at a national qualifying event and earned medals as indicated in the table below.

Division	**# of Medals**
Team	6
All-Around	3
Bars	4
Beam	3
Floor	3
Vault	5

13. What is the mode of all medals earned?

A. 3
B. 4
C. 5
D. 6

14. What is the difference between the median and the mean of all medals earned?

A. 0
B. 0.5
C. 3.5
D. 4

15. Boris owns four dogs: a schnauzer, a poodle, a Labrador, and a Great Dane. If the schnauzer weighs 41 pounds, the poodle weighs 56 pounds, the Labrador weighs 78 pounds, and the Great Dane weighs 133 pounds, what is the average weight of all four dogs?

41	49	56	64
77	78	106	133

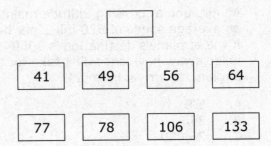

Ratios and Proportions Drill

1. An airplane at cruising altitude maintains an average speed of 520 miles per hour. If the airplane's destination is 3000 miles away, how long will it take for the airplane to arrive, in hours?

   A. 5.8
   B. 346
   C. 26,000
   D. 1,560,000

2. In Mrs. Carlton's class, the ratio of boys to girls is 3 to 5. If there are 15 boys in her class, how many are girls?

   [ ]

3. Choose two numbers below and place them in the boxes to the right so that the two ratios are equal.

3:5	[ ] :	[ ]
6	9	12
20	25	30

4. At a certain college event, there are 640 undergraduates and 296 alumnae in attendance. What is the ratio of undergraduate to alumnae in attendance?

   A. 41:35
   B. 37:80
   C. 80:37
   D. 35:41

5. John is baking cupcakes for his sister's birthday party. One box of cake mix will make 6 cupcakes. If John expects 25 people to attend his sister's birthday party, how many boxes of cake mix should he purchase to ensure that there is at least one cupcake for every person who comes?

   A. 4
   B. 4.17
   C. 4.83
   D. 5

6. Paige is setting up a new fish tank in her classroom. This new tank has a capacity of 90 gallons. The instructions on the algae preventative agent that Paige wants to use say to add 8 drops of agent for every 5 gallons of water. If a bottle contains 60 drops of the agent, how many bottles of the agent must Paige purchase for the new tank?

   A. 2
   B. 2.4
   C. 2.8
   D. 3

7. On a certain map, the distance between City A and City B is 3 inches. If the distance between the two cities is really 276 miles, how many miles does one inch represent on the map?

[ ]

8. A truck driver must stop to sleep 6 hours for every 8 hours he drives. If he must travel 3,080 miles and he travels at an average speed of 55 miles per hour, how many total hours must the driver sleep over the course of the trip?

A. 42
B. 48
C. 55
D. 56

9. In a surfing class, there are 30 men and 25 women. What is the ratio of men to women?

[ ] : [ ]

2	3	4
5	6	7

10. Jenny is very particular about making peanut butter and jelly sandwiches. She contends that the best ratio of peanut butter to jelly to use is 2 tbsp. of peanut butter to 1 tbsp. of jelly. If she needs to prepare 7 sandwiches this week, how many tablespoons of peanut butter and jelly will she use, combined?

A. 7
B. 14
C. 21
D. 28

11. For a dinner party, Joe is preparing grilled fish. For every 6 ounces of fish, he uses 1 tsp. of seasoning. If Joe must prepare 5 pounds of fish, how many teaspoons of seasoning will he use? (1 pound = 16 ounces)

A. 13
B. 13.3
C. 13.6
D. 14

12. Alayna calculated that for every hour she spent studying for her final, she earned 14 points on the final. If she spent 6 hours studying, how many total points did she earn on the final?

[ ]

Rate Drill

1. Tristan runs at an average speed of 5 miles per hour. If he ran for 4 hours, how many miles did he run?

   [ ]

2. A tourist visiting Los Angeles determined that it took him 1.5 hours to travel 17 miles. What was his average speed during his trip, in miles per hour?

   A. 11.3
   B. 17.5
   C. 22.4
   D. 25.5

3. A certain machine can produce 1 donut every 3 minutes. If the machine operated for 8 hours, how many donuts did it produce?

   A. $\frac{3}{8}$

   B. $\frac{8}{3}$

   C. 20

   D. 160

4. Over the course of a month, Heidi biked at a rate of 5 miles per hour for 75 hours. Put the appropriate numbers below into the boxes to show the equation that represents Heidi's total distance for the month.

   [ ] = [ ] × [ ]

5	15	75
375	1125	

5. A plane travels at a rate of 520 miles per hour for 7 hours. How far did the plane travel, in miles?

   A. 74
   B. 230
   C. 520
   D. 3,640

6. Driving at an average speed of 55 miles per hour, how many hours will it take Shanay to get from her home to her friend's home, which is 330 miles away?

   A. 5
   B. 6
   C. 66
   D. 1650

7. Quinton can type 94 words per minute. Approximately how long, in minutes, will it take him to type an essay that must be 2,500 words long?

25	25.5	26
26.5	27	

8. How many pages are there in a book that takes a student 7 days to read if he reads at an average rate of 23 pages per day?

A. 3
B. 3.3
C. 30
D. 161

9. A bicyclist travels at a rate of 15.5 km/h for 3.5 hours. How far, in kilometers, did the bicyclist travel?

A. 5
B. 18.5
C. 54.25
D. 56.75

10. Alicia can serve 4 customers every 10 minutes. At this rate, how many customers can she serve per hour?

11. An athlete can perform 20 pull-ups in 15 seconds. What is his rate of pull-ups per second?

A. $\frac{4}{3}$

B. $\frac{3}{4}$

C. $\frac{3}{5}$

D. $\frac{5}{3}$

12. A teacher who writes her own exams can write questions at a rate of 3 every 10 minutes. If she wants to write a final that has 50 questions on it, about how long should she plan to spend writing questions, in minutes?

A. 15
B. 30
C. 150
D. 167

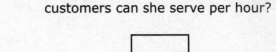

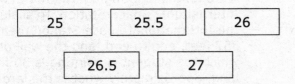

Scale and Unit Conversion Drill

1. Darnell is creating a scaled model of the solar system. If the sun's diameter is 109 times larger than the Earth's diameter, and if Darnell represents Earth with a ball that has a diameter of 2 mm, what will be the diameter of the ball that represents the sun, in millimeters?

   A. 2
   B. 54.5
   C. 109
   D. 218

2. A certain map has a legend that indicates one inch on the map is equal to $\frac{1}{2}$ mile. If two towns are 3 inches apart on the map, how far apart are the towns, in miles?

   A. 0.5
   B. 1
   C. 1.5
   D. 2

3. A sketch of a butterfly is drawn with a 1:7 scale. On the drawing, the butterfly's wing is 12 mm wide. How many millimeters wide is the wing on the butterfly itself?

   [ ]

4. A student is painting a large mural of the International Space Station, to scale. If the International Space Station measures 357 feet, end to end, and the wall on which the student is painting is 30 feet long, approximately what is the largest scale the student can use to accurately represent the station?

   A. $\frac{1}{12}$
   B. $\frac{1}{20}$
   C. $\frac{3}{20}$
   D. $\frac{7}{30}$

5. Evan is training for a weight-lifting competition, at which he hopes to lift a personal best of 150 kg. The weights at the gym where he trains are measured in pounds. How many pounds must he lift in order to attain his goal, to the nearest whole pound? (Note: 1 pound = 0.453592 kg)

   [ ]

6. Dan plans to travel to British Columbia for a cycling race, and is researching the average high and low temperatures during July. He finds that the average high temperature is 25°C and the average low temperature is 14°C. Which values below indicate the estimated average high and low temperatures in Vancouver in July, in degrees Fahrenheit?

$$\left(°F = °C\left(\frac{9}{5}\right) + 32 \right)$$

High	Low

37	47	57
67	77	
87	97	

7. Jessica plans to run a half marathon this summer, which is 13.1 miles. If she knows that one stride is roughly 3 feet long, approximately how many strides will she take during the entire half marathon? (Note: 1 mile = 5,280 feet)

A. 39.3
B. 15,840
C. 23,056
D. 69,168

8. Andrea is planning to move from Los Angeles, California, to Boston, Massachusetts. She estimates the total distance is about 3,000 miles. If she estimates that she can drive at an average speed of 55 miles per hour, including rest stops, approximately how many minutes will the trip take?

A. 16,500
B. 3,300
C. 3,273
D. 2,750

Charts and Graphs Drill

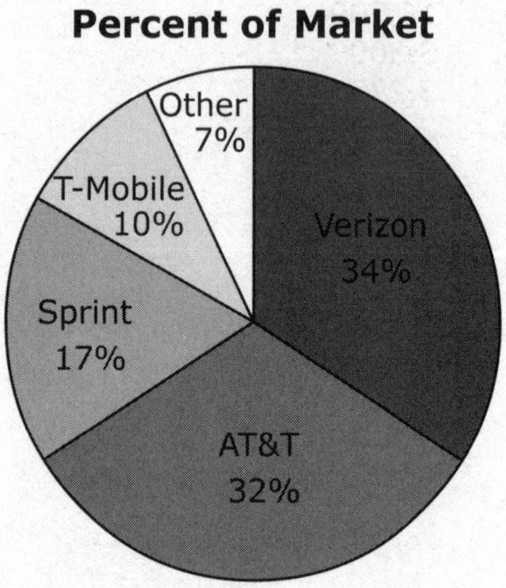

1. The pie graph above represents the percent of market share that some of the primary cell phone service providers captured during the second quarter of 2012. If this data was consistent in every geographic area of the US, and if there are an estimated 650,000 people living in Seattle, how many people lived in Seattle and used Sprint cell phone service during the second quarter of 2012?

Questions 2 and 3 refer to the chart below.

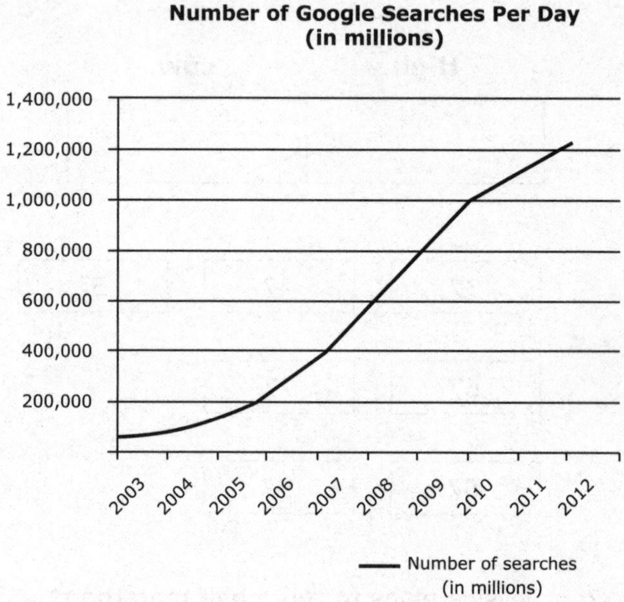

2. The chart above shows the increase in the number of searches on Google, per day, for the years 2003 through 2012. By approximately what percent did the number of searches increase between 2006 and 2010?

   A. 20%
   B. 40%
   C. 200%
   D. 400%

3. The chart above shows the increase in the number of searches on Google, per day, for the years 2003 through 2012. Approximately how many fewer daily searches were conducted, in millions, in 2005 than in 2008?

   A. 400,000
   B. 300,000
   C. 250,000
   D. 200,000

Questions 4 and 5 refer to the chart below.

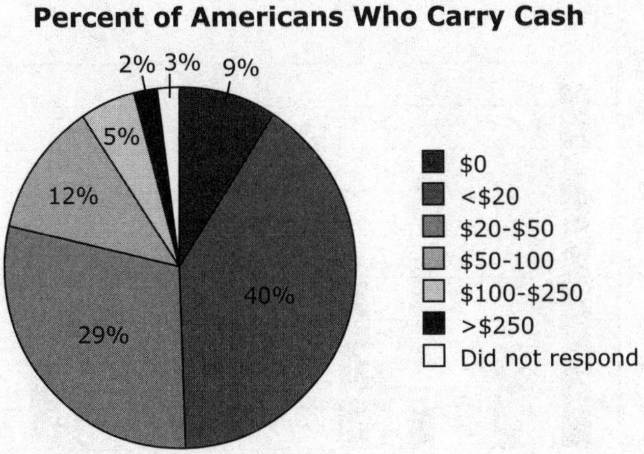

4. The pie chart above indicates the percentage of Americans who carry cash. If the population of the United States is roughly 319 million people, approximately how many Americans carry between $20 and $50 in cash?

   A. 1,595,000
   B. 28,710,000
   C. 92,510,000
   D. 127,600,000

5. The pie chart above indicates the percentage of Americans who carry cash. If the population of the United States is roughly 319 million people, how many more Americans carry less than $20 than carry no cash?

   A. 28,710,000
   B. 98,890,000
   C. 113,245,000
   D. 127,600,000

Questions 6 and 7 refer to the chart below.

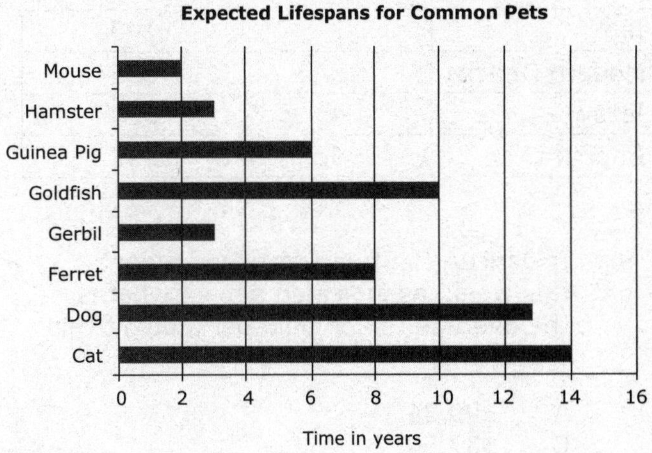

6. What is the average expected lifespan of all animals listed?

   A. 7.25
   B. 7.375
   C. 7.75
   D. 7.875

7. What is the median expected lifespan of all animals listed?

   A. 3
   B. 6
   C. 7
   D. 8

Class	Enrollment	Tuition (per student)
Ballet	3	$35
Tap	2	$40
Modern Dance	5	$35
Jazz	4	$30
Improv	6	$45

8. If DanceArts Studio enrolled students this week, as indicated above, what is the average tuition paid per student this week?

   A. $29.25
   B. $37.50
   C. $39.75
   D. $117.00

Questions 9 and 10 refer to the chart below.

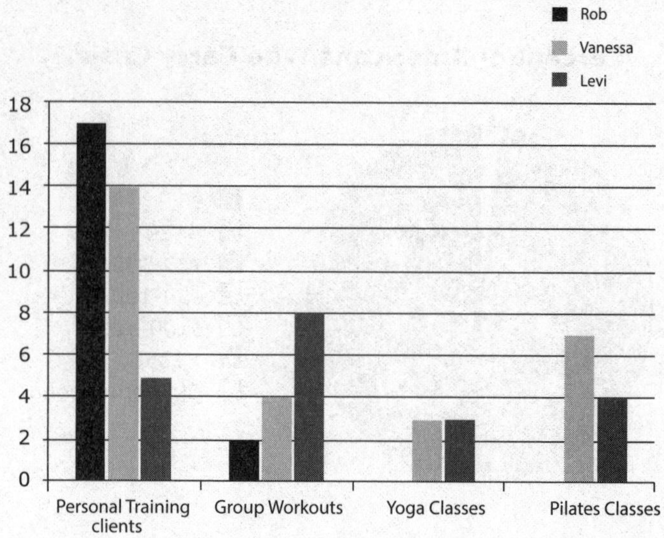

9. The table above represents the number of Personal Training Clients, Group Workouts, Yoga Classes and Pilates Classes that Rob, Vanessa and Levi each taught last week. What was the average number of Personal Training clients that the three coaches trained?

   [ ]

10. If each session represented above was an hour long, what was the median number of hours that the coaches spent with clients or teaching classes?

   A. 19
   B. 20
   C. 22
   D. 28

Questions 11 and 12 refer to the chart below.

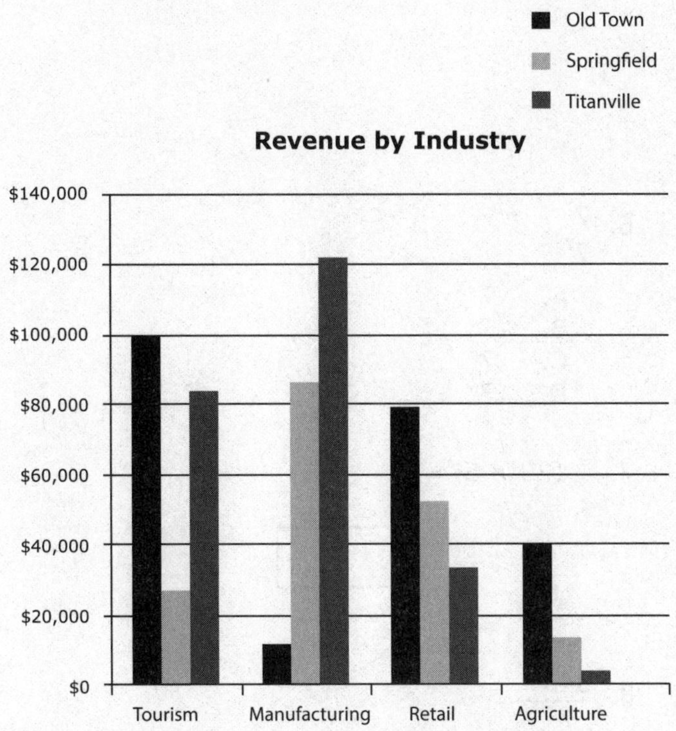

11. The graph above indicates the revenue earned in four different industries by three different towns last month. Which industry earned the most revenue last month?

    A. Tourism
    B. Manufacturing
    C. Retail
    D. Agriculture

12. Approximately what was the average amount of revenue earned across all four industries in Springfield last month?

    A. $43,750
    B. $50,625
    C. $58,000
    D. $65,500

Exponents and Roots Drill

1. Mark on the number line below approximately where the value of $2^3 \times 2^5$ would be.

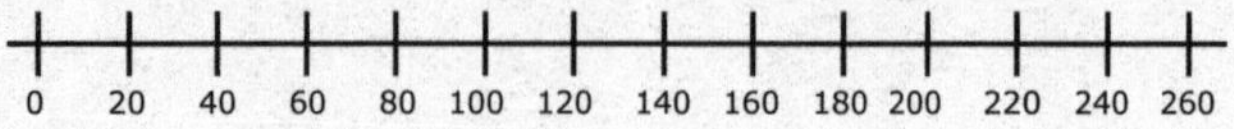

2. $3^4 \times 3^2 \times 3^3 =$

   A. 3^3
   B. 3^6
   C. 3^8
   D. 3^9

3. $5^2 \times 5^7 \times 5^2 =$

4. $\frac{3^3}{3^2} =$

   A. 3^1
   B. 3^2
   C. 3^3
   D. 3^5

5. $\frac{64^3}{4^4} =$

   A. 4^1
   B. 4^2
   C. 4^3
   D. 4^5

6. $\frac{7^7}{7^2} =$

   A. 7^3
   B. 7^4
   C. 7^5
   D. 7^6

7. $125 \times 5^2 =$

8. $\frac{343^4}{7^3} =$

   A. 7^{15}
   B. 7^{12}
   C. 7^9
   D. 7^7

9. $(7^3)^2 =$

   A. 7^2
   B. 7^3
   C. 7^5
   D. 7^6

10. $\frac{2^4}{4^2} =$

A. 0
B. 1
C. 2^2
D. 2^4

11. $\frac{3^3}{3^2} =$

A. 0
B. 1
C. 3
D. 3^3

12. $\sqrt{36} - \sqrt{4} =$

A. $\sqrt{32}$

B. 2

C. 4

D. 6

13. $\left(\frac{\sqrt{12}}{\sqrt{3}}\right) =$

A. 2
B. 3
C. 4
D. 5

14. $\left(\sqrt{48}\right) - \left(\sqrt{12}\right) =$

A. 2

B. $2\sqrt{3}$

C. 4

D. $4\sqrt{3}$

15. $\left(\sqrt{16} \times \sqrt{64}\right)^3 = 2^{\square}$

2	6	3
8	4	15

Scientific Notation Drill

1. $3.5 \times 10^6 =$

   A. 3,500,000
   B. 350,000
   C. 35,000
   D. 3,500

2. $4.01 \times 10^3 =$

   A. 401
   B. 4,010
   C. 40,100
   D. 401,000

3. $9.2 \times 10^8 + 6.5 \times 10^7 =$

   A. 9.265×10^7
   B. 9.265×10^8
   C. 9.85×10^7
   D. 9.85×10^8

4. $7.2 \times 10^{-4} =$

   A. 0.000072
   B. 0.00072
   C. 0.0072
   D. 0.072

5. $5.3 \times 10^{-2} =$

   A. 0.00053
   B. 0.0053
   C. 0.053
   D. 0.53

6. $4.4 \times 10^{-4} =$

   A. 0.00044
   B. 0.0044
   C. 0.044
   D. 0.44

7. 32,450,000 =

   A. 3.245×10^5
   B. 3.245×10^6
   C. 3.245×10^7
   D. 3.245×10^8

8. 7,200 =

   A. 7.2×10^{-3}
   B. 7.2×10^{-2}
   C. 7.2×10^2
   D. 7.2×10^3

9. 29,000 + 2400 =

   A. 3.14×10^3
   B. 3.14×10^4
   C. 3.14×10^5
   D. 3.14×10^6

10. 0.00045 =

    A. 4.5×10^{-4}
    B. 4.5×10^{-5}
    C. 4.5×10^{-6}
    D. 4.5×10^{-7}

11. 0.032 – 0.005 =

    A. 2.7×10^{-5}
    B. 2.7×10^{-4}
    C. 2.7×10^{-3}
    D. 2.7×10^{-2}

12. 0.00000078 =

    A. 7.8×10^{-5}
    B. 7.8×10^{-6}
    C. 7.8×10^{-7}
    D. 7.8×10^{-8}

Probability Drill

1. A deck of cards has four suits: hearts, diamonds, spades, and clubs. Each suit has 13 cards, numbered 1 to 13. If Leslie picks one card at random, what is the likelihood that she will draw a spade with a value of 5 or less?

   A. $\frac{1}{52}$

   B. $\frac{5}{52}$

   C. $\frac{5}{13}$

   D. $\frac{1}{13}$

2. Megan has 2 pairs of sneakers, 3 pairs of high-heeled shoes, 5 pairs of sandals, and a pair of boots. What is the probability that she will choose the boots if she selects a pair of shoes at random?

   $\frac{\square}{\square}$

1	2	3	4
5	6	7	8
9	10	11	

3. A jar has been filled with equal portions of various flavors of jellybeans: strawberry, orange, lemon, apple, and blueberry. If one jellybean is selected at random, what is the likelihood it will be lemon?

   $\frac{\square}{\square}$

4. McKenzi rolls a six-sided die. What is the likelihood that she will roll an odd number?

   A. $\frac{1}{2}$

   B. $\frac{1}{3}$

   C. $\frac{2}{3}$

   D. $\frac{3}{4}$

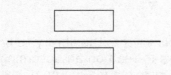

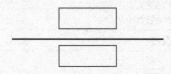

5. Los Ranchos Middle School students are selling tickets to a carnival. For every $15 in tickets sold, a student will receive one entry in a grand prize drawing. The table below shows the total carnival ticket sales for five students at Los Ranchos Middle School. What is the probability that Matthew will win the grand prize?

Student	Total Ticket Sales
Amanda	$105
Danya	$60
Jorge	$180
Matthew	$120
Zoe	$90

A. $\frac{4}{37}$

B. $\frac{6}{37}$

C. $\frac{8}{37}$

D. $\frac{12}{37}$

6. Barbi is selecting her classes for next year and has one space left to fill with an elective. She can choose from three language classes, two art classes, or physical education. If Barbi chooses randomly, what is the probability that she will select an art class?

A. $\frac{2}{5}$

B. $\frac{3}{5}$

C. $\frac{1}{3}$

D. $\frac{1}{2}$

7. Joe wants to adopt a pet from the humane society. When he visits, there are 7 cats, 12 dogs, 3 birds, and 5 guinea pigs available. Of the dogs, 5 are less than a year old. If he chooses at random, what is the probability that Joe will adopt a dog that is at least one year old?

$$\frac{\square}{\square}$$

8. Sally is planning to attend a seminar on college majors at a local university. She's most interested in one of the three business programs or one of the five pre-law programs. If her seminar is assigned at random, what is the probability that she will attend a seminar on one of these programs out of the 138 available on campus?

A. $\frac{4}{69}$

B. $\frac{3}{138}$

C. $\frac{5}{138}$

D. $\frac{1}{23}$

9. Caroline visits the library to borrow some books to read on an upcoming trip. She can borrow a maximum of six books, and has already selected five. For her remaining choice, she's deciding among four novels, three poetry books and four non-fiction books. If she chooses at random, what is the probability that she will select a non-fiction book as her last choice?

A. $\frac{3}{11}$

B. $\frac{4}{11}$

C. $\frac{7}{11}$

D. $\frac{8}{11}$

10. Raquel is connecting a new DVD player to her entertainment system. There are 7 wires in the box: 2 red, 2 blue, 2 green and 1 white. If the first wire that she needs to connect is white, what is the probability that she will select it when she reaches into the box without looking?

A. $\frac{6}{7}$

B. $\frac{4}{7}$

C. $\frac{2}{7}$

D. $\frac{1}{7}$

11. Darla is deciding what kind of dessert to bring to a potluck dinner with friends. She's considering five types of cookies, two kinds of after-dinner mints, four flavors of ice cream, and a fruit bowl. What is the probability that she will NOT choose to bring the fruit bowl?

$$\frac{\square}{\square}$$

1	2	3	4
5	6	7	8
9	10	11	12

12. Emma is deciding which picture to put on the last page of a photo album. She has two pictures of her whole family, three of her with her siblings, and one of her with her dog. What is the probability that she will use one of the pictures of her whole family?

A. $\frac{1}{2}$

B. $\frac{1}{3}$

C. $\frac{2}{3}$

D. $\frac{5}{6}$

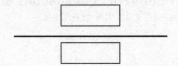

Counting Drill

1. A local bank is encouraging its customers to update their Personal Identification Numbers (PINs) after a recent series of debit card thefts. The bank suggests that each of the four digits in a PIN be unique. How many different PINs can be created using the bank's suggestion?

   [ ]

2. Sheila is hiring for three positions in her company: a marketing specialist, an operations manager, and an administrative assistant. She has three qualified applicants for each position, and no applicant has applied for more than one position. How many different combinations of new employees could she hire?

   A. 3
   B. 9
   C. 27
   D. 81

3. Lisa has twelve race medals she wants to display but only has five places to hang them. How many different combinations of race medals can she display?

   A. 12
   B. 792
   C. 59,400
   D. 95,040

4. Vivian is playing a game with tiles that have letters on them. If Vivian has seven tiles in her hand, how many different arrangements of letters can she create?

   A. 504
   B. 720
   C. 2,520
   D. 5,040

5. Horace is purchasing ingredients to make dinner. He needs to purchase one side dish, one vegetable, one entrée and one beverage. He has narrowed his choices down to four side dishes, six vegetables, three entrees and three beverages. How many different combinations of food and beverage can he create?

   [ ]

36	54	72	216

6. Mary Ruth is creating a gift basket to donate to a local non-profit organization's fundraiser. She plans to include 6 items, and has ten to choose from. How many different combinations of items can she include in the gift basket?

   A. 60
   B. 210
   C. 25,200
   D. 151,200

7. A dog enthusiasts' club is hosting its annual dog show. In the final round, judges will select the Best in Class in the following categories: Sporting, Hound, Working, Terrier, Toy, Non-Sporting, and Herding. If there are three semi-finalists in each category, how many different combinations of Best in Class winners can there be?

   A. 12
   B. 21
   C. 2,187
   D. 19,683

8. Five athletes are competing in an obstacle course. The first three to finish the course win gift cards to the local running store: first place wins $100, second wins $50, and third wins $25. How many different arrangements of winners from first to third are possible?

   A. 120
   B. 60
   C. 20
   D. 12

9. Walter is planning a trip for his family. He is deciding a single final destination, what mode of travel to use, and how long to stay. His choices include three destinations, two modes of travel, and either 4, 5 or 6 nights in a hotel. How many different combinations of destination, mode of travel, and trip duration are possible for Walter to determine?

   A. 8
   B. 12
   C. 16
   D. 18

10. Barb has ten credit cards, but only wants to keep two of them in her wallet. How many different combinations of credit cards can she keep in her wallet?

11. The local pizza shop is offering a special on one medium pizza with two toppings for $5.99. Joy is selecting which toppings to include from 5 meats, 8 vegetables, and 3 sauces. How many unique pizzas could she create?

    A. 16
    B. 234
    C. 468
    D. 936

12. Allison is deciding which movies to watch with her friends this weekend. They'll have time to watch three movies, and she has twenty to choose from. How many combinations of movies can they watch?

Applied Arithmetic: Answers and Explanations

APPLIED ARITHMETIC: ANSWERS AND EXPLANATIONS

Setup Questions Drill

1. **A** The first step is to figure out how much *more* Megan must save, which would be represented by the total amount she needs ($560) minus the amount she has already saved ($140). So that would look like $560 – $140, together, in the answers. That allows us to eliminate everything except choice (A). To finish the setup, take the amount that Megan still has to save and divide it by the amount of money she saves out of each paycheck ($20) to figure out how many more weeks she has to save.

2. **C** First, remember that 'per cent' literally means 'out of every 100.' So, anytime the word 'percent' or the symbol '%' shows up, rewrite it as a fraction with 100 in the denominator. So, if Joe's account yields 2%, rewrite it to say $\frac{2}{100}$. That translates into .02 in decimal format, so you know your answer must be (C).

3. **D** This one is a straightforward multiplication setup. To figure out the maximum amount of money she could earn in one day, multiply the maximum number of dogs times the amount she charges, or 10 × 50. Then, multiply that by 14 days (the equivalent of two weeks) to establish a total.

4. **$900 \geq 390 + 16x$**

   Since Bob can't spend more than $900, that value must be **greater than or equal to** all of the other manipulations. The $390 charge for the bounce house doesn't change, so start with that and then add the food & beverage expense to it. Using x to represent the cost per person, multiply that by 16 people to get the total food and beverage expense ($16x$).

5. **C** '15 more than' means to add 15, which is represented in all answer choices. '4 times' the number of lampposts translates to '$4s$.' The final expression should be $4s + 15$.

6. **B** Start by determining the amount he earns for the first 40 hours of his work week: 40 hours × $22. Then, multiply the number of extra hours (6) by his overtime rate, which is represented by 1.5 × 22, 22 × 1.5 × 6. Last, add those together.

7. **B** Begin by determining 60% of today's price, or $45 \times \frac{60}{100}$. Then, add that to today's price, since the price seven years ago was 60% MORE than today's price.

8. **C** Begin by determining the amount of the discount, or $200 \times \frac{15}{100}$. Since it is a discount, or percent decrease, subtract that value from the starting value of $200.

9. **173/7** Be careful when counting the hours: 10AM-11AM is the first hour, 11AM-12PM is the second, 12PM-1PM is the third, etc. Don't count 10AM as an hour! From 10AM-5PM is a total of 7 hours, so divide the total cost by the total number of hours to get the hourly rate.

10. **B** Tackle this question step by step instead of trying to deal with all of it at once. Start by figuring out how much would be in the account at the end of the first year: Start with $300, and then add 5% of 300 to it: 300 + $\left(\frac{5}{100}\right)$(300). Then, subtract the $100 she withdrew at the end of the first year.

11. **B** First, determine how many points Antonio needs in order to get an A: 1400 × $\frac{90}{100}$. Then, subtract the number of points he's already earned (940) to figure out how many more points he needs.

12. **C** Start by figuring out how much will be taken out in taxes (500,000 × $\frac{18}{100}$). and then subtract that from 500,000 to determine how much the group will be splitting. Then, divide that amount be 10 to figure out how much each friend will take home.

Mean, Median, and Mode Drill

1. **D** Start by determining how many total points Brady must earn in order to have an average of 91: 5 × 91. Then, subtract his total earned already (86 + 90 + 84 + 95) to establish how many points he must earn on his next exam.

2. **B** When reading word questions, be careful about determining what information is actually relevant to the question being asked. In this case, the information in the first sentence doesn't apply so don't get sucked into thinking that it has to be included in the correct answer. To find the average number of photographs taken, simply divide the total number of pictures by the number of weddings.

3. **1020** To find the total number of hours, multiply the average by the number of members: 85 × 12.

4. **X**

32, 6, 11, 12, 0, 16, 14, 7, 28

First, rewrite the values in order (0, 6, 7, 11, 12, 14, 16, 28, 32). Then identify the one that is in the middle.

5. **C** Write out all of the values that represent the number of courses taught in each semester (2, 3, 3, 4, 4, 4, 5, 5). Then identify the one that occurs the most.

6. **92.7** Because different components of the grade weigh more heavily, this is a weighted average question, and each component needs to be multiplied by the appropriate percentage. Take it step by step. First, multiply her perfect attendance by 10% (100 × .15); next multiply her quiz score by 25% (95 × .25); then multiply her test average by 35% (87 × .35); lastly multiply her final score by 25% (94 × .25). Then, add all of those values together.

7. **B** Add all of the values together (28 + 29+ 29 + 10 + 10 + 10 + 7 + 11 + 10 + 7 + 9 + 8) and divide by 3, because there are three symphonies represented.

8. **D** Subtract the median number of cellos (10) from the mode of the violas (10).

9. **D** Multiply the average cost times the number of citations to find the total value: $237 \times 38 = 9{,}006$.

10. **3.75** Write out the values represented in the chart, in order: 2.5, 3.5, 3.5, 4, 4.5, 5. Since there is an even number of values, find the average of the middle two: $\frac{3.5 + 4}{2} = 3.75$

11. **\$37,143**

If 15 employees earn an average of \$40,000, multiply those two figures to determine the total value of their salaries: $15 \times 40{,}000 = \$600{,}000$. Do the same for the other two subgroups: $3 \times 80{,}000 = \$240{,}000$ and $5 \times 20{,}000 = \$100{,}000$. These two subgroups, therefore, account for \$340,000 of the \$600,000 that all 15 employees earn. Subtract the two subgroups' income from the total to get the total income of the remaining employees: \$600,000 - \$340,000 = \$260,000. That \$260,000 is earned by a total of 7 employees (15 total, minus the 8 already accounted for). Divide \$260,000 by 7 to get the average of their income: $\frac{\$260{,}000}{7} = \$37{,}142.86$. The question asks for the value rounded to the nearest dollar, or \$37,143.

12. **B** This is a weighted average question – it won't work to just take an average of the two speeds given. First, find the total time of each trip, using Distance = Rate × Time. For the trip to Palm Desert: $125 = 55 \times t$. Solve to determine the time to get to Palm Desert was 2.3 hours. Use the same formula for the return trip: $125 = 72 \times t$. Her return trip took 1.7 hours. Now, use the same formula, with the total distance traveled and the total time it took: $250 = r \times 4$. Solve to find the total average speed she drove was 62.5 miles per hour.

13. **A** The mode of a set of values is the one that appears the most frequently. The team won 3 medals in 3 divisions, which is the number of medals that appears most frequently.

14. **B** The median of a set of values is the one in the middle, when the numbers are in order. Start by writing out the values presented: 3, 3, 3, 4, 5, 6. Since there is an even number of values presented, take the average of the middle two: $\frac{(3 + 4)}{2} = 3.5$. Next, find the mean of all the values by adding all six values together to get a total of 24. Divide by 6 to get a mean of 4. Subtract the median, 3.5, from the mean, 4, to get a difference of 0.5.

15. **77** To find the average, add all four dogs' weights and then divide by 4: $\frac{(41 + 56 + 78 + 133)}{4} = 77$

Ratios and Proportions Drill

1. **A** When setting up a proportion, start with the relationship that is given: in this case, $\frac{520 \text{ miles}}{1 \text{ hour}}$. Set that equal to the relationship involving the unknown part, using a variable to represent the unknown: in this case, the known distance is 3000 miles and the unknown piece is the time. So, the proportion should be $\frac{520 \text{ miles}}{1 \text{ hour}} = \frac{3{,}000 \text{ miles}}{x \text{ hours}}$. Remember to always set up a proportion so that the same units are on the top (in this case, miles) and the same units are on the bottom (here, hours). Once the proportion is set up, cross multiply and solve for x. $3000 = 520x$. Divide both sides by 520 to get x alone: $x = 5.8$.

2. **25** This question can also be solved with a proportion, because the relationship presented is between two parts (boys and girls). So, $\frac{3 \text{ boys}}{5 \text{ girls}} = \frac{15 \text{ boys}}{x \text{ girls}}$. Cross multiply and solve to find that $x = 25$.

3. **12, 20** This question requires a bit of testing the values presented, using proportions. The given relationship is 3:5, and the question is asking for two values that would reduce to the same. Since the first value in the given relationship is 3, the first number in the unknown relationship must also be a multiple of 3. Try 6: to get from 3 to 6, you'd have to multiply by 2, and then you'd have to do the same thing to the 5, which would be 10. But there is no 10 available, so 6 won't work. Next, try 9: to get from 3 to 9, you'd multiply by 3. So, multiply 5 by 3 to get 15, but there's no 15 available, so eliminate the 9. Start again with 12: multiply 3 by 4 to get 12, so multiply 5 by 4 to get 20. The good news is there's a 20, so put the 12 in the first space and 20 in the second. 12:20 is the same relationship as 3:5.

4. **C** Set this up as a fraction to make it easier to reduce the values: $\frac{640}{296}$. Divide the numerator and denominator by 2 to get $\frac{320}{148}$. Since both values are even, divide by 2 again: $\frac{160}{74}$. Again, they're both even, so keep dividing by 2: $\frac{80}{37}$. Now, there's a prime number in the denominator, so it can't be reduced any more. When selecting an answer, be sure to reference the question again: it's asking for the ratio of undergraduates to alumnae, so be sure to select the answer that matches that order. Choice (B) actually reverses it.

5. **D** Start this question with a proportion: $\frac{1 \text{ box}}{6 \text{ cupcakes}} = \frac{x \text{ boxes}}{25 \text{ cupcakes}}$. Cross multiply and solve to find that $x = 4.167$. Be careful though: it's not possible to buy .167 box of cake mix. So, in order to ensure that everyone has a cupcake, John would need to round up and buy 5 boxes.

6. **D** Set up a proportion to determine how drops are needed: $\frac{8 \text{ drops}}{5 \text{ gallons}} = \frac{x \text{ drops}}{90 \text{ gallons}}$. Cross-multiply and solve to find $x = 144$ drops. Set up another proportion to determine how many bottles Paige will need to purchase: $\frac{1 \text{ bottle}}{60 \text{ drops}} = \frac{x \text{ bottles}}{144 \text{ drops}}$. Cross-multiply and solve to find that $x = 2.4$. That means that 2 bottles will not supply as much of the agent as Paige needs, so she'll need to buy 3 bottles.

7. **92** Set up a proportion with the known relationship: $\frac{3 \text{ inches}}{276 \text{ miles}} = \frac{1 \text{ inch}}{x \text{ miles}}$. Cross-multiply and solve to find $x = 92$ miles.

8. **A** This question requires multiple steps. In order to use a proportion relating hours to sleep, first determine how many hours the trip will take. Set up a proportion to figure that out: $\frac{1 \text{ hour}}{55 \text{ miles}} = \frac{x \text{ hours}}{3{,}080 \text{ miles}}$. Cross-multiply and solve to find the trip will take 56 hours. Now set up another proportion to determine hours of sleep required: $\frac{6 \text{ hours sleep}}{8 \text{ hours driving}} = \frac{x \text{ hours sleep}}{56 \text{ hours driving}}$. Cross-multiply and solve to find that the driver will be required to sleep 42 hours.

9. **6, 5** When looking for the ratio between two given numbers, start by asking if the two numbers have a factor in common. In this case, both 30 and 25 are multiples of 5. Divide both numbers by 5, resulting in 6 and 5. These two values don't have any factors in common, so this is as far as we can reduce them.

10. **C** This question can be approached two ways. The first is to solve for the number tablespoons of peanut butter and jelly independently, and then add them together. That would require the use of two proportions: $\frac{1 \text{ sandwich}}{2 \text{ tbsp. peanut butter}} = \frac{7 \text{ sandwiches}}{x \text{ tbsp. peanut butter}}$. Cross-multiply and solve to find that Jenny needs 14 tablespoons of peanut butter. Then do the same for jelly:

$\frac{\text{1 sandwich}}{\text{1 tbsp. jelly}} = \frac{\text{7 sandwiches}}{x\text{ tbsp. jelly}}$. Cross-multiply and solve to find that Jenny needs 7 tablespoons of peanut butter. Add them together, and Jenny needs 21 tablespoons of peanut butter and jelly, combined. Alternatively, use one proportion that relates the number of sandwiches to the total number of tablespoons: $\frac{\text{1 sandwich}}{\text{3 tablespoons}} = \frac{\text{7 sandwiches}}{x\text{ tablespoons}}$. Cross-multiply and solve to find Jenny needs 21 tablespoons of peanut butter and jelly, combined.

11. **B** To figure out the relationship of ounces of fish to teaspoons of seasoning, first figure out how many total ounces of fish Joe plans to grill: $\frac{\text{1 pound}}{\text{16 ounces}} = \frac{\text{5 pounds}}{x\text{ ounces}}$. Cross-multiply to find that Joe plans to grill 80 ounces. Now set up another proportion to figure out how much seasoning he needs: $\frac{\text{6 ounces fish}}{\text{1 tsp. seasoning}} = \frac{\text{80 ounces fish}}{x\text{ tsp. seasoning}}$. Cross-multiply to find that Joe needs 13.3 teaspoons of seasoning.

12. **84** Set up a proportion between the number of points and the number of hours spent studying: $\frac{\text{1 hour}}{\text{14 points}} = \frac{\text{6 hours}}{x\text{ points}}$. Cross-multiply and find that Alayna earned 84 points.

Rate Drill

1. **20** Remember to use the formula Distance = Rate × Time. Then plug in the information that's been provided and solve. D = 5 × 4 = 20 miles.

2. **A** Use Distance = Rate × Time: 17 = r × 1.5. Solve to find r = 11.3 miles per hour.

3. **D** The same rate formula applies to work accomplished: Work = Rate × Time. Be careful, though, to pay attention to the fact that the question gives the rate in MINUTES and asks for the donuts produced in 8 HOURS. So, first, convert the rate to hours with a proportion: $\frac{\text{1 donut}}{\text{3 minutes}} = \frac{x\text{ donuts}}{\text{60 minutes}}$. Cross-multiply and solve to find that the machine creates 20 donuts per hour. Then, use the rate formula Work = Rate × Time: W = 20 × 8 = 160 donuts.

4. $375 = 5 \times 75$ or $375 = 75 \times 5$

Use Distance = Rate × Time. The rate and time are given: $5 \times 75 = 375$.

5. **D** Distance = Rate × Time. The rate and time are given: $520 \times 7 = 3{,}640$.

6. **B** Distance = Rate × Time. The rate and distance are given: $330 = 55 \times t$. Solve to find $t = 6$.

7. **26.5** Use Work = Rate × Time. In this case, the work is the 2500 words to be typed: $2500 = 94 \times t$. Solve to find $t = 26.6$. Since the question asks approximately how long it will take Quinton to type the paper, choose the value that is closest rather than rounding up.

8. **D** Work = Rate × Time. In this case, the work is the total number of questions that the student reads. $W = 23 \times 7 = 161$

9. **C** Distance = Rate × Time. $D = 15.5 \times 3.5 = 54.25$

10. **24** Use Work = Rate × Time, and consider the number of customers the 'work.' $W = \frac{4 \text{ customers}}{10 \text{ minutes}} \times 60 \text{ minutes} = 24$.

11. **A** This question actually gives the ratio – all that needs to happen is to simplify it! So take $\frac{20 \text{ pull-ups}}{15 \text{ seconds}}$ and look for a common factor – 5. Divide both the numerator and the denominator by 5, and the result is $\frac{4}{3}$.

12. **D** Use Work = Rate × Time: $50 = \left(\frac{3}{10}\right) \times t$. Solve to find $t = 166.67$ minutes.

Scale and Unit Conversion Drill

1. **D** The key to this question is the phrase '109 times larger.' So, take the dimension of the ball Darnell will use for the Earth (2mm) and multiply it by 109.

2. **C** Set this up as a proportion: $\frac{1 \text{ inch}}{.5 \text{ mile}} = \frac{3 \text{ inches}}{x \text{ miles}}$. (Remember to keep the same units on the top and the same units on the bottom when setting up the proportion.) Cross-multiply to find that $x = 1.5$.

3. **84** Set this up as a proportion: $\frac{1}{7} = \frac{12 \text{ mm}}{x}$. (Remember to keep the same units on the top and the same units on the bottom when setting up the proportion.) Cross-multiply to find that $x = 84$.

4. **A** Because this question asks for an 'approximate' scale, round 357 to 360. Then, set it up as a fraction and reduce it: $\frac{30}{360} = \frac{1}{12}$.

5. **331** Set this up as a proportion: $\frac{1\text{ pound}}{0.453592\text{ kg}} = \frac{x\text{ pounds}}{150\text{ kg}}$. (Remember to keep the same units on the top and the same units on the bottom when setting up the proportion.) Cross-multiply to find that $x = 330.6937$. The question indicates that this should be rounded to the nearest whole pound.

6. **77, 57** Plug the given °C values in to the formula: $°F = 25\left(\frac{9}{5}\right) + 32 = 45 + 32 = 77°F$ for a high; $°F = 14\left(\frac{9}{5}\right) + 32 = 25.2 + 32 = 57.2°F$ for a low. Because the question says 'estimated,' choose the values that are closest.

7. **C** This question requires the use of two proportions: the first one to convert miles to feet, and the second to convert feet to strides:

$$\frac{1\text{ mile}}{5{,}280\text{ feet}} = \frac{13.1\text{ miles}}{x\text{ feet}}$$

(Remember to keep the same units on the top and the same units on the bottom when setting up the proportion.) Cross-multiply to find that $x = 69{,}168$.

$$\frac{1\text{ stride}}{3\text{ feet}} = \frac{x\text{ strides}}{69{,}168\text{ feet}}$$

Cross-multiply to find that $x = 23{,}056$ strides.

8. **C** Set this up as a proportion: $\frac{55\text{ miles}}{1\text{ hour}} = \frac{3{,}000\text{ miles}}{x\text{ hours}}$. (Remember to keep the same units on the top and the same units on the bottom when setting up the proportion.) Cross-multiply to find that $x = 54.55$. Be careful, though! Pay attention to what the question is asking! It's not asking for the time in HOURS, it's asking for the time in MINUTES. So that means to use another proportion: $\frac{60\text{ minutes}}{1\text{ hour}} = \frac{x\text{ minutes}}{54.55\text{ hours}}$. $x = 3{,}273$.

Charts and Graphs Drill

1. **110,500**

Take the percentage indicated for Sprint (17%) and multiply it by the estimated 650,000 people living in Seattle: $650{,}000 \times \frac{17}{100} = 110{,}500$.

2. **D** Percent Change = $\frac{\text{Difference between two values}}{\text{Starting Value}}$. To find the percent increase, find the difference between the number of searches performed in 2006 and the number of searches performed in 2010: 1,000,000 – 200,000 = 800,000. Divide that value by the starting number (the question is asking for the percent INCREASE, so use the smaller value), 200,000: $\frac{800{,}000}{200{,}000} = 4$. Last, multiply the answer by 100 to make it a percent. That means the number of daily Google searches increased by 400%.

3. **A** Estimate the number of searches per day in 2005 (180,000) and in 2008 (580,000). Find the difference: 580,000 – 180,000 = 400,000.

4. **C** The chart indicates that 29% of Americans carry between \$20 and \$50 in cash. Translate that into math: $\frac{29}{100} \times 319{,}000{,}000 = x$. Solve for x to find that 92,510,000 Americans carry between \$20 and \$50 in cash.

5. **B** The chart indicates that 40% of Americans carry less than \$20. Translate that into math: $\frac{40}{100} \times 319{,}000{,}000 = x$. Solve for x to find that 127,600,000 Americans carry less than \$20. The chart also indicates that 9% of Americans carry no cash. Translate that into math: $\frac{9}{100} \times 319{,}000{,}000 = x$. Solve for x to find that 28,710,000 Americans carry no cash. Subtract that number from the number of Americans who carry less than \$20: 127,600,000 – 28,710,000 = 98,890,000. Another option is to subtract the percents since they come from the same total. 40% – 9% = 31%. 31% of 319,000,000 is 98,890,000.

6. **B** Add the ages of all of the animals and divide by the number of ages: 2 + 3 + 6 + 10 + 3 + 8 + 13 + 14 = 59. $\frac{59}{8} = 7.375$

7. **C** List the values in order: 2, 3, 3, 6, 8, 10, 13, 14. Since there is an even number of values in the list, take the average of the middle two: $\frac{6+8}{2} = 7$.

8. **B** Start by determining the total tuition paid, by class: Ballet, \$105; Tap, \$80; Modern Dance, \$175; Jazz, \$120; Improv, \$270. Add them all together (\$750) and divide by the total number of students (20). This gives the average tuition payment per student: \$37.50.

9. **12** Add the number of Personal Training Clients that the three coaches trained (17 + 14 + 5 = 36) and divide it by 3. The average is 12.

10. **B** Start by writing out a list of the number of hours each coach spent with clients or teaching classes, in total: Rob, 19; Vanessa, 28; Levi, 20. Put these values in order: 19, 20, 28. The median, or middle number, is 20.

11. **B** Add the revenue amounts in each column to determine the one with the greatest total revenue. Estimate amounts if exact values are difficult to determine. Tourism: \$100,000 + \$25,000 + \$82,000 = \$207,000. Manufacturing: \$12,000 + \$85,000 + \$121,000 = \$218,000. Retail: \$79,000 + \$52,000 + \$35,000 = \$166,000. Agriculture: \$41,000 + \$13,000 + \$5,000 = \$59,000. Manufacturing has the highest total revenue.

12. **A** Add the approximate revenue earned in each industry in Springfield last month: \$25,000 + \$85,000 + \$52,000 + \$13,000 = \$175,000. Divide that amount by 4: $\frac{175{,}000}{4} = \$43{,}750$.

Exponents and Roots Drill

1. When multiplying the same base, add the exponents: $2^3 \times 2^5 = 2^8$. $2^8 = 256$.

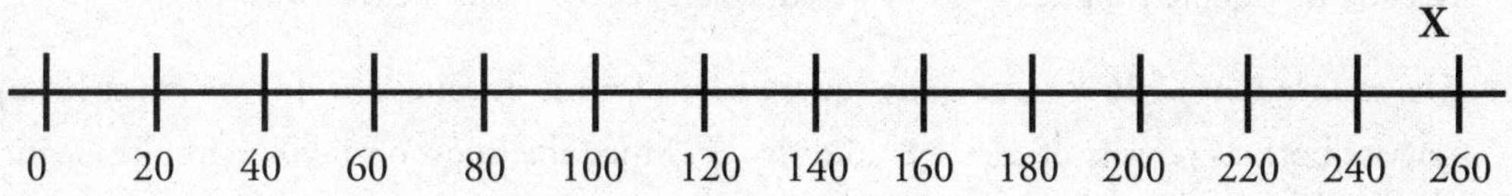

2. **D** When multiplying the same base, add the exponents: 4 + 2 + 3 = 9.

3. **5^{11}** When multiplying the same base, add the exponents: 2 + 7 + 2 = 11.

4. **A** When dividing the same base, subtract the exponents: 3 – 2 = 1.

5. **D** If the bases are not the same, convert them to the same bases. Since 64 is a power of 4, rewrite it as such: $64 = 4^3$. Since the 64 was raised to the third power, raise 4^3 to the third power as well, by multiplying the exponents: 4^9. This gives $\frac{4^9}{4^4}$.

   Now that the bases are the same and are in a division question, subtract the exponents: 9 – 4 = 5.

6. **C** To divide the same base, subtract the exponents: 7 – 2 = 5.

7. **3,125** Multiply 125 by 25.

8. **C** If the bases are not the same, convert them to the same bases. Since 343 is a power of 7, rewrite it as such: $343 = 7^3$. Since that is raised to the fourth power, multiply the exponents, resulting in 7^{12}. Dividing 7^{12} by 7^3 results in subtracting the exponents, or 7^9.

9. **D** To raise a power to another power, multiply the exponents: 3 × 2 = 6.

10. **B** When bases are not the same, convert them to the same bases: 4 is a power of 2, so convert it to 2^2. Since that is then raised to the second power, multiply the exponents, resulting in 2^4 in the denominator. Since the question is dividing, subtract the exponents, resulting in 2^0. Anything to the 0 power is equal to 1.

11. **C** To divide, subtract the bases: 3^1. Any value raised to the first power is equal to itself.

12. **C** Take the square root of each value first, then subtract: $\sqrt{36} = 6$; $\sqrt{4} = 2$; $6 - 2 = 4$.

13. **A** Since the question is dividing two roots, combine both values under the same square root sign: $\sqrt{\frac{12}{3}}$. Then, divide 12 by 3 to get 4. The square root of 4 is 2.

14. **B** To find the roots of numbers that aren't perfect squares, look for factors that are perfect squares. So, to find $\sqrt{48}$, look for factors of 48 that are perfect squares: 16. Rewrite the value using these factors: $\sqrt{16 \times 3}$. Since 16 is a perfect square, it can move out of the square root sign and sit in front of it as its root: $4\sqrt{3}$. Repeat with $\sqrt{12}$, which can be written as $\sqrt{4 \times 3}$. The 4 can move outside the square root, leaving $2\sqrt{3}$. Subtract: $4\sqrt{3} - 2\sqrt{3}$ leaves $2\sqrt{3}$.

15. **2, 24** The square root of 16 is 4, and the square root of 64 is 8. Since the answer must be a power of 2, rewrite both as powers of 2: $4 = 2^2$ and $8 = 2^3$. Since the question involves multiplication, add the exponents ($2 + 3 = 5$), and then raise that to the power of 3: 2^{15}.

Scientific Notation Drill

1. **A** When a question has scientific notation with a positive exponent, move the decimal to the right the same number of spaces as the exponent. So, since the exponent here is 6, move the decimal to the right 6 spaces: from 3.5 to 3,500,000.

2. **B** When a question has scientific notation with a positive exponent, move the decimal to the right the same number of spaces as the exponent. So, since the exponent here is 3, move the decimal to the right 3 spaces: from 4.01 to 4,010.

3. **D** The first exponent is 8, so convert 9.2 into 920,000,000; then, since the second exponent is 7, convert 6.5 into 65,000,000. Add the results together: 985,000,000. Then, count back from the right until there is only one digit left – that's 8 spaces. So, written in scientific notation: 9.85×10^8.

4. **B** When a question has scientific notation with a negative exponent, move the decimal to the left the same number of spaces as the exponent. Since the exponent here is -4, move the decimal to the left 4 spaces: from 7.2 to 0.00072.

5. **C** When a question has scientific notation with a negative exponent, move the decimal to the left the same number of spaces as the exponent. Since the exponent here is -2, move the decimal to the left 2 spaces: from 5.3 to 0.053.

6. **A** Since the exponent here is 4, move the decimal to the left 4 spaces: from 4.4 to 0.00044.

7. **C** When converting a value to scientific notation, always leave one digit in front of the decimal. Then, count how many spaces there are between where the decimal started and where it ended. If it moved to the left, use a positive exponent; if the decimal moved to the right, use a negative exponent. So, starting with 32,450,000, move the decimal to the left until it says 3.245. Then, count how many spaces the decimal moved (7) and in which direction (left). That means it becomes 3.245×10^7.

8. **D** When converting a value to scientific notation, always leave one digit in front of the decimal. Then, count how many spaces there are between where the decimal started and where it ended. If it moved to the left, use a positive exponent; if the decimal moved to the right, use a negative exponent. So, starting with 7,200, move the decimal to the left until it says 7.2. Then, count how many spaces the decimal moved (3) and in which direction (left). That means it becomes 7.2×10^3.

9. **B** Add the values together: 31,400. When converting a value to scientific notation, always leave one digit in front of the decimal. Then, count how many spaces there are between where the decimal started and where it ended. If it moved to the left, use a positive exponent; if the decimal moved to the right, use a negative exponent. So, starting with 31,400, move the decimal to the left until it says 3.14. Then, count how many spaces the decimal moved (4) and in which direction (left). That means it becomes 3.14×10^4.

10. **A** When converting a value to scientific notation, always leave one digit in front of the decimal. Then, count how many spaces there are between where the decimal started and where it ended. If it moved to the left, use a positive exponent; if the decimal moved to the right, use a negative exponent. So, starting with 0.00045, move the decimal to the left until it says 4.5. Then, count how many spaces the decimal moved (4) and in which direction (right). That means it becomes 4.5×10^{-4}.

11. **D** Subtract: $0.032 - 0.005 = 0.027$. When converting a value to scientific notation, always leave one digit in front of the decimal. Then, count how many spaces there are between where the decimal started and where it ended. If it moved to the left, use a positive exponent; if the decimal moved to the right, use a negative exponent. So, starting with 0.027, move the decimal to the left until it says 2.7. Then, count how many spaces the decimal moved (2) and in which direction (right). That means it becomes 2.7×10^{-2}.

12. **C** When converting a value to scientific notation, always leave one digit in front of the decimal. Then, count how many spaces there are between where the decimal started and where it ended. If it moved to the left, use a positive exponent; if the decimal moved to the right, use a negative exponent. So, starting with 0.00000078, move the decimal to the left until it says 7.8. Then, count how many spaces the decimal moved (7) and in which direction (right). That means it becomes 7.8×10^{-7}.

Probability Drill

1. **B** Probability is always a representation of the number of results that satisfy what you WANT out of the total number of results you could GET. In this case, you WANT a spade numbered 1, 2, 3, 4 or 5, which would be 5 cards that satisfy what you want. With a total of 52 cards in a deck, the probability of pulling a spade with a value of 5 or less would be 5 out of 52, or $\frac{5}{52}$.

2. $\mathbf{\frac{1}{11}}$ Probability is always a representation of the number of results that satisfy what you WANT out of the total number of results you could GET. It's often easiest to count the total number of options first, which gives the denominator. In this case, Megan can choose from 11 different pairs of shoes (2 sneakers, 3 high-heeled, 5 sandals, 1 boots). With only one pair of boots to select, the resulting probability is $\frac{1}{11}$.

3. $\mathbf{\frac{1}{5}}$ At first, it seems like there isn't enough information to answer the question. The key is in the first sentence: A jar has been filled with **equal portions** of various flavors of jellybeans: **strawberry, orange, lemon, apple, and blueberry**. Because there are equal portions of five flavors, the probability of picking ANY flavor is equal to the probability of picking any other flavor: 1 flavor picked out of 5 available flavors, or $\frac{1}{5}$.

4. **A** In this question, the total number of results that McKenzi could roll would be 6, so that's the denominator. Out of the six possible results, 3 are odd, which would be the numerator. The probability of rolling an odd number is $\frac{3}{6}$, or $\frac{1}{2}$.

5. **C** The first step in tackling this question is to divide the total ticket sales by $15 to determine how many tickets each student sold: Amanda, 7; Danya, 4; Jorge, 12; Matthew, 8; Zoe, 6. Add all of the tickets up to find the total number sold: 37. Matthew sold 8 of them, so the probability of him winning the prize is $\frac{8}{37}$. Alternatively, add all of the total ticket sales together ($555) – that's the denominator. Then, Matthew's ticket sales ($120) would be the numerator. Then, that will reduce to $\frac{8}{37}$.

6. **C** Probability is always a representation of the number of results that satisfy what you WANT out of the total number of results you could GET. Barbi WANTS an art class, of which there are 2 available – that's the numerator. Barbi can choose from a total of 6 classes – that's the denominator. $\frac{2}{6}$ reduces to $\frac{1}{3}$.

7. $\frac{7}{27}$ This question doesn't directly give you the number of results that satisfy what Joe WANTS: 12 dogs, but 5 are less than a year old. That means that 7 are at least a year old – that's what Joe wants, so that's the numerator. Then, add all of the animals together to figure out how many different animals he could adopt – 27. That's the denominator. Therefore, the probability that Joe will adopt a dog that is at least one year old is $\frac{7}{27}$.

8. **A** Probability is always a representation of the number of results that satisfy what you WANT out of the total number of results you could GET. Sally WANTS one of the 8 programs (3 business or 5 law – she'd be happy with any of them) out of the 138 available. So that means the probability that she'll attend one of those is $\frac{8}{138}$; or $\frac{4}{69}$.

9. **B** The question calls for a non-fiction selection – there are 4 options that satisfy that requirement, out of 11 total books. The probability that she will select a non-fiction book is $\frac{4}{11}$.

10. **D** The question asks for the likelihood of choosing the one white wire out of all 7 available: $\frac{1}{7}$.

11. $\frac{11}{12}$ This question asks what the likelihood is that Darla will NOT choose the fruit bowl; there are 11 options that satisfy this requirement, out of a total of 12 options she could select. That means the probability that she won't bring the fruit bowl is $\frac{11}{12}$.

12. **B** There are 2 pictures that satisfy the question's request of a picture of the whole family, out of 6 total pictures available: $\frac{2}{6}$, or $\frac{1}{3}$

Counting Drill

1. **5,040** This question has a couple of potentially tricky pieces to be aware of. First, remember that the digits to consider include all digits from 0 through 9, which is a total of ten digits. Then, because the question indicates that none of the digits can be repeated, treat this question as if order DOES matter. So, write out four blanks to represent the four spaces that need to be filled. Then, consider the number of digits available for the first space: 10. For the second space, regardless of which digit was used in the first space, there are 9 digits available for the second space. Then there will be 8 left for the third space, and 7 left for the fourth space. Multiply all values together for a product of 5,040.

2. **C** Think about whether these selections are being made from the same source or different sources: the question indicates that no applicant has applied for more than one position, so that confirms different sources. Next, draw a blank for each position that is being filled. Each one has three applicants, so write 3 in each space and then multiply.

3. **B** Consider whether these selections are being made from the same source or different sources: Lisa has the same group of twelve medals from which she is selecting ones to display, so that confirms same source. Next, draw a blank for each space being filled. For the first space, Lisa could select any of the 12 medals; for the second, she could select any of the remaining 11; for the third, she could select any of the remaining 10; for the fourth, she could select any of the remaining 9; for the last space, she could select any of the remaining 8. Multiply all of these together. Lastly, consider whether the question asks for all of the ARRANGEMENTS of the medals, or the COMBINATIONS of medals. Since it calls for combinations, eliminate repeat combinations by dividing by the factorial of the number of spaces being filled:

$$\frac{12 \times 11 \times 10 \times 9 \times 8}{5!} = \frac{12 \times 11 \times 10 \times 9 \times 8}{5 \times 4 \times 3 \times 2 \times 1}$$

Before multiplying, cancel out values from the top and bottom. For example, 12 on top will cancel with the 4 × 3 on the bottom. The 10 on top will cancel with the 5 × 2 on the bottom:

$$\frac{\cancel{12} \times 11 \times \cancel{10} \times 9 \times 8}{\cancel{5} \times \cancel{4} \times \cancel{3} \times \cancel{2} \times 1}$$

This makes the math much easier, with simply 11 × 9 × 8 remaining.

4. **D** Are these selections being made from the same source or different sources? Since all seven tiles are already in her hand, she'll be choosing from the same group of seven. Draw seven blanks, one for each space being filled. For the first space, Vivian can choose from 7 tiles; for the second, 6; for the third, 5; etc., all the way to 1 tile option for the final space. Multiply these together. Lastly, consider whether the question asks for all of the ARRANGEMENTS of the tiles, or the COMBINATIONS of tiles. Since it asks for arrangements, do not try to remove any duplicates by dividing – just leave the product alone.

5. **216** Check to see whether these selections are being made from the same source or different sources: there are three different components of dinner, Horace will be selecting from different sources for each. Draw three blanks, one for each space being filled. For the first space, he can choose from 4 side dishes; he can choose from 6 vegetables for the next space. He can also choose from 3 entrees for the third space and 3 beverages for the last space. Multiply these together. Because all choices are from different sources, no further work is needed.

6. **B** Consider whether these selections are being made from the same source or different sources: Mary Ruth is choosing from the same group of ten items, so that confirms same source. Next, draw a blank for each space being filled. For the first space, she could select any of the 10 items; for the second, she could select any of the remaining 9; for the third, she could select any of the remaining 8; continue with this thought process down to 5 items available for the last space. Multiply all of these together. Lastly, consider whether the question asks for all of the ARRANGEMENTS of the items, or the COMBINATIONS of items. Since it calls for combinations, eliminate repeat combinations by dividing by the factorial of the number of spaces being filled:

$$\frac{10 \times 9 \times 8 \times 7 \times 6 \times 5}{6!} = \frac{10 \times 9 \times 8 \times 7 \times 6 \times 5}{6 \times 5 \times 4 \times 3 \times 2 \times 1}$$

Again, simplify by cancelling values in the numerator and the denominator before you multiply. The 6 & 5 on the top will cancel with the 6 & 5 on the bottom. The 8 on top will cancel with the 4 & 2 on the bottom. And the 9 on top will cancel with the 3 on the bottom, leaving 10 × 3 × 7.

$$\frac{10 \times \overset{3}{\cancel{9}} \times \cancel{8} \times 7 \times \cancel{6} \times \cancel{5}}{\cancel{6} \times \cancel{5} \times \cancel{4} \times \cancel{3} \times \cancel{2} \times 1}$$

7. **C** Think about whether these selections are being made from the same source or different sources: there are seven different categories with unique semi-finalists in each, which indicates different sources for each category. Draw seven blanks, one for each space being filled. For each space, there are 3 possible winners. Multiply these together. Because all choices are from different sources, no further work is needed.

8. **B** Are these selections being made from the same source or different sources? There are five different athletes, and the winners will come out of this group of five. This indicates same source. Draw three blanks, one for each space being filled, first through third. For the first space, there are 5 athletes who could place first. Once one athlete has crossed the finish line, there are 4 remaining athletes who could take second place. Then, there are 3 athletes who could claim third place. Multiply these together. Lastly, consider whether the question asks for all of the ARRANGEMENTS of the tiles, or the COMBINATIONS of tiles. Since it asks for arrangements, do not try to remove any duplicates by dividing – just leave the product alone. Note that the prize amounts are extra information not relevant to the question.

9. **D** Look at whether these selections are being made from the same source or different sources: there are three different categories with distinct options for each, which indicates different sources for each category. Draw three blanks, one for each space being filled. For the first space, there are 3 destinations to consider; for the second, there are 2 modes of travel; for the last, there are 3 options for the length of the stay. (Be careful not to get confused by the '4, 5 or 6 nights' – those are really THREE different durations!) Multiply these together. Because all choices are from different sources, no further work is needed.

10. **45** Think about whether these selections are being made from the same source or different sources: Barb is selecting from one group of 10 cards, which confirms same source. Next, draw a blank for each space being filled. For the first space, she could select any of the 10 items; for the second, she could select any of the remaining 9. Multiply these together. Lastly, consider whether the question asks for all of the ARRANGEMENTS of the items, or the COMBINATIONS of items. Since it calls for combinations, eliminate repeat combinations by dividing by the factorial of the number of spaces being filled:

$$\frac{10 \times 9}{2 \times 1}$$

Again, simplify the 10 on top & 2 on the bottom, then multiply:

$$\frac{\overset{5}{\cancel{10}} \times 9}{\cancel{2} \times 1}$$

11. **B** Do we know whether these selections are being made from the same source or different sources? There are three different categories of choices to be made (meats, vegetables and sauces), which indicates different sources. However, also consider the two choices of toppings (meats & vegetables): does it matter whether the pizza shop puts pepperoni on before onions, or onions before pepperoni? Nope! So...be careful with how to deal with that. First, draw a blank for each space being filled (two for toppings and one for sauce). For the first space, there are 13 toppings to choose from; for the second, there are 12. Multiply these together. Here's how to deal with the pepperoni/onion aspect. Since it doesn't matter which of these two spaces is filled first, divide by the factorial of the number of spaces:

$$\frac{13 \times 12}{2 \times 1}$$

Then, put a 3 in for the number of sauce options:

$$\frac{13 \times 12 \times 3}{2 \times 1}$$

Simplify the 12 in the numerator with the 2 in the denominator and multiply.

$$\frac{13 \times \overset{6}{\cancel{12}} \times 3}{\cancel{2} \times 1}$$

12. **1,140** Consider whether these selections are being made from the same source or different sources: Allison is selecting from one large group of 20 movies, which confirms same source. Next, draw a blank for each space being filled. For the first space, she could select any of the 20 movies; for the second, she could select any of the remaining 19 movies; for the last she could choose any of the remaining 18. Multiply these together. Lastly, consider whether the question asks for all of the ARRANGEMENTS of the items, or the COMBINATIONS of items. Since it calls for combinations, eliminate repeat combinations by dividing by the factorial of the number of spaces being filled:

$$\frac{20 \times 19 \times 18}{3 \times 2 \times 1}$$

As always, simplify values from the numerator and the denominator to make the math easier:

$$\frac{20 \times 19 \times \overset{3}{\cancel{18}}}{\cancel{3} \times \cancel{2} \times 1}$$

Part IV
Algebra

As you work through this section, remember that you can refer to the Mathematics Formula Sheet if you need to. It's printed at the very back of this book, and you can also download it when you register your book online.

Simple Equations Drill

1. If $4x - 6 = 30$, then what is the value of x?

   A. 6
   B. 9
   C. 12
   D. 18

2. If $5c + 9 = 6c$, then $c =$

   A. −9
   B. $-\frac{9}{11}$
   C. $\frac{9}{11}$
   D. 9

3. If $2y + 3 = -3y - 2$, then $y =$

   A. −1
   B. $\frac{1}{5}$
   C. 1
   D. 5

4. If $8z - 7 = 5z + 11$, then what is the value of z?

   A. 3
   B. 6
   C. 12
   D. 18

5. If $4(d + 7) = 8$, then $d =$

   A. −5
   B. 2
   C. 7
   D. 9

6. If $-3(2x - 1) = -x - 2$, then $x =$

   [ ]

7. If $7(r - 3) = 21$, what is the value of $r - 3$?

   A. 3
   B. 6
   C. 9
   D. 27

8. If $6s + 8 = 26$, then $3s + 4 =$

   A. 3
   B. 10
   C. 13
   D. 17

9. If $\frac{6}{13} = \frac{18}{x}$, then $x =$

   A. $4\frac{1}{3}$
   B. 25
   C. $27\frac{2}{3}$
   D. 39

10. If $\frac{2m}{3} = \frac{8}{3m}$, then which of the following could be the value of m?

A. −4
B. −2
C. 4
D. 6

11. If $5cy = 10$, then $y =$

A. $2c$

B. $\frac{c}{2}$

C. $\frac{2}{c}$

D. $5c$

12. If $3ax = \frac{42a}{5}$, then what is the value of x?

A. $\frac{14}{5}$

B. $\frac{14a}{5}$

C. $\frac{14}{5a}$

D. $\frac{14a^2}{5}$

13. If $r = -2$ and $s = 3$, what is the value of $4r - 3s$?

A. −17
B. −1
C. 1
D. 17

14. If $m = 3$ and $n = 4$, what is the value of $m + 4n$?

[ ]

15. If $p = -3$ and $5p + 11 = 2q$, then what is the value of q?

A. −6
B. −4
C. −3
D. −2

16. If $c = 2$ and $2c - 3d = 4d$, then $d =$

A. $\frac{4}{7}$

B. $\frac{7}{2}$

C. 4

D. 7

Inequalities Drill

1. If $3x + 5 \geq 23$, then which of the following expressions gives all possible values of x?

   A. $x \geq 8$
   B. $x \geq 6$
   C. $x \geq 4$
   D. $x \geq 2$

2. If $-4y - 8 < 12$, then which of the following expressions gives all possible values of y?

   A. $y > -5$
   B. $y > 5$
   C. $y < 5$
   D. $y < -5$

3. If $5z + 17 \leq 6z$, what is the least possible value of z?

4. If $2n + 4 > 5n + 13$, then which of the following expressions gives all possible values of n?

   A. $n < -9$
   B. $n > -3$
   C. $n < -3$
   D. $n > -9$

5. If $7m + 5 < 19$, then which of the following is a possible value of m?

   A. 1
   B. 2
   C. 3
   D. 4

6. For which of the following values of a is the inequality $-3a - 5 \leq 4a + 7$ true?

   A. -4
   B. -3
   C. -2
   D. -1

7. If $c = 3$, which of the following inequalities contains the value of c?

   A. $x > 4$
   B. $x > 2$
   C. $x < -2$
   D. $x < -4$

8. If p is the integer -2, which of the following inequalities could be true?

   A. $2p + 4 < -3$
   B. $4p - 4 > -4$
   C. $-3p + 2 > 7$
   D. $-5p - 3 < 6$

9. If three more than x is less than four times x, which of the following is a possible value of x?

   A. -1
   B. 0
   C. 1
   D. 2

10. If three less than twice p is greater than or equal to eight times p, then which of the following inequalities must be true?

A. $p \leq -\frac{1}{2}$

B. $p \geq -\frac{1}{2}$

C. $p \geq -2$

D. $p \leq -2$

11. Shelton is more than five years older than twice Roberta's age. If Shelton is s years old and Roberta is r years old, which of the following inequalities must be true?

A. $s > 2r + 5$

B. $s > 2(r + 5)$

C. $s + 5 > 2r$

D. $2s > r + 5$

12. A pretzel stand pays $100 to rent a spot in a park for a day. It also pays 50 cents per pretzel. If the pretzel stand charges $2 per pretzels and the stand only needs to pay for the pretzels it sells, which of the following inequalities can be used to determine how many pretzels p the pretzel stand must sell for the revenues to be greater than the costs?

A. $2p < 0.50p + 100$

B. $2p < 0.50(p + 100)$

C. $2p > 0.50(p + 100)$

D. $2p > 0.50p + 100$

13. In order for a college club to retain certification, the number of members must be at least two-thirds the number of members in the previous year. If a club of 90 members lost m members, which of the following expresses the possible values of m that would allow the club to retain certification.

A. $m \geq 30$

B. $m \leq 30$

C. $m \leq 60$

D. $m \geq 60$

14. In order to be considered an antique, an item must be at least 100 years old. Which of the following expresses the age of all items that *are* considered antiques?

A. $x > 100$

B. $x < 100$

C. $x \geq 100$

D. $x \leq 100$

15. In order for a boxer to qualify as a welterweight, he cannot weigh more than 147 pounds. Which of the following inequalities expresses the weight of a boxer who does qualify as a welterweight?

A. $w > 147$

B. $w < 147$

C. $w \geq 147$

D. $w \leq 147$

16. The weight of the legal soccer ball must be within the range of 14 to 16 ounces. Which of the following expresses the possible weight of a ball that is NOT legal?

A. $14 < b < 16$

B. $b < 14$ or $b > 16$

C. $b = 15$

D. $15 > b > 14$

Translating Words into Math Drill

1. Morgan is eight years older than her cousin Lawrence. If Morgan is m years old, how old is Lawrence?

   A. $m + 8$

   B. $m - 8$

   C. $8m$

   D. $\frac{m}{8}$

2. Virgil has half as many baseball cards as his sister Cheryl. If Cheryl has c baseball cards, how many baseball cards does Virgil have?

   A. $2c$

   B. $c + \frac{1}{2}$

   C. $c - \frac{1}{2}$

   D. $\frac{1}{2}c$

3. Brad has five dollars less than four times the amount of money that Georgia has. If Georgia has d dollars, how many dollars does Brad have?

   A. $4d - 5$
   B. $4(d - 5)$
   C. $5d - 4$
   D. $5(d - 4)$

4. Bartolo decides to begin a record collection. He starts by buying a set of r records. Three years later, he increases his collection to five times what it was originally. What is the number of records in his collection three years after he began?

   A. $3r - 5$
   B. $5r - 3$
   C. $5r$
   D. $5r + 3$

5. A piano store doubles its inventory. After doing so, it sells five pianos. If the store had p pianos originally and buys no additional pianos, how many pianos does it currently have?

   A. $p - 10$

   B. $\frac{p - 5}{2}$

   C. $2(p - 5)$

   D. $2p - 5$

6. The population of a city doubles every five years. If the city's current population is p, which of the following given the population of the city in 10 years?

   A. $2p$
   B. $4p$
   C. $10p$
   D. $25p$

7. Booker is three times as old as Ken was four years ago. If Ken is k years old now, how old is Booker?

A. $\frac{k - 4}{3}$

B. $\frac{k + 4}{3}$

C. $3k - 4$

D. $3(k - 4)$

8. If four more than m is two less than three times n, which of the following must be true?

A. $4 + m = 2 - 3n$
B. $m + 4 = 3n - 2$
C. $m + 4 = 3(n - 2)$
D. $m = 3(n - 2) + 4$

9. Triple x is equal to the positive difference between x and y. If $x < y$, which of the following must be true?

A. $3x = y - x$

B. $3x = \frac{y}{x}$

C. $x = y - 3x$

D. $x = 3(y - x)$

10. Twice the square of x is the square root of twice y. Which of the following equations best expresses this relationship?

A. $(2x)^2 = \sqrt{2y}$

B. $(2x)^2 = 2\sqrt{y}$

C. $2x^2 = 2\sqrt{y}$

D. $2x^2 = \sqrt{2y}$

11. Jon is twelve years older than Fiona. In four years, Jon will be twice as old as Fiona. If Jon and Fiona's current ages, in years, are j and f, respectively, which of the following equations could be used to determine their current ages?

A. $j = f + 12$
$2j = f$
B. $f = j + 12$
$2(j + 4) = f + 4$
C. $j = f + 12$
$j + 4 = 2(f + 4)$
D. $f = j + 12$
$j + 4 = 2(f + 4)$

12. A local post office sells two denominations of stamps: postcard stamps that cost 34 cents and first class stamps that cost 49 cents. Hector went to the post office and bought x postcard stamps and y first class stamps for a total of $5.17. If Hector bought a total of thirteen stamps, which of the following is true?

A. $x + y = 5.17$
$0.34x + 0.49y = 13$
B. $x + y = 13$
$0.34x + 0.49y = 5.17$
C. $x + y = 13$
$0.49x + 0.34y = 5.17$
D. $x + y = 5.17$
$0.49x + 0.34y = 13$

13. A troop of a summer camp serves only seven- and eight-year-olds. The sum of the ages of the twenty children in the troop is 149. If there are *a* seven-year-olds and *b* eight-year-olds in the troop, what equation could be used to determine the number of children of each age?

[ ] a + [ ] b = [ ]

$a + b$ = [ ]

7 8 15

20 129 149

14. What is forty percent of 30?

A. 6
B. 12
C. 24
D. 75

15. Twenty-five percent of what number is 20?

[ ]

16. What percent of eighty is 24?

A. 19.2
B. 30
C. 64
D. 76

17. Sixty percent of seventy-five percent of what number is equal to one hundred thirty-five?

A. 60.75
B. 81
C. 300
D. 540

18. Twenty percent of x is eighty percent of y. Which of the following is the value of x in terms of y?

A. $4y$
B. $5y$
C. $10y$
D. $20y$

19. Khalil has eight percent as many gumballs as Jacob. If Khalil has k gumballs and Jacob has j, which of the following equations is true?

A. $j = \frac{8k}{100}$

B. $k = 1.08j$

C. $j = 1.08k$

D. $k = \frac{8j}{100}$

20. Naomi has \$8,000 in the bank. She withdraws thirty-five percent of her money to spend on her vacation. After this withdrawal, her bank pays interest equal to 5% of what she has in the bank. How much does she currently have in the bank?

A. \$4,800
B. \$4,940
C. \$5,460
D. \$5,880

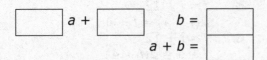

Polynomials Drill

1. What is the result of $4y + 2(x + 3y) - 5x$?

   A. $x + 6y$
   B. $6x + y$
   C. $-3x + 10y$
   D. $7xy$

2. Which of the following is equivalent to $x^2 + 2x - 3x^2 + 9 + 6x$?

   A. $2x^2 - 4x + 9$
   B. $-2x^2 + 8x + 9$
   C. $-3x^2 + 8x - 9$
   D. $-2x^2 + 4x + 9$

3. Simplify the expression $5x^2 - 2x(x + 5) - 9(x + y^2) + 10y(y + 1) - 5y$.

   A. $5x^2 - 9x + 10y^2 - 5y$
   B. $5x^2 - 19x + 10y^2 + 5y$
   C. $3x^2 + 9x + 2y^2 + 5y$
   D. $3x^2 - 19x + y^2 + 5y$

4. Simplify.

   $(x^2y^3)^4(x^3y^{-2})^2$

   A. $x^{11}y^0$
   B. $x^{48}y^{-48}$
   C. $x^{14}y^8$
   D. $x^{24}y^{12}$

5. Simplify.

   $$\frac{a^6b^8c^{10}}{a^2b^4c^5}$$

   A. $a^4b^4c^5$
   B. $a^3b^2c^2$
   C. $a^8b^{12}c^{15}$
   D. $a^{12}b^{32}c^{50}$

6. Multiply.

   $(x + 3)(x - 7)$

   A. $x^2 - 4x - 21$
   B. $x^2 - 21x - 4$
   C. $x^2 + 4x - 21$
   D. $x^2 - 21x + 21$

7. Which of the following is equivalent to $(2y + 4)(y + 2)$?

   A. $2y^2 + 6y + 8$
   B. $2y^2 + 8y + 8$
   C. $2y^2 + 8y + 6$
   D. $2y^2 + 6y + 6$

8. Multiply.

   $(2z - 3)(3z + 4)$

   A. $5z^2 - z - 12$
   B. $5z^2 - 12z + 1$
   C. $6z^2 - 12z + 1$
   D. $6z^2 -z - 12$

9. Which of the following is the factored form of $x^2 + 8x + 15$?

   A. $(x + 1)(x + 15)$
   B. $(x + 8)(x + 15)$
   C. $(x + 3)(x + 5)$
   D. $(x + 2)(x + 6)$

10. Which of the following is a factor of $x^2 - 6x + 2x - 12$?

    A. $(x + 12)$
    B. $(x + 6)$
    C. $(x - 2)$
    D. $(x - 6)$

11. Factor the expression $3x^2 + 9x - 2x - 6$.

A. $(3x - 1)(x + 6)$
B. $(3x - 2)(x + 3)$
C. $(3x + 2)(x - 3)$
D. $(3x + 2)(x - 6)$

12. Which of the following is the factored form of the expression $2c^2 - 3c + 4cd - 6d$?

A. $(c - 2d)(2c + 3)$
B. $(c + 3d)(2c - 2)$
C. $(c - 3d)(2c + 2)$
D. $(c + 2d)(2c - 3)$

13. Solve the equation for x.

$x^2 + 4x = 32$

A. $x = -4$ and $x = 8$

B. $x = 4$ and $x = -8$

C. $x = \frac{-4 \pm \sqrt{48}}{2}$

D. $x = \frac{-4 \pm \sqrt{48}}{4}$

14. Solve the equation for x.

$3x^2 + 6x = -2$

A. $x = \frac{-6 \pm \sqrt{12}}{3}$

B. $x = \frac{-6 \pm \sqrt{12}}{6}$

C. $x = 6$ and $x = -1$

D. $x = -6$ and $x = 1$

15. What is the sum of the solutions to $x^2 - 7x + 12 = 0$?

[ ]

16. What is the product of the solutions to $2x^2 + 6x = 80$?

A. 80
B. 40
C. -40
D. -80

Simultaneous Equations Drill

1. If $2x + y = 12$ and $y = 4x$, then what is the value of x?

   A. 1
   B. 2
   C. 4
   D. 6

2. If $3x - 2y = -21$ and $y = 5x$, then what is the value of y?

   A. −15
   B. −3
   C. 3
   D. 15

3. If $5x + 2y = 7$ and $-4x - 2y = 5$, then what is the value of x?

   A. 2
   B. 6
   C. 9
   D. 12

4. If $-3x + 4y = 22$ and $-3x + y = 13$, then what is the value of y?

   A. 3
   B. 7
   C. 9
   D. 35

5. If $2x + 3y = 7$ and $3x - 3y = 3$, then what is the value of y?

   A. −1
   B. 1
   C. 2
   D. 3

6. If $3x + 4y = 10$ and $x - 8y = 6$, then what is the value of $4x - 4y$?

   A. 1
   B. 8
   C. 16
   D. 32

7. If $8a + 2b = 4$ and $2a + 4b = 8$, then what is the value of $20a + 12b$?

   A. 0
   B. 2
   C. 12
   D. 24

8. If $-6x + 5y = 10$ and $8x = 3y - 4$, then what is the sum of x and y?

9. If $y = x^2 + 1$ and $y = 2x$, then which of the following is the value of $x - 1$?

   A. −1
   B. 0
   C. 1
   D. 2

10. If $p + q = r$, $q = p - 7$, and $r = p + 1$, what is the value of p?

    A. −5
    B. −1
    C. 2
    D. 8

11. If $3a + 2b + 4c = 12$, $b = -4c + 2$, and $a = 6 - b$, select values for a, b, and c.

a	
b	
c	

−3	−0.5	0.5	1
2	3.5	4	

12. If the sum of x and twice y is 14 and x is one less than y, what is the value of y?

A. 2
B. 3
C. 4
D. 5

13. If x is two more than y and the product of x and y is 48, then which of the following could be the sum of x and y?

A. −16
B. −14
C. 10
D. 16

14. Hendrick's Hardware Supplies sells boxes of nails in two different sizes. Large boxes cost three dollars each and small boxes cost two dollars each. If Yolanda goes into the Hendrick's Hardware Supplies and buys seven boxes of nails for a total of nineteen dollars, then how many small boxes did she buy?

A. 2
B. 3
C. 5
D. 7

15. Natasha is three years younger than twice her brother's age. If Natasha's brother is seven years younger than she is, how old is Natasha?

A. 10
B. 14
C. 17
D. 21

16. A printing company is printing rectangular posters for which the width is four inches longer than the length. If the area of each of the posters is 96 square inches, select the values for the length and the width of each poster in inches.

Width	**Length**

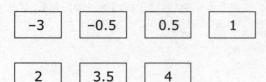

Functions Drill

1. Which of the following relations is a function of *x*?

A.

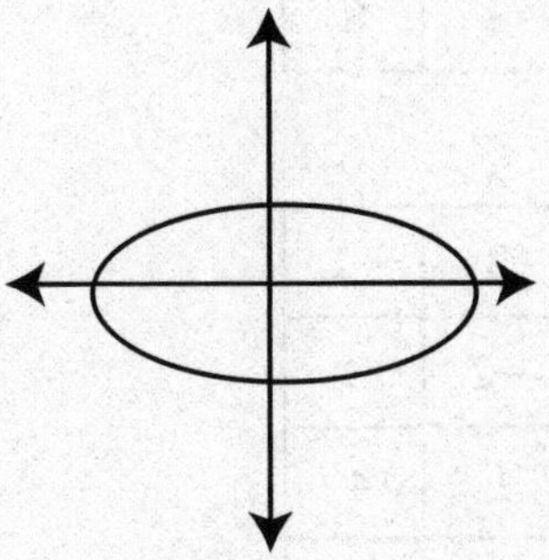

B.

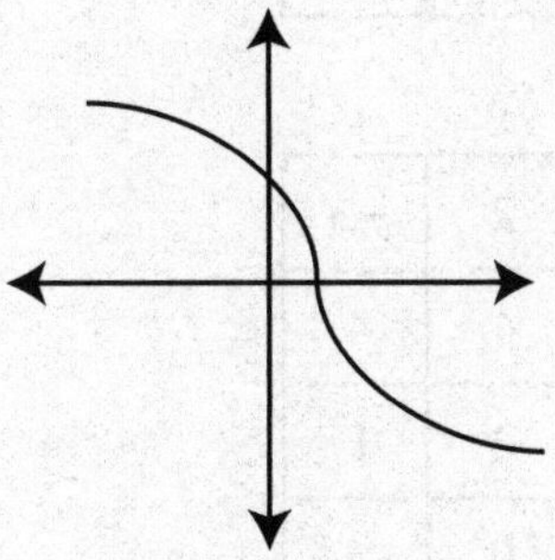

C.

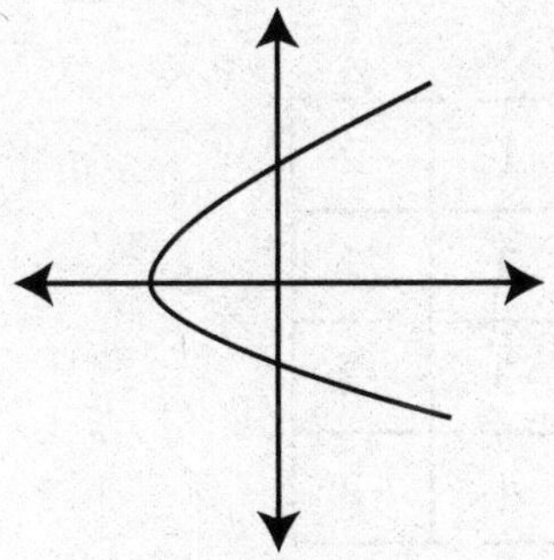

D.

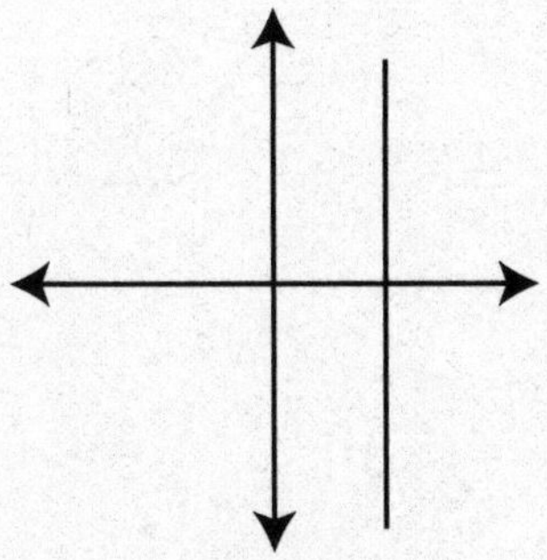

2. Which of the following relations is NOT a function?

A.

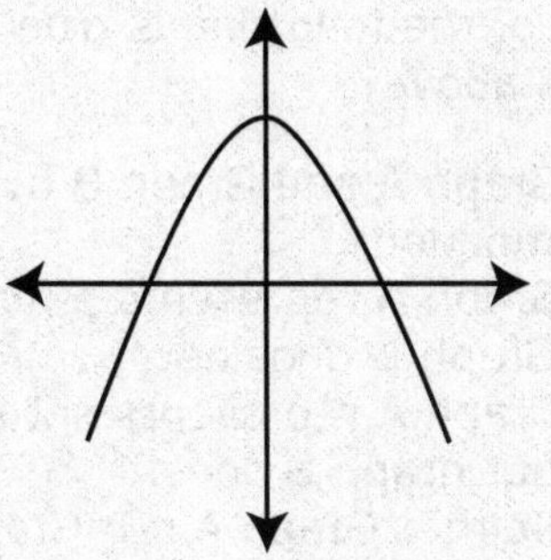

B.

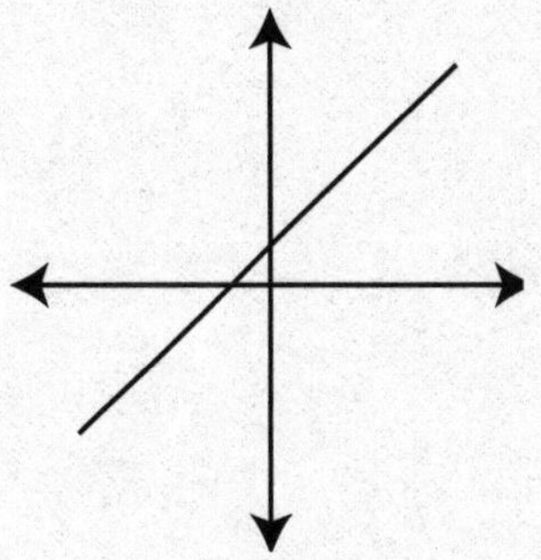

C.

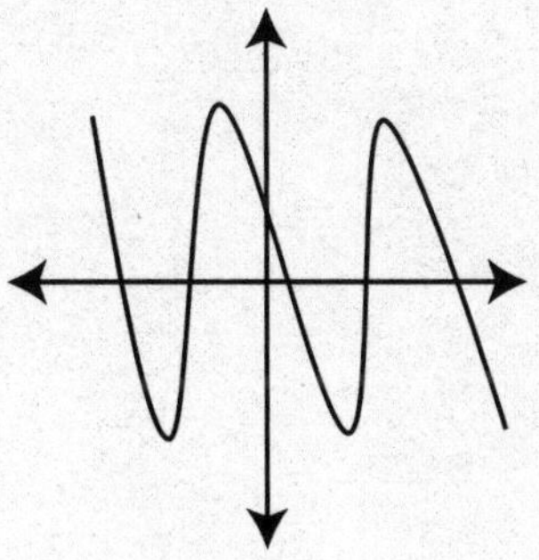

D.

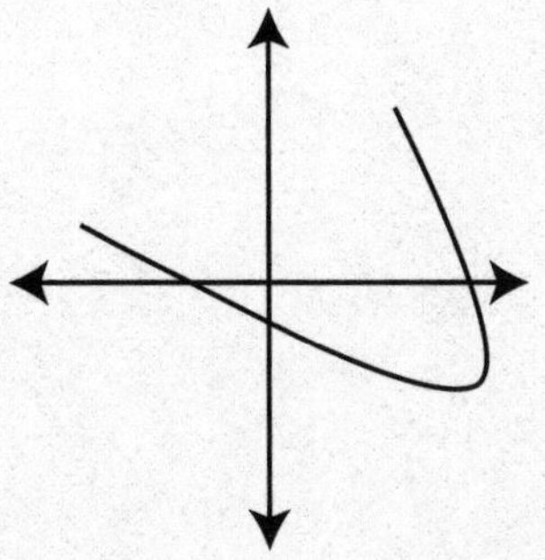

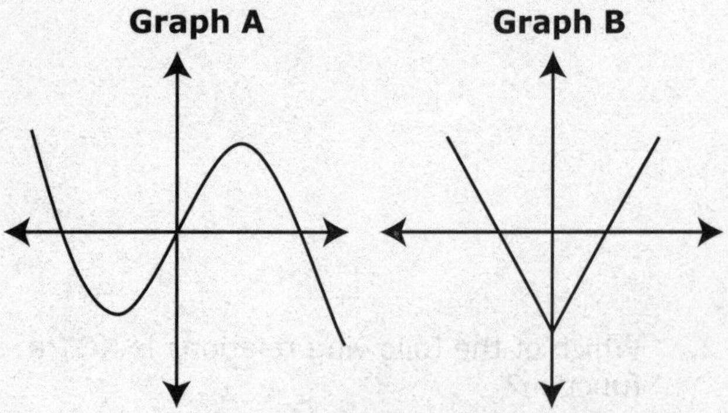

3. Which of the following is true of the graphs above?

   A. Graph A and Graph B both represent functions.
   B. Graph A represents a function but Graph B does not.
   C. Graph A represents not a function but graph B does.
   D. Neither Graph A nor Graph B represents a function.

4. Which of the following tables does NOT represent a function of *x* on *y*?

A.

x	*y*
2	4
5	2
−1	4
3	8

B.

x	*y*
3	−1
−2	3
1	4
0	0

C.

x	*y*
2	−3
4	4
2	1
0	8

D.

x	*y*
1	−2
2	−2
3	−2
4	−2

5. Which of the following tables represents a function of x on y?

A.

x	y
3	2
2	2
1	−4
3	−4

B.

x	y
4	1
2	1
5	1
2	1

C.

x	y
6	−3
5	9
−2	−4
5	7

D.

x	y
5	−5
3	−3
3	2
4	6

6. Select one number for each column so that it contains a function. Do not repeat an ordered pair from the table.

x	y
8	9
6	1
9	9
13	5

1 6 8

9 13

7. If $f(x) = 2x - 4$, what is the value of $f(3)$?

A. 2
B. 3
C. 6
D. 10

8. If $g(x) = 3x^3 - 2x^2 + 8$, what is the value of $g(4)$?

A. 126
B. 144
C. 168
D. 188

9. If $h(x) = 2x^2 + 3x - 4$ and $h(t) = 86$, what is the value of t?

A. 3
B. 4
C. 5
D. 6

10. A coffee shop tracks its expenses in dollars by the function $E(c) = .50c + 1{,}000$, where c represents the number of cups of coffee sold. It also tracks the revenues in dollars by the function $R(c) = 1.25c$, where c is the number of cups of coffee sold. What are the revenues for the coffee shop when its expenses are $3,000?

A. $2,200
B. $3,700
C. $4,800
D. $5,000

11. If selected values of $f(x)$ are displayed in the table below, which of the following could be the equation for $f(x)$?

x	$f(x)$
−1	1
1	5
3	9
5	13

A. $f(x) = 2x + 3$
B. $f(x) = 5x - 2$
C. $f(x) = 4x + 5$
D. $f(x) = 3x + 2$

12. If values of the quadratic function $g(x)$ are displayed in the table below, which of the following could be the equation of $g(x)$?

x	$g(x)$
1	0
2	9
3	22
4	39

A. $g(x) = x^2 - 2x + 6$
B. $g(x) = 2x^2 + 3x - 5$
C. $g(x) = 4x^2 - 8x + 4$
D. $g(x) = 3x^2 + 4x + 7$

13. If values of the function $h(x)$ are displayed in the table below, which of the following could be the equation of $h(x)$?

x	$h(x)$
−2	22
−1	−10
0	−4
1	4

A. $h(x) = x^3 + 2x^2 - 4x + 8$
B. $h(x) = x^4 - 4x^3 + 2x^2 + 7x - 4$
C. $h(x) = 4x^4 + 2x^3 - 3x^2 + 5x - 4$
D. $h(x) = 3x^3 + 7x^2 - 4x$

14. Which of the following tables accurately represents selected values of the function $f(x) = x^2 - 4x - 12$?

A.

x	$f(x)$
−2	0
0	−12
3	−15
6	0

B.

x	$f(x)$
−2	8
0	12
3	33
6	72

C.

x	$f(x)$
−2	24
0	12
3	9
6	24

D.

x	$f(x)$
−2	−16
0	−12
3	9
6	48

15. If $m(x)$ is a linear function that has a slope of −3 and a y-intercept of 10, select the values that fill the table below.

x	$m(x)$
0	
1	
2	
3	

−3	−1	1	3
4	5	7	10

16. If $g(x) = (x - 3)^2$, select the values that fill the table below.

x	$g(x)$
−1	
0	9
1	4
2	

−16	−5	−1	1
3	5	16	25

17. A toy store always keeps red and blue marbles in its inventory using a particular function. The number of red marbles is always 3 greater than twice the number of blue marbles. If r is a function determining the number and b is the number of blue marbles, what is $r(b)$?

A. $r(b) = 3b + 2$
B. $r(b) = 2(b + 3)$
C. $r(b) = 2b + 3$
D. $r(b) = 3(b + 2)$

18. Two linear functions, $f(x)$ and $g(x)$ are defined as follows: f has a slope of 2 and a y-intercept of −1 and g has slope of −4 and an x-intercept of 3. Select the correct answers for f and g from the choices below and write them into the boxes.

$f(x)$	
$g(x)$	

$-x + 2$	$2x - 1$	$3x - 4$
$4x + 1$	$-4x + 12$	$-4x + 3$

19. A sporting goods store staffs a number of employees each day based on the expected number of customers it has. The company needs one sales representative for every ten customers and also needs three managers regardless of the number of customers for the day. If the store staffs only these employees and the number of employees staffed in a given day, E, is a function of the number of customers, c, which of the following could be $E(c)$?

A. $E(c) = 10c + 3$

B. $E(c) = 10(c + 3)$

C. $E(c) = \frac{c + 3}{10}$

D. $E(c) = \frac{c}{10} + 3$

20. Stuart uses a function to determine the cost of his vacation to Calgary. Including hotel, he will spend \$200 each day. In addition to that, the round trip flight to Calgary will cost \$650 dollars, regardless of the amount of time he spends in Calgary. If the cost of the vacation, C, is given as a function of d, the length of the vacation in days, which of the following could be $C(d)$?

A. $C(d) = 650d$
B. $C(d) = 650 + 200d$
C. $C(d) = 200 + 650d$
D. $C(d) = 200d$

Algebra: Answers and Explanations

ALGEBRA: ANSWERS AND EXPLANATIONS

Simple Equations Drill

1. **B** Set up the equation $4x - 6 = 30$. Isolate x. Perform the reverse operation of what is in the equation. Whatever you to do one side of the equation, do to the other, as well. Since the equation subtracts 6, add 6 to both sides to get $4x = 36$. Since x is multiplied by 4, divide both sides by 4 to get $x = 9$. The correct answer is choice (B).

2. **D** When there are multiple terms with the same variable, bring them all to the same side of the equation. In this case, subtract $5c$ from both sides to get $9 = c$. The correct answer is choice (D).

3. **A** First bring the y terms together. Add $3y$ to both sides to get $5y + 3 = -2$. Subtract 3 from both sides to get $5y = -5$. Divide both sides by 5 to get $y = -1$. The correct answer is choice (A).

4. **B** Subtract $5z$ from both sides to get $3z - 7 = 11$. Add 7 to both sides to get $3z = 18$. Divide both sides by 3 to get $z = 6$. The correct answer is choice (B).

5. **A** There are two ways to solve this problem. One way is to distribute the 4 on the left side to get $4d + 28 = 8$. Subtract 28 from both sides to get $4d = -20$. Divide both sides by 4 to get $d = -5$. Alternatively, rather than distribute, divide both sides by 4 immediately to get d + 7 = 2. Subtract 7 from both sides to get $d = -5$. The correct answer is choice (A).

6. **1** Distribute –3 on the left side to get $-6x + 3 = -x - 2$. Add x to both sides to get $-5x + 3 = -2$. Subtract 3 from both sides to get $-5x = -5$. Divide both sides by –5 to get $x = 1$.

7. **A** There are two ways to solve this problem. One way is to distribute the 7 on the left sides to get $7r - 21 = 21$. Add 21 to both sides to get $7r = 42$. Divide both sides by 7 to get $r = 6$. However, this is not the answer, since the question asks for $r - 3 = 6 - 3 = 3$. Alternatively, rather than distributing the 7, divide by 7 to get $r - 3 = 3$. Since this is what the questions asks for, there is no need to solve for r. The correct answer is choice (A).

8. **C** There are two ways to solve this problem. One is to solve for s first. Subtract 8 from both sides to get $6s = 18$. Divide by 6 to get $s = 3$. This is not the answer, since the question asks from $3s + 4 = 3(3) + 4 = 9 + 4 = 13$. Alternatively, factor a 2 from the left side to get $2(3s + 4) = 26$. Divide both sides by 2 to get $3s + 4 = 13$. The correct answer is choice (C).

9. **D** When an equation has two fraction sets equal to each other, cross-multiply to solve for x: multiply the denominator of the first equation by the numerator of the second, multiply the denominator of the second equation by the numerator of the first, then set the two products equal to each other. In this case, the result is $(18)(13) = (6)(x)$. You can multiply the left side and then divide by 6. However, notice that 18 is a multiple of 6. Because of this, it is easier to divide first. This makes the

equation $\frac{(18)(13)}{6} = x$. Reduce this fraction. Since 18 ÷ 6 = 3, this equation becomes (3)(13) = x and 39 = x. The correct answer is choice (D).

10. **B** Once again, two fractions are set equal to each other, so cross-multiply. The result of the cross-multiplication is (2m)(3m) = (8)(3), so $6m^2 = 24$. Divide both sides by 6 to get $m^2 = 4$. Now, take the square root of both sides. The square root of 4 is 2, but remember that while $2^2 = 4$, it is also true that $(-2)^2 = 4$, so $m = \pm 2$. –2 is an answer choice, so the correct answer is choice (B).

11. **C** Although this looks different from the previous problems because of the extra variable, it's the same procedure as the other problems. The question asks for y. On the left side of the equation, y is multiplied by $5c$, so divide both sides by $5c$. Thus, the equation becomes $y = \frac{10}{5c}$. However, $\frac{10}{5c}$ is not an answer choice. Since 10 is a multiple of 5, reduce this fraction by dividing the numerator and denominator by 5 to get $\frac{2}{c}$. The correct answer is choice (C).

12. **A** The question asks for the value of x. The variable x is on the left side and is being multiplied by $3a$, so divide both sides by $3a$. This isolates x on the left sides and leaves $\frac{42a}{5} \div 3a$ on the right. When doing fraction division, multiply the first fraction by the reciprocal of the second to get $\frac{42a}{5} \times \frac{1}{3a} = \frac{42a}{15a}$. This is not an answer choice, so reduce this fraction. Cancel the a's to get $\frac{42}{15}$. Since both the numerator and denominator are multiples of 3, divide both by 3 to get $\frac{14}{5}$. The correct answer is choice (A).

13. **A** The question asks for $4r - 3s$. Plug the given values of r and s, $r = -2$ and $s = 3$, into the expression and solve. $4r - 3s = 4(-2) - 3(3) = -8 - 9 = -17$. The correct answer is choice (A).

14. **19** Substitute the given values of m and n into the given expression for m and n. $m + 4n = 3 + 4(4) = 3 + 16 = 19$. The correct answer is 19.

15. **D** Substitute the given value of p in the equation, and solve for q. Since $p = -3$, $5p + 11 = 2q$ is equivalent to $5(-3) + 11 = 2q$ and $-15 + 11 = 2q$, so $-4 = 2q$. Divide both sides by 2 to get $-2 = q$. The correct answer is choice (D).

16. **A** Substitute the given value of c in the equation, and solve for d. $2c - 3d = 4d$ becomes $2(2) - 3d = 4d$, which is equivalent to $4 - 3d = 4d$. Add $3d$ to both sides to get $4 = 7d$. Divide by 7 to get $\frac{4}{7} = d$. The correct answer is choice (A).

Inequalities Drill

1. **B** To solve an inequality, follow the same procedure as you would to solve an equation. Isolate x. Subtract 5 from both sides to get $3x \geq 18$. Divide both sides by 3 to get $x \geq 6$. The correct answer is choice (B).

2. **A** Once again, to solve an inequality, follow largely the same procedure as you would to solve an equation. Isolate x. Add 8 to both sides to get $-4y < 20$. Now, divide both sides by -4. The difference between solving an inequality and solving an equation is that there is an extra rule for inequalities: when you multiply or divide by a negative, flip the inequality. Therefore, when you divide both sides by -4, you get $y > -5$. The correct answer is choice (A).

3. **17** To solve this inequality, bring all the z's to one side and everything else to the other side. Subtract $5z$ from both sides to get $17 \leq z$. Therefore, all values of z are either greater than or equal to 17, and the least possible value of z is 17. The correct answer is 17.

4. **C** Again, bring all the n's to one side and everything else to the other. Subtract $5n$ from both sides to get $-3n + 4 > 13$. Subtract 4 from both sides to get $-3n > 9$. Divide both sides by -3 and flip the inequality to get $n < -3$. The correct answer is choice (C).

5. **A** Rather than solving this inequality, try using a strategic shortcut we call Plugging In the Answers. This entails substituting—or "plugging in"—each of the answer choices for the variable m, starting with choice (C). Eliminate any answer choice that makes the inequality false. If $m = 3$, the $7(2) + 5 < 19$. $7(3) + 5 = 26$. Since it is not the case that $26 < 19$, this choice is not correct. Eliminate choice (C). The value of m needs to be less, so eliminate choice (D), as well. Now, try choice (B). If $m = 2$, then $7(2) + 5 < 19$. $7(2) + 5 = 19$. Since it is not the case that $19 < 19$, this choice is not correct. (When the two sides of an inequality are equal, double check to see whether the inequality sign is $<$ or $\leq$.) Eliminate choice (B). Only one answer remains. The correct answer is choice (A).

6. **D** Once again, plug in the answer choices, starting with choice (C). If $a = -2$, then $-3(-2) - 5 \leq 4(-2) + 7$. $-3(-2) - 5 = 6 - 5 = 4$, and $4(-2) + 7 = -8 + 7 = -1$. Therefore, if $a = -2$, $1 \leq -1$. Since this is false, eliminate choice (C). Now determine whether the correct answer should be greater or less. If a is less, the $-3a$ would be greater, making the left side of the inequality greater. Also, $4a$ would be less, making the right side less. Since the left side of the inequality is already greater, decreasing the value of a will only increase this gap rather than reverse it. Therefore, any value of a that makes the inequality true would have to be greater than -2. Therefore, eliminate choices (A) and (B). Only one choice remains. The correct answer is choice (D).

7. **B** Plug 3 into each of the answer choices and eliminate any choice that is false. Don't worry about the change from c to x, as c is a constant that refers to a particular value of x. Choice (A) says $x > 4$. Since it's not true that $3 > 4$, eliminate choice (A). Choice (B) says $x > 2$. Since it is true that $3 > 2$, keep choice (B). Choice (C) says that $x < -2$. Since it is not true that $3 < -2$, eliminate choice (C). Choice (D) says that $x < -4$. Since it is not true that $3 < -4$, eliminate choice (D). The correct answer is choice (B).

8. **C** Plug –2 into each of the answer choices and eliminate any answer choice that is false. Choice (A) says $2p + 4 < -3$. Plug in $p = -2$ to get $2(-2) + 4 < -3$. Simplify to get $-4 + 4 < -3$ and $0 < -3$. Since this is false, eliminate choice (A). Choice (B) says $4p - 4 > -4$. Plug in –2 for p to get $4(-2) - 4 > -4$. Simplify to get $-8 - 4 > -4$ and $-12 > -4$. Since this is false, eliminate choice (B). Choice (C) says $-3p + 2 > 7$. Plug in –2 for p to get $-3(-2) + 2 > 7$. Simplify to get $6 + 2 > 7$ and $8 > 7$. Since this is true, keep choice (C). Choice (D) says $-5p - 3 < 6$. Plug in –2 for p to get $-5(-2) - 3 < 6$. Simplify to get $10 - 3 < 6$ and $7 < 6$. Since this is false, eliminate choice (D). The correct answer is choice (C).

9. **D** First, translate the sentence into an inequality. Three more than x is less than four times x. "Three more than x" translates to $x + 3$, and "four times x" translates to $4x$. Therefore, $x + 3 < 4x$. Now, plug the answer choices into this inequality. Choice (A) is –1, so plug this in to get $-1 + 3 < 4(-1)$. This simplifies to $2 < -4$. Since this is false, eliminate choice (A). Choice (B) is 0. Plug this is to get $0 + 3 < 4(0)$, which simplifies to $3 < 0$. Since this is false, eliminate choice (B). Choice (C) is 1. Plug this is to get $1 + 3 < 4(1)$, which simplifies to $4 < 4$. Since this is false (it's less than, not less than or equal to), eliminate choice (C). Choice (D) is 2. Plug this is to get $2 + 3 < 4(2)$, which simplifies to $5 < 8$. Since this is true, the correct answer is choice (D).

10. **A** First, get an inequality from the first clause: three less than twice p is greater than or equal to eight times p. "Three less than" translates to "__– 3", leaving some room to the left for whatever follows. What follows is twice p, which translates to $2p$, leaving you with $2p - 3$. "Is greater than or equal to" translates to ≥. Finally, "eight times p" translates to $8p$. Thus the inequality is $2p - 3 \geq 8p$. This is not an answer choice. Instead, the answer choices have p isolated, so isolate p. First subtract $2p$ from both sides to get $-3 \geq 6p$. Divide both sides by 6 to get $-\frac{1}{2} \geq p$, so $p \leq -\frac{1}{2}$. The correct answer is choice (A).

11. **A** Translate the statement into an inequality. Shelton is more than five years older than twice Roberta's age. "Twice Roberta's age" is $2r$. "Five years older" than this is $2r + 5$. Shelton's age is more than this, so $s > 2r + 5$. The correct answer is choice (A).

12. **D** The question asks for the revenues to be greater than the costs. Come up with an expression for each of these individually. The store charges \$2 per pretzel, so the revenues are $2p$. The costs are the \$100 for rent plus 50 cents for each pretzel sold. 50 cents for each pretzel sold is $0.50p$. Add this to the \$100 for rent to get $0.50p + 100$. Since the revenues have to be greater, $2p > 0.50p + 100$. The correct answer is choice (D).

13. **B** The question says that in order to retain certification, the club has to have at least two-thirds of the number of members of the previous year. In the previous year, the club had 90 members, so the club must have at least $\frac{2}{3}(90)$. The club lost m members, so it currently has $90 - m$. This has to be

at least $\frac{2}{3}(90)$, so $90 - m \geq \frac{2}{3}(90)$. This is not an answer choice. In each of the answer choices, m is isolated, so do that here. First, simplify the right side to get $\frac{2}{3}(90) = \frac{2}{3} \times \frac{90}{1} = \frac{180}{3} = 60$, leaving $90 - m \geq 60$. Subtract 90 from both sides to get $-m \geq -30$. Divide both sides by –1 and flip the inequality to get $m \leq 30$. The correct answer is choice (B).

14. **C** In order to be an antique, an item must be "at least 100 years old". The term "at least" translates to greater than or equal to. Therefore, if the age of an item is x (use the variable from the answer choices), then $x \geq 100$. The correct answer is choice (C).

15. **D** In order for a boxer to qualify as a welterweight, he cannot weigh more than 147 pounds. "Cannot weigh more than 147" means that his weight can be less 147. Since 147 is not more than 147, his weight can also be 147. Therefore, if a welterweight boxer weighs w pounds, $w \leq 147$. The correct answer is choice (D).

16. **B** The question says that a legal ball must be from 14 to 16 ounces, so, if the weight of the ball is b, $14 \leq b \leq 16$. However, the questions for the weight of a ball that is NOT legal, so choice (A) is a trap answer. In order for a ball to be illegal it must be outside this range, so it must be either less than 14 or greater than 16. Therefore $b < 14$ or $b > 16$. The correct answer is choice (B).

Translating Words into Math Drill

1. **B** Translate the first sentence. Morgan is eight years older than her cousin Lawrence. Morgan is m years old. The word "is" translates to "=". "Eight years older than" translates to "__+ 8", leaving yourself some room to the left. Finally, "Lawrence" can be called "L". Fill the space to the left of "+ 8" with L. Therefore, $m = L + 8$. The question, however, asks for L. Subtract 8 from both sides to get $m - 8 = L$. The correct answer is choice (B).

2. **D** Translate the first sentence. Virgil has half as many baseball cards as his sister Cheryl. We'll say that Virgil has V baseball cards. The word "has" translates to "=". The phrase "half as many" translates to $\frac{1}{2}(\quad)$, filling the parentheses with whatever follows. What follows is "baseball cards as his sister Cheryl". The next sentence says to call this c, so "half as many baseball cards as his sister Cheryl" translates to $\frac{1}{2}(c)$. Therefore the sentence translates to $V = \frac{1}{2}c$. The question asks for how many cards Virgil has, which is V. Since this is already isolated, the correct answer is choice (D).

3. **A** Translate the first sentence. Brad has five dollars less than four times the amount of money that Georgia has. Call the amount of money that Brad has B. The word "has" translate to "=". "Five dollars less than" translates to "– 5", leaving yourself some room to the left. Fill this space with "four times the amount of money that Georgia has." Georgia has d dollars, so four times this amount is

$4d$. Therefore, the sentence can be translated to $B = 4d - 5$. Since the question asks for B, the correct answer is choice (A).

4. **C** Bartolo begins with r records. Three years later, he increases his collection to five times what it was originally. Therefore, three years later, he has $5r$ records. The question asks for what he had three years after he began, so the correct answer is (C).

5. **D** The piano store has p pianos. It doubles its inventory, so it now has $2p$ pianos. It sells five. Subtract 5 from the present number to get $2p - 5$. The correct answer is choice (D).

6. **B** The sentence says that the population of the city doubles every five years. If the city's current population is p, then in 5 years, the city's population will have doubled and thus be $2p$, which is choice (A). However, the question asks for this city's population in ten years not five. Eliminate choice (A). To get the population after 10 years, another five years will have passed, so the population will have doubled again. Thus, the population will be double $2p$, which is $2(2p) = 4p$. The correct answer is choice (B).

7. **D** Translate the first sentence. Booker is three times as old as Ken was four years ago. Call Booker B years old. The word "is" translates to "=". The term "three times as old as" translates to "3(   )", leaving room inside the parentheses for what's mentioned next, which is "Ken was four years ago". If Ken is k years old now, then four years ago, Ken was $k - 4$. Fill this into the parentheses. Therefore, the sentence translates to $B = 3(k - 4)$. The question asks for Booker's age, so the correct answer is choice (D).

8. **B** Translate the key clause: four more than m is two less than three times n. "Four more than m" translates to "$m + 4$". "Is" translates to "=". "Three times n" translates to "$3n$". Two less than this is "$3n - 2$". Therefore, this clause translates to "$m + 4 = 3n - 2$". The correct answer is choice (B).

9. **A** Translate the first sentence. Triple x is equal to the positive difference between x and y. "Triple x" translates to $3x$. "Is equal to" translates to "=". "Difference" translates to subtraction. Since $x < y$, $x - y$ is negative. Therefore, "the positive difference between x and y" translates to "$y - x$". Thus, the sentence translates to "$3x = y - x$". The correct answer is choice (A).

10. **D** Translate the sentence. Twice the square of x is the square root of twice y. "Twice" translates to "2 times". The phrase "the square of x" translates to x^2, so the first part of the sentence translates to $2x^2$. The word "is" translates to "=". The phrase "the square root of" translates to $\sqrt{\ }$, writing whatever follows under the square root sign. What follows is "twice y", which translates to $2y$. Therefore, the sentence translates to $2x^2 = \sqrt{2y}$. The correct answer is choice (D).

11. **C** Translate each sentence, one at a time. The first sentence says "Jon is twelve years older than Fiona." Jon is j years old. The word "is" translates to "=". The phrase "twelve years older than" translates to "__+ 12", leaving room to the left for whatever follows. What follows is "Fiona", who is f years old. Thus, the first sentence translates to $j = f + 12$. Eliminate any answer that does not include this: choices (B) and (D). Now translate the second sentence: "In four years, Jon will be twice as old as Fiona." The clause "Jon is twice as old as Fiona" would normally translate to $j = 2f$. However,

in this case, the sentence begins with "in four years". Therefore, 4 needs to be add to each person's age, making the equation $j + 4 = 2(f + 4)$. Choice (A) does not have the amended version of the equation, so eliminate choice (A). The correct answer is choice (C).

12. **B** Each of the answer choices has two equations, so that will be what you need to look for. There are a total of 13 stamps. Since there are x postcard stamps and y standard stamps, there are a total of $x + y$ stamps. Therefore, $x + y = 13$. Eliminate any answer choices that does not include this equation: choices (A) and (D). The x postcard stamps cost 34 cents each, so the total cost of the x stamps is $0.34x$. The y standard stamps cost 49 cents each, so the total cost of the y stamps is $0.49y$. Therefore, the total cost of all the stamps is $0.34x + 0.49y$. Since the question says that the total cost was \$5.17, eliminate any answer choice that does not include the equation $0.34x + 0.49y = 5.17$: choice (C). The correct answer is choice (B).

13. **$7a + 8b = 149$; $a + b = 20$**

There are a total of 20 children, so $a + b = 20$. Drop 20 into the right side of the second equation. The sum of the ages is 149. The sum of the ages of the a seven-year-olds is $7a$, and the sum of the ages of the b eight-year-olds is $8b$. Therefore, $7a + 8b = 149$. Drag the 7 to the first box of the first equation, the 8 to the second, and the 149 to the third.

14. **B** Translate the question: "What is forty percent of 30?" The word "what" translates to the variable. We'll use x. The word "is" translates to "=". "Forty percent" translates to "$\frac{40}{100}$". The word "of" translates to "×". Therefore, the question translates to the equation $x = \frac{40}{100} \times 30$. Simplify the right side to get $x = 12$. The correct answer is choice (B).

15. **80** Translate the question: "Twenty-five percent of what number is 20?" The term "twenty-five percent" translates to "$\frac{25}{100}$". The word "of" translates to "×". The term "what number" translates to the variable. We'll use y. The word "is" translates to "=". Therefore, the question translates to "$\frac{25}{100}y = 20$". Reduce the fraction on the left side by 25 to get $\frac{1}{4}y = 20$. Multiply both sides by 4 to get $y = 80$. The correct answer is 80.

16. **B** Translate the question: What percent of eighty is 24? The word "what" translates to the variable. We'll use z. The word "percent" translates to "÷ 100". The word "of" translates to "×". The word "is" translates to "=". Therefore, the question translates to $\frac{z}{100} \times 80 = 24$. Multiply both sides by 100 to get $80z = 2400$. Divide both sides by 80 to get $z = 30$. The correct answer is choice (B).

17. **C** Sixty percent of seventy-five percent of what number is equal to one hundred thirty-five? Even though it looks more complex, it's the same idea as in previous questions. "Sixty percent" translates to $\frac{60}{100}$. The word "of" translates to "×". "Seventy-five percent" translates to $\frac{75}{100}$. Again, the word "of" translates to "×". The term "what number" translates to the variable. We'll use *n*. The term "is equal to" translates to "=". Therefore, the question translates to $\frac{60}{100} \times \frac{75}{100} \times n = 135$. First, reduce the fractions on the right side to get $\frac{3}{5} \times \frac{3}{4} \times n = 135$. Now, multiply the fractions to get $\frac{9}{20} \times n = 135$. Multiply both sides by 20 to get $9n = 2{,}700$. Divide both sides by 9 to get $n = 300$. The correct answer is choice (C).

18. **A** Translate the first sentence: Twenty percent of *x* is eighty percent of *y*. "Twenty percent" translates to $\frac{20}{100}$, and "of" translates to multiplication, so the first part of the sentence translates to $\frac{20}{100}(x)$. Similarly, "eighty percent of *y*" translates to $\frac{80}{100}(y)$. Since "is" translates to "=", the whole sentence translates to $\frac{20}{100}x = \frac{80}{100}y$. Reduce the two fractions to get $\frac{1}{5}x = \frac{4}{5}y$. The question asks for *x*, so isolate this variable. Since *x* is multiplied by $\frac{1}{5}$, divide both sides by $\frac{1}{5}$, which is the same as multiplying by 5. The result is $x = 4y$. The correct answer is choice (A).

19. **D** Translate the first sentence: Khalil has eight percent as many gumballs as Jacob. The next sentence says that Khalil has *k* gumballs, so "Khalil" translates to *k*. The word "has" translates to "=". "Eight percent" translates to $\frac{8}{100}$. The term "as many as" translates to "×". Since the next sentence says that Jacob has *j* gumballs, "Jacob" translates to *j*. Therefore, the sentence translates to $k = \frac{8}{100} \times j$. Simplify this a bit to get $k = \frac{8j}{100}$. The correct answer is choice (D).

20. **C** Go through this one step at a time. The question says that Naomi withdraws thirty-five percent of her money. Since she has \$8,000 in the bank, "thirty-five percent of her money" translates to $\frac{35}{100} \times 8{,}000$, which equals \$2,800. Since she withdraws this amount, she is left with \$8,000 – \$2,800 = \$5,200. Her bank then pays interest equal to "5% of what she has in the bank". This can be translated to $\frac{5}{100} \times 5{,}200$, which is equal to \$260. This amount is added to her bank account to get \$5,460. The correct answer is choice (C).

Polynomials Drill

1. **C** First, distribute the 2 to get $4y + 2x + 6y - 5x$. Now combine like terms: $2x - 5x = -3x$ and $4y + 6y = 10y$. Therefore, the expression simplifies to $-3x + 10y$. The correct answer is choice (C).

2. **B** Combine like terms. Note that even if two terms have the same variables, they are not like terms unless they are the same degree (e.g. x^3 and x^2 are not like terms). $x^2 - 3x^2 = -2x^2$, and $2x + 6x = 8x$. Therefore, the simplified expression is $-2x^2 + 8x + 9$. The correct answer is choice (B).

3. **D** First, distribute. $-2x(x + 5) = -2x^2 - 10x$, $-9(x + y^2) = -9x - 9y^2$, and $10y(y + 1) = 10y^2 + 10y$, so the expression is equal to $5x^2 - 2x^2 - 10x - 9x - 9y^2 + 10y^2 + 10y - 5y$. Now combine like terms: $5x^2 - 2x^2 = 3x^2$, $-10x - 9x = -19x$, $-9y^2 + 10y^2 = y^2$, and $10y - 5y = 5y$. Therefore, the expression is equivalent to $3x^2 - 19x + y^2 + 5y$. The correct answer is choice (D).

4. **C** $(x^2y^3)^4(x^3y^{-2})^2$. When a number with an exponent is raised to an exponent, multiply the exponents. Therefore, $(x^2y^3)^4 = (x^8y^{12})$ and $(x^3y^{-2})^2 = (x^6y^{-4})$. Now, when multiplying numbers with the same base, add the exponents, so $(x^8y^{12})(x^6y^{-4}) = x^{14}y^8$. The correct answer is choice (C).

5. **A** $\frac{a^6b^8c^{10}}{a^2b^4c^5}$ When dividing by numbers with exponents and the same base, subtract the exponents. Therefore, $a^6 \div a^2 = a^4$, $b^8 \div b^4 = b^4$, and $c^{10} \div c^5 = c^5$. Therefore, the correct answer is choice (A).

6. **A** Expand the expression. When there are two binomial factors (i.e. two factors with two terms each), expanding using the FOIL method. FOIL stands for first, outer, inner, last. Begin by multiplying the first terms of each binomial, x and x, to get x^2. Then, multiply the outer terms, x and -7, to get $-7x$. Next, multiply inner terms, 3 and x, to get $3x$. Finally, multiply last terms of each binomial, 3 and -7, to get -21. Now add the terms to get $x^2 - 7x + 3x - 21$. Combine like terms to get $x^2 - 4x - 21$. The correct answer is choice (A).

7. **B** Just like in Question 6, FOIL. Multiply the first terms to get $2y^2$, outer terms to get $4y$, inner terms to get $4y$, and last terms to get 8. Add these four to get $2y^2 + 4y + 4y + 8$. Combine like terms to get $2y^2 + 8y + 8$. The correct answer is choice (B).

8. **D** Once again, FOIL. Multiply the first terms to get $6z^2$, outer terms to get $8z$, inner terms to get $-9z$, and last terms to get -12. Add these four and combine like terms to get $6z^2 - z - 12$. The correct answer is choice (D).

9. **C** In order factor a quadratic expression in the form $x^2 + bx + c$, do FOIL in reverse. First, come up with two number that have a product of c and a sum of b. Since $c = 15$, the factors of c are 1 and 15 and 3 and 5. The sum of 1 and 15 is 16, which is not b. However, the sum of 3 and 5 is 8, which is equal to b. Therefore, the factored form of $x^2 + 8x + 15$ is $(x + 3)(x + 5)$. The correct answer is choice (C).

10. **D** Though the tempting first step would be to combine like term, when an expression is presented in this form on the GED®, there is likely a reason. Factor the terms in pairs. Factor an x from $x^2 - 6x$ to get $x(x - 6)$, and factor a 2 from $2x - 12$ to get $2(x - 6)$. Thus, the original expression can be

rewritten as $x(x - 6) + 2(x - 6)$. Since both terms have a factor of $(x - 6)$, this can be factored out to get $(x - 6)(x + 2)$. The first of these two factors is an answer choice. Another way to think about this is that the inner and outer terms must equal the O and the I of FOIL. Therefore, the outer term must be $-6x$, and therefore the terms must be x and -6. The same is true for the $2x$, where the inner terms multiplied together must be 2 and x. The correct answer is choice (D).

11. **B** Just like in Question 10, factor in pairs. Factor a $3x$ from $3x^2 + 9x$ to get $3x(x + 3)$, and factor a -2 from $-2x - 6$ to get $-2(x + 3)$, resulting in an expression of $3x(x + 3) - 2(x + 3)$. Factor $(x + 3)$ to get $(3x - 2)(x + 3)$. The correct answer is choice (B).

12. **D** Again, factor in pairs. Factor c from $2c^2 - 3c$ to get $c(2c - 3)$. Factor $2d$ from $4cd - 6d$ to get $2d(2c - 3)$. Add these to get $c(2c - 3) + 2d(2c - 3)$. Factor $(2c - 3)$ to get $(c + 2d)(2c - 3)$. Another way to approach this problem is to FOIL out the answer choices to see which equals the original equation. The correct answer is choice (D).

13. **B** $x^2 + 4x = 32$. To solve a quadratic equation with an x^2 term and an x term, start by getting one side equal to 0 to get an equation in the form $ax^2 + bx + c = 0$. Subtract 32 from both sides to get $x^2 + 4x - 32 = 0$, so $a = 1$, $b = 4$, and $c = -32$. Now factor, which is basically FOIL in reverse. To do this, you need two factors of the c that have a sum of b: in this case two factors of -32 that have a sum of $+4$. The factors of 32 are 1 and 32, 2 and 16, and 4 and 8. For factors of -32, use the same pair but make one in each pair negative: 1 and -32, -1 and 32, 2 and -16, -2 and 16, 4 and -8, and -4 and 8. The pair with a sum of 4 is -4 and 8. (Alternatively, since the sign of -32 is negative, find a pair of factors of 32 with a difference of 4, making sure the sign of the larger factor matches the sign of $4x$.) Use these factors of -32 to factor the left side of the left side of the equation to get $(x - 4)(x + 8) = 0$. Remember that a product is 0 if either factor is equal to 0. Thus, you need to set both factors equal to 0. If $x - 4 = 0$, then $x = 4$. If $x + 8 = 0$, then $x = -8$. The correct answer is choice (B).

14. **B** $3x^2 + 6x = -2$. First set one side of the equation equal to 0 by adding 2 to both sides to get $3x^2 + 6x + 2 = 0$. This equation is difficult to factor, so use the quadratic formula. When an equation is in the form $ax^2 + bx + c = 0$, the values of x can be determined using the equation $x = \dfrac{-b \pm \sqrt{b^2 - 4ac}}{2a}$.

In the equation $3x^2 + 6x + 2$, $a = 3$, $b = 6$, and $c = 2$. Plug these into the quadratic formula to get $x = \dfrac{-6 \pm \sqrt{6^2 - 4(3)(2)}}{2(3)} = \dfrac{-6 \pm \sqrt{36 - 24}}{6} = \dfrac{-6 \pm \sqrt{12}}{6}$. The correct answer is choice (B).

15. **7** There are two possible approaches to this problem. One is to find the two solutions to the equation and add them. For this approach, factor $x^2 - 7x + 12 = 0$, find two factors of 12 with a sum of -7. The positive factors of 12 are 1 and 12, 2 and 6, and 3 and 4. The pair 3 and 4 has a sum of

7. Therefore, –3 and –4 have a sum of –7 (and a product of 12), so the equation factors into $(x-3)(x-4)=0$. Set each factor equal to 0. If $x-3=0$, then $x=3$. If $x-4=0$, then $x=4$. Therefore, the solutions are 3 and 4 and the sum is 7. Alternatively, the sum of the solutions to an equation $ax^2+bx+c=0$ is $-\frac{b}{a}$. In this case, $-\frac{b}{a}=-\frac{-7}{1}=7$. Either way, the correct answer is 7.

16. **C** Similar to the previous problem, there are two possible approaches. One is to find the two solutions. If $2x^2+6x=80$, then $2x^2+6x-80=0$. Factor the 2 to get $2(x^2+3x-40)=0$. Divide by 2 to get $x^2+3x-40=0$. Factor the left side to get $(x-8)(x+5)=0$. Set both factors equal to 0 to get $x=8$ and $x=-5$. The product is $(8)(-5)=-40$. Alternatively, the product of the solutions to an equation $ax^2+bx+c=0$ is $\frac{c}{a}$. In this case, $\frac{c}{a}=-\frac{-80}{2}=-40$. Either way, the correct answer is choice (C).

Simultaneous Equations Drill

1. **B** Since y is isolated in the second equation, substitute its value into the first equation. Thus, $2x+y=12$ is equivalent to $2x+4x=12$. Combine like terms to get $6x=12$. Divide both sides by 6 to get $x=2$. The correct answer is choice (B).

2. **D** Once again, y is isolated in the second equation, so substitute its value into the first equation, giving you $3x-2(5x)=-21$. Since $-2(5x)=-10x$, the equation becomes $3x-10x=-21$. Combine like terms to get $-7x=-21$. Divide both sides by –7 to get $x=3$. However, the question asks for the value of y, so this is not the final answer. Take this value of x and substitute it into one of the two equations. The second equation is simpler, so use that one. $y=5x=5(3)=15$. The correct answer is choice (D).

3. **D** Neither of the two equations is isolated for either variable. However, the first equation includes the term $2y$ and the second equation includes the term $-2y$. The question asks for x, so you'll want to eliminate the y terms. To do this, stack the two equations and add. When you stack, make sure to line up like terms: put $5x$ above $-4x$, $2y$ above $-2y$, and 7 above 5. Add the two equations: $5x-4x=x$, $2y-2y=0$, and $7+5=12$. The result is $x+0=12$ or $x=12$. The correct answer is choice (D).

4. **A** Again, neither equation is isolated for either variable. This time, though, both equations are have a $-3x$ term. To solve for y, eliminate the x terms by subtracting the two equations. Line up the two equations. $-3x-(-3x)=0$. $4y-y=3y$. $22-13=9$. Therefore $3y=9$. Divide both sides by 3 to get $y=3$. The correct answer is choice (A).

5. **B** Adding the two equations will eliminate the y term. However, the question asks for the value of y. This is fine. Add the two equations to solve for x, and then use that value to solve for y. Add the two equations to get $5x=10$. Divide both sides by 5 to get $x=2$. Plug this value of x into one of the

original equations. Let's use the first. Substitute $x = 2$ into $2x + 3y = 7$ to get $2(2) + 3y = 7$. Therefore, $4 + 3y = 7$. Subtract 4 from both sides to get $3y = 3$. Divide both sides by 3 to get $y = 1$. The correct answer is choice (B).

6. **C** Neither variable in the two equations can be easily cancelled through the stack and add/subtract method. However, the question doesn't ask for either variable individually but rather an expression involving both. When this is the case, don't worry above solving for either individual variable and just add or subtract the two without cancelling. If the two equations are added, the result is $4x - 4y = 16$. Since this is what the question asks for, the correct answer is choice (C).

7. **D** Once again, the question doesn't ask for either variable individually, so don't worry about trying to cancel. Try adding the two equations. $8a + 2b = 4$ and $2a + 4b = 8$. Add the two to get $10a + 6b = 12$. This is not what the questions is asking for. The question asks for $20a + 12b$, which is $2(10a + 6b)$. Therefore $20a + 12b = 2(10a + 6b) = 2(12) = 24$. The correct answer is choice (D).

8. **3** The question asks for the sum of x and y, which translates to $x + y$. Since, once again, the question doesn't ask for the value of x or y but rather for an expression involving both, it may not be necessary to solve for either variable individually. Try adding the two equations. First, though, put the two equations in the same form. In the second equation, subtract $3y$ from both sides to get $8x - 3y = -4$. Now, stack the two equations and add to get $2x + 2y = 6$. Although the question does not ask for the value of $2x + 2y$, this was still helpful, because it is a multiple of what the question asks for. Factor a 2 from the left side of the equation to get $2(x + y) = 6$. Divide both sides by 2 to get $x + y = 3$.

9. **B** Find a way to combine the two equations in the question: $y = x^2 + 1$ and $y = 2x$. Since both are isolated for y, set them equal to each other to get $x^2 + 1 = 2x$. This is a quadratic, so get one side of the equation equal to 0. Subtract $2x$ from both sides to get $x^2 - 2x + 1 = 0$. Factor the left sides. You need two factors of 1 with a sum of -2. These are -1 and -1, making the equation $(x - 1)(x - 1) = 0$, or $(x - 1)^2 = 0$. You could solve for x but you don't need to, since the question simply asks for $x - 1$. Take the square root of both sides to get $x - 1 = 0$. The correct answer is choice (B).

10. **D** $p + q = r$, $q = p - 7$, and $r = p + 1$. The question asks for the value of p. Two of the questions are one of the other variables in terms of p, so substitute these expressions into the first equation, $p + q = r$. Since $q = p - 7$, $p + (p - 7) = -r$. Since $r = p + 1$, $p + (p - 7) = -(p + 1)$. Combine like terms on the left side to get $2p - 7 = (p + 1)$. Distribute the negative on the right side to get $2p - 7 = p + 1$. Subtract p from both sides to get $p - 7 = 1$. Add 7 to both sides to get $p = 8$. The correct answer is choice (D).

11. **a = 2, b = 4, c = –0.5**

There are three equations and three variables. Though this looks like a more complicated problem than one with two equations and two variables, it requires a very similar method. First get all the equations in the same form. The first equation has all the variables on the left side of the equation, so do the same for the other two. In the second equation, add $4c$ to both sides to get $b + 4c = 2$. In the third equation add b to both sides to get $a + b = 6$. Stack the three equations, so that like terms line up. If it helps, rewrite the second equation as $0a + b + 4c = 2$ and the third as $a + b + 0c = 6$. Now determine how to combine these equations. The question asks for the values of the three variables individually, so find a way to cancel variables. Notice that the first two equations each has a $4c$ term, so subtracting the second equation will cancel these terms. Furthermore, the first equation has a $2b$ term and the second and third equation each have a b term. Therefore, subtracting these equations will cancel out b, resulting in an equation for a. Subtract the second and third equation from the first term by term. $3a - 0a - a = 2a$, $2b - b - b = 0$, $4c - 4c - 0c = 0$, and $12 - 2 - 6 = 4$. The result is $2a = 4$. Divide both sides by 2 to get $a = 2$. Plug this value into the third equation to get $2 + b = 6$. Subtract 2 from both sides to get $b = 4$. Plug this value in to the third equation to get $4 + 4c = 2$. Subtract 4 from both sides to get $4c = -2$. Divide both sides by 4 to get $c = -0.5$.

12. **D** Translate the statements into equations. The first statement says the sum of x and twice y is 14. The word "sum" translates to addition and "twice y" translates to $2y$. Therefore, "the sum of x and twice y" translates to $x + 2y$. The word "is" translates to "=", so the whole statement translates to $x + 2y = 14$. The second statement is x is one less than y. The phrase "one less than" translates to "– 1", leaving some room to the left for whatever follows. Since what follows is y, fill this in to get "$y - 1$". Thus, the second statement translates to $x = y - 1$. Since this second statement is isolated for x, substitute this value into the first equation to get $(y - 1) + 2y = 14$. Combine like terms to get $3y - 1 = 14$. Add 1 to both sides to get $3y = 15$. Divide both sides by 3 to get $y = 5$. The correct answer is choice (D).

13. **B** Translate the statements into equations. The first statement says that x is two more than y. This translates to $x = y + 2$. The second statement says that product of x and y is 48. This translates to $xy = 48$. Since the first equation is isolated for x, substitute this value into the second equation to get $(y + 2)y = 48$. Distribute the y to get $y^2 + 2y = 48$. Since this is a quadratic, get one side equal to zero by subtracting 48 from both sides to get $y^2 + 2y - 48 = 0$. Factor the left side. You need two numbers that have a product of –48 and a sum of 2: these are 8 and –6. Therefore, the equation factors to $(y + 8)(y - 6) = 0$. Set both factors equal to 0. If $y + 8 = 0$, then $y = -8$. If $y - 6 = 0$, then $y = 6$. Since x is two more than y, if y is 8, then x is 6, and the sum is 14. However, this is not an answer choice, so try the other possible value of y. If y is –8, then x is –6. The sum is –14. This is an answer choice. The correct answer is choice (B).

14. **A** Translate the information in the question into equations. Let L represent the number of large boxes Yolanda buys and S represent the number of small boxes she buys. She buys a total of seven boxes. Since total translates to addition, $S + L = 7$. Also, she spends a total of nineteen dollars. Since small boxes cost two dollars each, she spends $2S$ dollars on small boxes. Since larges boxes cost three dollars each, she spends $3L$ dollars on large boxes. Therefore, she spends a total of $2S + 3L$ on all seven boxes and $2S + 3L = 19$. The question asks for the number of small boxes, so you'll want to cancel the L terms. Do this by multiplying the first equation by –3 to get $-3S - 3L = -21$. Add this equation to $2S + 3L = 19$ to get $S = 2$. The correct answer is choice (A).

15. **C** Translate the information in the question into equations. The first sentence says that Natasha is three years younger than twice her brother's age. Let Natasha's age be n and her brother's age be b. This sentence translates to $n = 2b - 3$. The next sentence says that Natasha's brother is seven years younger than she is. This translates to $b = n - 7$. The question asks for n, so find a way to eliminate b. Since b is isolated in the second equation, substitute its value into the first to get $n = 2(n - 7) - 3$. Distribute the 2 on the right side of the equation to get $n = 2n - 14 - 3$. Combine like terms on the right to get $n = 2n - 17$. Subtract $2n$ from both sides to get $-n = -17$. Divide both sides by -1 to get $n = 17$. The correct answer is choice (C).

16. **Width = 12, Length = 8.**

Translate the information in the question into equations. The question says that the width is four inches longer than the length. This translates to $w = l + 4$. The question also says that the area of each poster is 96. Since the area of a rectangle is determined by the formula $A = lw$, this information translates to $lw = 96$. Substitute the value of w from the first equation into the second to get $l(l + 4) = 96$. Distribute to get $l^2 + 4l = 96$. Subtract 96 from both sides to get $l^2 + 4l - 96 = 0$. Factor the left side of the equation. Find to numbers with a product of -96 and a sum of 4: these are 12 and -8. Therefore, the equation factors into $(l + 12)(l - 8) = 0$. Set both factor equal to 0. If $l + 12 = 0$, the $l = -12$. Since lengths can't be negative, ignore this possibility. If $l - 8 = 0$, then $l = 8$, so select this value for the length. The width is four inches longer than the length, so $w = l + 4 = 8 + 4 = 12$. Select this value for this length. Another way to look at this problem is to think of all the possible factor pairs for 96: 1 and 96, 2 and 24, 3 and 32, 4 and 24, 6 and 16, and 8 and 12. Since 8 and 12 have a difference of 4, and w is four more than l, the width must be 12 and the length must be 8.

Functions Drill

1. **B** When you're given the graph of a relation, use the vertical line test to determine whether it is a function. The vertical line test means that if any vertical line can be drawn so that it touches the curve at more than one point, then the relation is not a function. In choice (A), a vertical line can be drawn at the y-axis that touches the curve at two points, so eliminate choice (A). In choice (B), any vertical line drawn appears to only touch the curve once, so keep this choice. In choice (C), a vertical line drawn at the y-axis touches the curve at two points, so eliminate choice (C). Choice (D) is itself a vertical line, so a vertical line could be drawn on top of it, so that it touches at infinitely many points. Eliminate choice (D). The correct answer is choice (B).

2. **D** Just like in Question 1, use the vertical line test. The difference is that, on this question, select the choice that is NOT a function. In choices (A), (B), and (C), any vertical line drawn only touches the curve at one point. In choice (D), a vertical line drawn towards the far right side of the curve will touch in two places, so this is not a function. The correct answer is choice (D).

3. **A** The question asks which is true of the graph above. This doesn't clarify what you need to do, so look at the answer choices. From the answer choices, it is clear that you need to determine whether these graphs represent a function. Once again, use the vertical line test. Work one graph one at a time, starting with Graph A. On graph A, any vertical line drawn only touches the curve at one point. Therefore, Graph A does represent a function. Eliminate choices (C) and (D). Go to Graph B. Any vertical line drawn in this graph as well will only touch the curve in one point. Therefore, this also represents a function. Eliminate choice (B). The correct answer is choice (A).

4. **C** A relation is a function if and only if every x value corresponds with a unique y value. Therefore, a relation is NOT a function if there is an x value that corresponds with more than one y value. In choices (A), (B), and (D), each x value corresponds with only one y value. Note that in choices (A) and (D), there are y values that correspond with multiple x values. This does not prevent the relation from being a function. In choice (C), $x = 2$ corresponds with both $y = -3$ and $y = 1$. Therefore, this is not a function. The correct answer is choice (C).

5. **B** Once again, a relation is not a function if there is an x value that corresponds with more than one y value. In choice (A), the x value 3 corresponds with both 2 and –4, so this is not a function. Eliminate choice (A). In choice (B), the x value 4 only corresponds with 1, the x value 2 only corresponds with 1, and the x value 5 only corresponds with 1. Although the y value 1 corresponds with multiple x values, this does not prevent the relation from being a function. Although the x value 2 appears on the table twice, it corresponds with 1 in both cases. Keep this choice. In choice (C), the x value 5 corresponds with both 9 and 7. Eliminate choice (C). In choice (D), the x value 3 corresponds with both –3 and 2. Eliminate choice (D). The correct answer is choice (B).

6. $\mathbf{x = 1}$ and $\mathbf{y = 6, 8, 9}$, or **13**

A relation is a function if and only if every x value corresponds with a unique y value. Also, according to the question, no ordered pair can be repeated. The x values on the table are 6, 8, 9, and 13. If any of these values are chosen for x, the corresponding y value would either repeat an ordered pair or make the relation not a function. Therefore, the only answer choice that could be x is 1. For the y value, there are no restrictions. Multiple x values could correspond with a single y value and this will not prevent the relation from being a function. Therefore, y could be any of the remaining choices: 6, 8, 9, or 13.

7. **A** To solve a function question, replace x with the number inside the parenthesis. Since $f(x) = 2x - 4$ and the question asks for $f(3)$, then $f(3) = 2(3) - 4 = 6 - 4 = 2$. The correct answer is choice (A).

8. **C** Just like in Question 7, replace x with the number inside the parenthesis. Since $g(x) = 3x^3 - 2x^2 + 8$, and the question asks for $g(4)$, then $g(4) = 3(4)^3 - 2(4)^2 + 8 = 3(64) - 2(16) + 8 = 192 - 32 + 8 = 168$. The correct answer is choice (C).

9. **D** Once again, whatever is inside the parentheses replaces x. Since t is inside the parentheses, $h(t) = 2t^2 + 3t - 4$. The question also says that $h(t) = 86$, so $2t^2 + 3t - 4 = 86$. One option is to set one side equal to 0, then factor and solve. However, since the question asks for a specific

number, try the numbers in the answer choices. Begin with one of the middle choices. Try choice (B), which is 4. If $t = 4$, then $h(t) = h(4) = 2(4)^2 + 3(4) - 4 = 2(16) + 12 - 4 = 32 + 8 = 40$. This is not 86, so eliminate choice (B). Since this is too small and a greater value of t will result in a greater value of $h(t)$, eliminate any answer choice that is less than 4. Eliminate choice (A). Now, try choice (C), which is 5. If $t = 5$, then $h(t) = f(5) = 2(5)^2 + 3(5) - 4 = 2(25) + 15 - 4 = 50 + 11 = 61$. This is closer but still too small, so eliminate choice (C). This leaves only one answer choice. The correct answer is choice (D).

10. **D** The expenses are $3,000, so set this equal to the expense function. $3{,}000 = 0.5c + 1{,}000$. Subtract 1,000 from both sides to get $2{,}000 = 0.5c$. Divide both sides by 0.5 to get $c = 4{,}000$. This is the number of cups of coffee sold, so plug this into the revenue function. $R(4{,}000) = 1.25(4{,}000) = 5{,}000$. The correct answer is choice (D).

11. **A** Plug the points from the table into the equations in the answer choices. Start with an easy point from the chart and let $x = 1$, where $y = 5$. Eliminate any choice in which $f(x)$ does not equal 5. In choice (A), $f(1) = 2(1) + 3 = 5$, so keep choice (A). In choice (B), $f(1) = 5(1) - 2 = 3$, so eliminate this choice. In choice (C), $f(1) = 4(1) + 5 = 9$, so eliminate this choice as well. In choice (D), $f(1) = 3(1) + 2 = 5$, so keep this choice. Now, try another point. Try $f(3) = 9$. In choice (A), $f(3) = 2(3) + 3 = 9$, so keep this choice. In choice (D), $f(3) = 3(3) + 2 = 11$, so eliminate this choice. The correct answer is choice (A).

12. **B** Plug the points from the table into the equations into the answer choices. Start with an easy point and let $x = 1$. Eliminate any choice in which $g(1)$ does not equal 0. In choice (A), $g(1) = (1)^2 - 2(1) + 6 = 5$, so eliminate choice (A). In choice (B), $g(1) = 2(1)^2 + 3(1) - 5 = 0$, so keep choice (B). In choice (C), $g(1) = 4(1)^2 - 8(1) + 4 = 0$, so keep this choice as well. In choice (D), $g(1) = 3(1)^2 + 4(1) + 7 = 14$, so eliminate choice (D). Now try $x = 2$, and eliminate any answer choice for which $g(2)$ does not equal 9. In choice (B), $g(2) = 2(2)^2 + 3(2) - 5 = 9$, so keep choice (B). In choice (C), $g(2) = 4(2)^2 - 8(2) + 4 = 4$, so eliminate this choice. The correct answer is choice (B).

13. **C** Once again, plug in points from the table into the equations in the answer choices. Since the equations are more complicated, it's especially important to start with easy answer choices. Start with $h(0) = -4$. In choice (A), $h(0) = (0)^3 + 2(0)^2 - 4(0) + 8 = 8$, so eliminate choice (A). In choice (B), $h(0) = (0)^4 - 4(0)^3 + 2(0)^2 + 7(0) - 4 = -4$, so keep choice (B). In choice (C), $h(0) = 4(0)^4 + 2(0)^3 - 3(0)^2 + 5(0) - 4 = -4$, so keep choice (C). In choice (D), $h(0) = 3(0)^3 + 7(0)^2 - 4(0) = 0$, so eliminate choice (D). Now try another easy point. Use $h(1) = 4$. Test the two remaining choices. In choice (B), $h(1) = (1)^4 - 4(1)^3 + 2(1)^2 + 7(1) - 4 = 2$, so eliminate choice (B). In choice (C), $h(0) = 4(1)^4 + 2(1)^3 - 3(1)^2 + 5(1) - 4 = 4$, so keep choice (C). The correct answer is choice (C).

14. **A** Plug in points from the table into the function. Start with the easiest value, $x = 0$. In the function equation, $f(0) = 0^2 - 4(0) - 12 = -12$. Eliminate any answer choice for which $f(0) \neq -12$: choices (B) and (C). Now try another point, $x = 3$. In the function equation, $f(3) = 3^2 - 4(3) - 12 = -15$. Eliminate the answer choice for which $f(3) \neq -15$: choice (D). The correct answer is choice (A).

15. $m(0) = \mathbf{10}$, $m(1) = 7$, $m(2) = \mathbf{4}$, and $m(3) = \mathbf{1}$

The question says that m is a linear function with a slope of –3 and a y-intercept of 10. If a function has a y-intercept of 10, then, by definition, $m(0) = 10$. Write the value 10 into the box next to the 0. The slope of a line is equal to $\frac{\textit{change in } y}{\textit{change in } x}$. Therefore, if the slope is –3 and x increases by 1, then y decreases by 3. Therefore, since $m(0) = 10$, $m(1) = 10 - 3 = 7$, $m(2) = 7 - 3 = 4$, and $m(3) = 4 - 3 = 1$.

Alternatively, a linear function can be put into the form $y = mx + b$, in which m represents the slope and b represents the y-intercept. Therefore $m(x)$ can be written as $m(x) = -3x + 10$. Plug in $m(0) = -3(0) + 10 = 10$, $m(1) = -3(1) + 10 = 7$, $m(2) = -3(2) + 10 = 4$, and $m(3) = -3(3) + 10 = 1$.

16. $g(-1) = \mathbf{16}$ and $g(2) = \mathbf{1}$

To fill in the table, determine the values of $g(-1)$ and $g(2)$. To do this, plug in –1 and 2 for x into $g(x) = (x - 3)^2$. $g(-1) = (-1 - 3)^2 = (-4)^2 = 16$, so drag this value into the table for $g(-1)$. $g(2) = (2 - 3)^2 = (-1)^2 = 1$, so drag this value into the table for $g(2)$.

17. **C** Translate the statement, "The number of red marbles is always 3 greater than twice the number of blue marbles." According to information presented later in the question, "The number of red marbles" translates to $r(b)$. The word "is" translates to "=". When you see "3 greater than" leave some space and write "+ 3". Fill the space with whatever follows: in this case, "twice the number of blue marbles". The word "twice" translates to "2 times", so "twice the number of blue marbles" translates to "$2b$". Therefore, the sentence translates to $r(b) = 2b + 3$. The correct answer is choice (C).

18. $f(x) = \mathbf{2x - 1}$ and $g(x) = \mathbf{-4x + 12}$

A linear equation can be put into the form $y = mx + b$, where m is the slope, and b is the y-intercept. For $f(x)$, the slope is 2 and the y-intercept is –1, so $m = 2$ and $b = -1$. Therefore $f(x) = 2x - 1$. Drag this expression into this box. For $g(x)$, the slope is –4, so $m = -4$. The question then says that the x-intercept is 3. The x-intercept is not b. The x-intercept is the x value for which y, or in this case $g(x)$, equals 0. Therefore, $g(3) = 0$. To determine the value of b, set $g(x) = -4x + b$ and $g(3) = -4(3) + b = 0$. Simplify $-4(3)$ to -12 to get $-12 + b = 0$. Add 12 to both sides to get $b = 12$. Therefore, $g(x) = -4x + 12$. Write this expression into this box.

19. **D** This question isn't a neat translation, so try particular numbers. Suppose 20 customers are expected in a particular day. Since a sales rep is need for each 10 customers, 2 sales reps are needed. Also three managers are needed, regardless of the number of customers. Therefore, there are a total of 5 employees needed and $E(20) = 5$. Go through each answer choice and eliminate any choice for

which this isn't true. In choice (A), $E(20) = 10(20) + 3 = 203$. Eliminate choice (A). In choice (B), $E(20) = 10(20 + 3) = 230$. Eliminate choice (B). In choice (C), $E(20) = \frac{20 + 3}{10} = 2.3$. Eliminate choice (C). In choice (D), $E(20) = \frac{20}{10} + 3 = 5$. The correct answer is choice (D).

20. **B** In Calgary, Stuart will spend \$200 each day. Therefore, over the course of *d* days, Stuart will spend \$200*d*. Now add the round trip airfare to get $C(d) = 200d + 650$. The correct answer is choice (B).

Part V
Geometry

For a bonus review of general geometry concepts and formulas, register your book online and download our free supplement: Geometry and the GED® Test.

You can also download the Mathematics Formula Sheet for reference as you work on this and other sections.

Lines and Angles Drill

<u>Question 1</u> refers to the following figure below:

DO NOT USE A CALCULATOR FOR QUESTION 1.

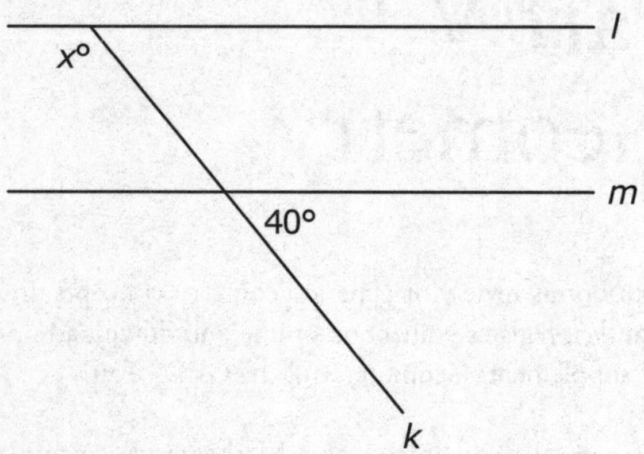

1. Lines l and m are parallel. If line k traverses the two lines, what is the measure of $x°$?

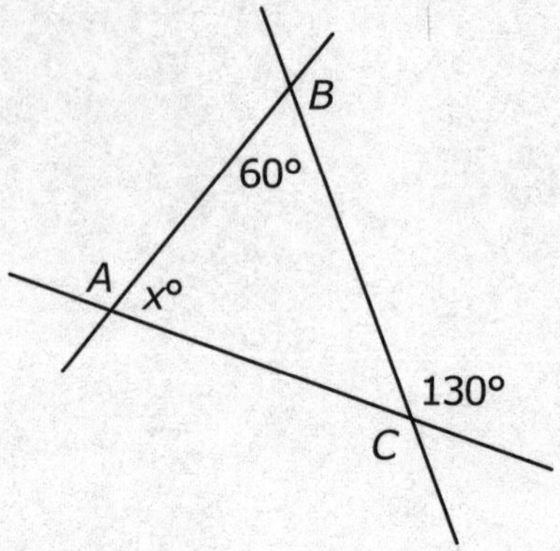

2. Three distinct lines cross as seen above to form points A, B, and C. What is the measure of $x°$?

   A. 50
   B. 60
   C. 70
   D. 130

DO NOT USE A CALCULATOR FOR QUESTIONS 3-5.

3. Based on the figure below, lines j and k are parallel. Lines h and g intersect j and k at points A, B, and C. The obtuse angle B is equal to 150° and the acute angle A is equal to 40°.

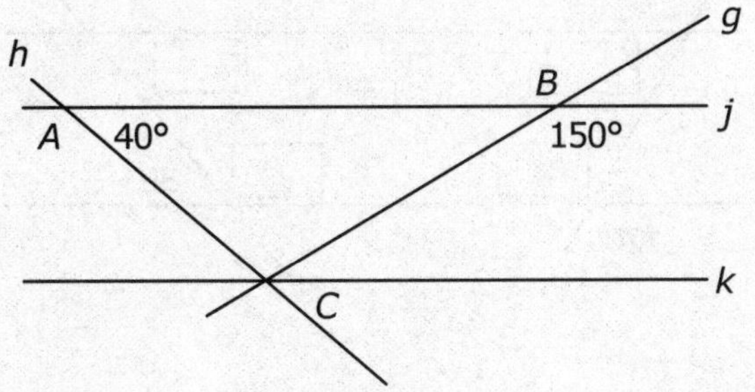

Lines j and k have [Select... ▼]

- slightly different
- the same
- negative reciprocal

slopes.

∠*CAB* is [Select... ▼] ∠*ABC*.

- greater than
- equal to
- less than

Line h is [Select... ▼] line g.

- perpendicular to
- parallel to
- intersecting

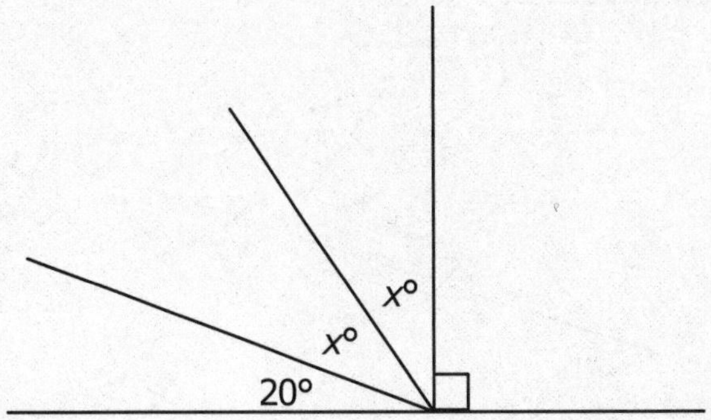

4. What is the value of $x°$ in the figure above?

5. In the figure below, what is the value of $y° + x°$?

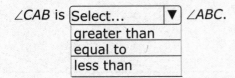

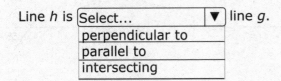

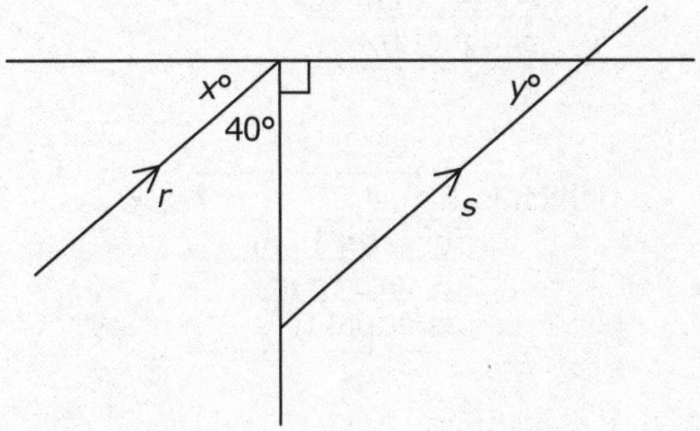

A. 40
B. 50
C. 90
D. 100

Questions 6–7 refer to the figure below:

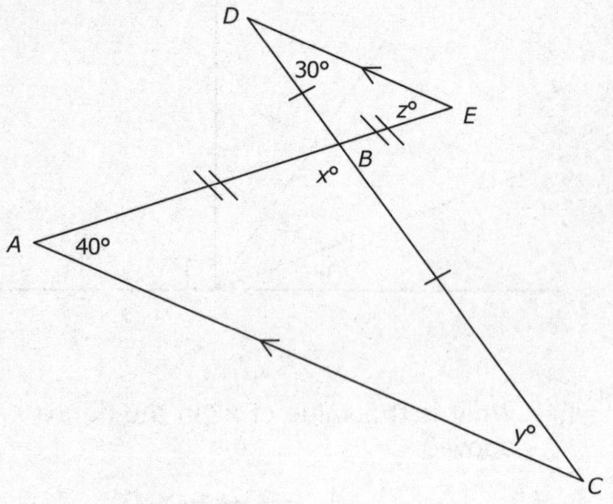

6. $\angle y$ [Select... ▼] $\angle z$,

- greater than
- is less than
- is equal to

which is [Select... ▼] $\angle x$,

- greater than
- is less than
- is equal to

which is [Select... ▼] $\angle y$.

- greater than
- is less than
- is equal to

7. $\angle y + \angle x - \angle z =$

DO NOT USE A CALCULATOR FOR QUESTIONS 8–9.

8. Lines *l* and *m* are parallel. Label the interior angle measurements of the trapezoid.

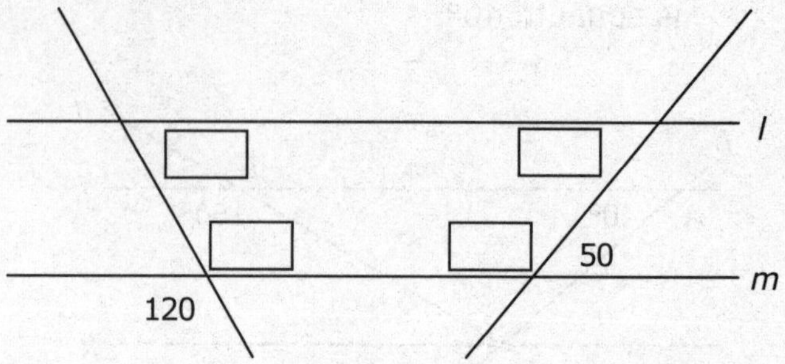

20	120	30	130
50	60	160	

9. Lines *m* and *n* are parallel. Given the information on the figure, what is the measure of $x°$?

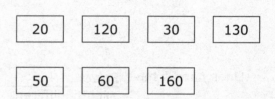

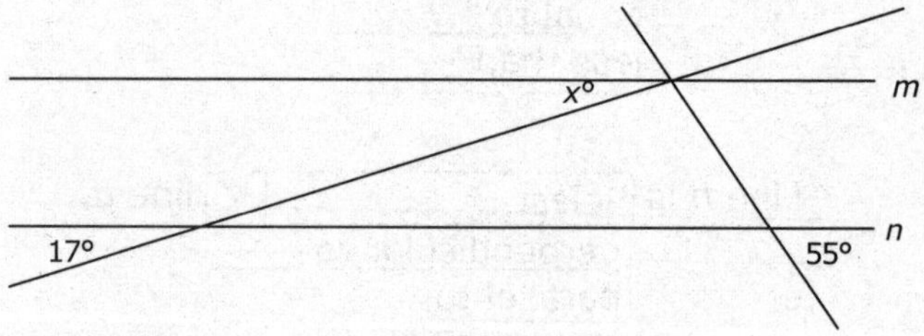

DO NOT USE A CALCULATOR FOR QUESTIONS 10–11.

10. Based on the information in the figure below, what is the measure of $y°$?

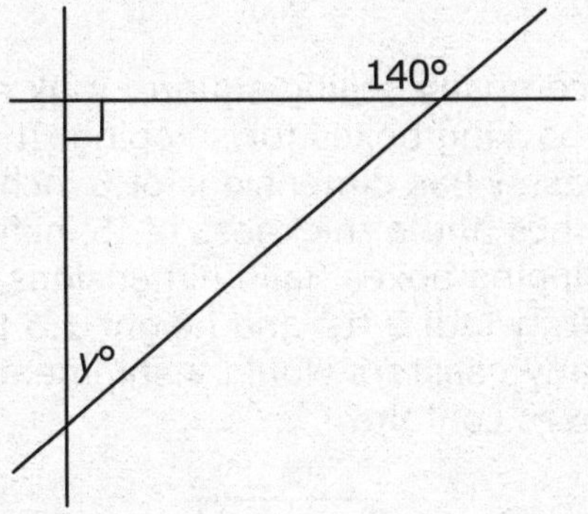

A. 40°
B. 50°
C. 60°
D. 90°

11. Find the measure of $\angle CGA$.

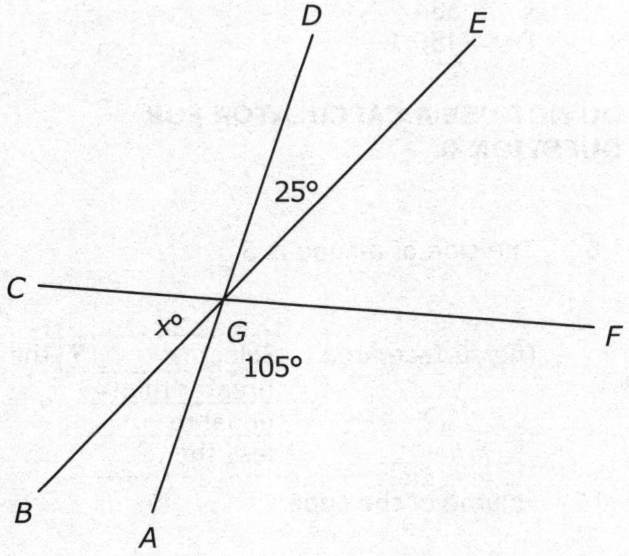

A. 25
B. 50
C. 75
D. 105

The following question refers to the figure below:

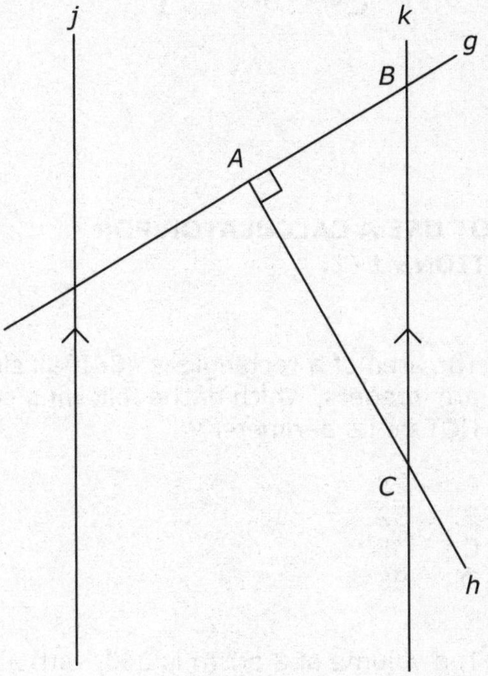

12. Line *j* is [Select... ▼] line *k*.
   - intersecting but not perpendicular to
   - perpendicular to
   - parallel to
   - cannot be determined from the information given

Line *g* is [Select... ▼] line *h*.
   - intersecting but not perpendicular to
   - perpendicular to
   - parallel to
   - cannot be determined from the information given

$\angle CBA$ [Select... ▼].
   - is equal to 40°
   - is equal to 45°
   - is equal to 50°
   - is a right angle
   - cannot be determined from the information given

Rectangles, Squares, and Prisms Drill

DO NOT USE A CALCULATOR FOR QUESTIONS 1–2.

1. The area of a rectangle is 48. If all sides are integers, which of the following could NOT be its perimeter?

   A. 28
   B. 32
   C. 35
   D. 98

2. The volume of a prism is 240, with a length of 12 and a width of 4. What is the height?

   [ ]

3. Andrea is fitting furniture in her living room. The coffee table is 52 inches by 26 inches, the television stand is 3.5 feet wide by 18 inches deep, and the couch is four feet long and two feet deep. If the entire room is 12 ft. by 14 ft., approximately how much open walking space, in square feet, will she have? (Note: 1 foot = 12 inches)

   A. 22.64
   B. 90.37
   C. 150.17
   D. 168

4. A company selling square drink coasters is packing boxes for shipping. If a single coaster has dimensions of 6 inches by 6 inches and a thickness of .5 inches, and shipping boxes have dimensions length 2 ft., width 3 ft., and height 1.5 ft., how many coasters would a shipment of 4 boxes contain?

   [ ]

5. A cube has a volume of 64 cubic units. What is the surface area of the figure?

   A. 16
   B. 96
   C. 384
   D. 455.1

DO NOT USE A CALCULATOR FOR QUESTION 6.

6. The side of a cube is 5.

   The surface area is [Select... ▼ | greater than | equal to | less than] the volume of the cube.

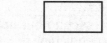

7. A trapezoid, *ABCD*, has a height of 4, and *AD* || *BC*. If $AB = 4\sqrt{2}$, *CD* = 5, and *AD* = 14, what is the area of the entire figure?

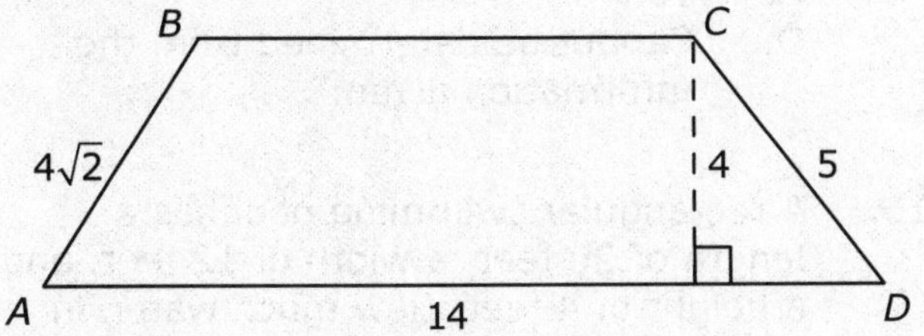

A. 40
B. 42
C. 44
D. 56

8. A parallelogram *CDEF* is shown below. If *CD* = 8 and *DE* = 12, what is the area of the parallelogram?

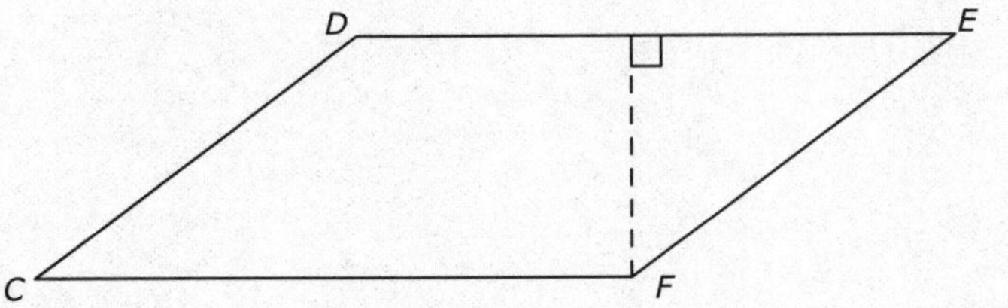

A. 40
B. 80
C. 96
D. Cannot be determined by the information given.

DO NOT USE A CALCULATOR FOR QUESTIONS 9-10.

9. *JKLM* is a parallelogram. What is the area of ΔJLM?

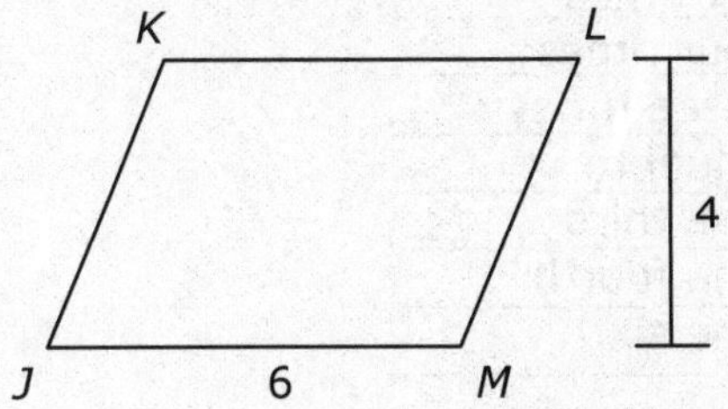

10. A rectangular box has a length of 4, a width of 20, and height of 2. The length is then decreased by 25%, the width decreased by 40%, and the height increased by 50%. What is the volume of the new box?

11. The radius of a circle and the diagonal of a rectangle are both 10.

If the width of the rectangle is 6, the area of the circle is approximately

Select... ▼
six times
four times
three times
equal to
one third
one fourth
one sixth

the area of the rectangle.

DO NOT USE A CALCULATOR FOR QUESTION 12.

12. A prism has a square base with an area of 3, and a height of 7. What is the volume of the prism?

13. A suitcase measures h inches high, 20 inches wide, and 18 inches deep. If maximum volume of a carry-on bag is 3307 in^3 and the height h is an integer, what is the maximum height the suitcase can be for it still to be a carry-on?

A. 7
B. 8
C. 8.5
D. 9

DO NOT USE A CALCULATOR FOR QUESTIONS 14-15.

14. A square has sides of $x + 1$ and $2x - 3$. What is the area of the square?

A. 4
B. 9
C. 16
D. Cannot be determined from the information given.

15. A rectangular swimming pool has a length of 20 feet, a width of 12 feet, and a height of 4 feet. How much water, in cubic feet, would be needed to fill 7/8ths of the pool?

Triangles and Pyramids Drill

1. ΔXYZ is a right triangle. What is the area of the triangle to the nearest hundredth?

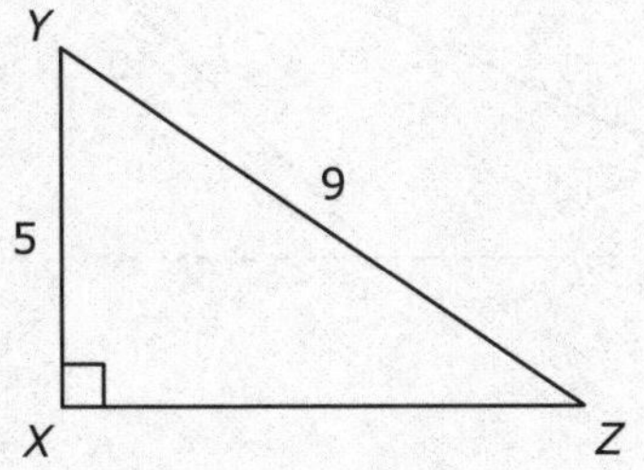

2. The perimeter of an equilateral triangle is 12. What is its area?

A. $2\sqrt{3}$

B. 8

C. $4\sqrt{3}$

D. $8\sqrt{3}$

DO NOT USE A CALCULATOR FOR QUESTION 3.

3. Which of the following could NOT be the third side of ΔABC?

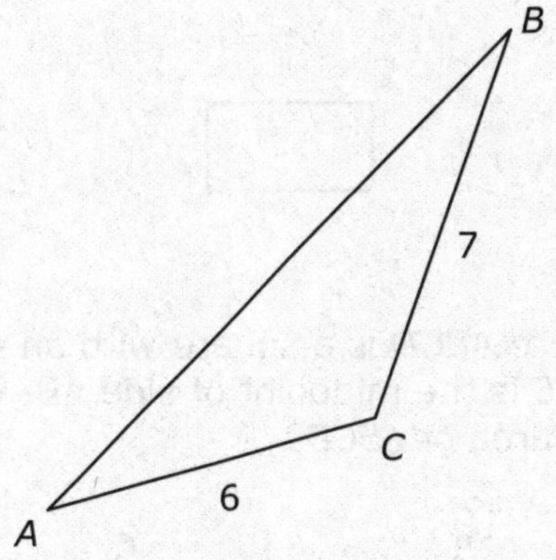

<u>Note</u>: Figure not drawn to scale.

A. 2
B. 12
C. 14
D. Cannot be determined from the information given

DO NOT USE A CALCULATOR FOR QUESTIONS 4-5.

4. ΔDEF is a right triangle. What is its perimeter?

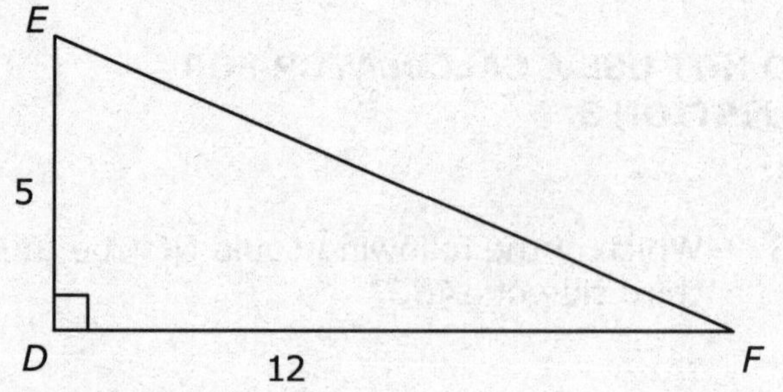

5. Figure *ABCD* is a square with an area of 16. *E* is the midpoint of side *AB*. What is the area of ΔECD?

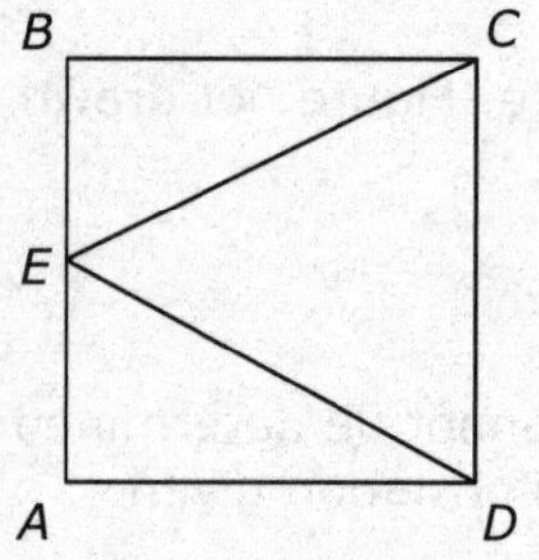

A. 6
B. 8
C. 12
D. 16

DO NOT USE A CALCULATOR FOR QUESTIONS 6-7.

6. The area of ΔABC is 32. What is the height?

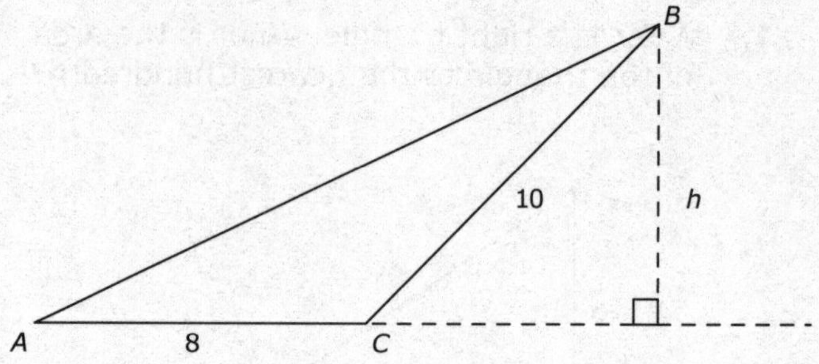

A. 4
B. 8
C. 10
D. 16

7. A rectangular pyramid has a base with a length of 5 cm and a width of 4 cm. If the volume of the pyramid is 180 cm^3, what is the height, in cm?

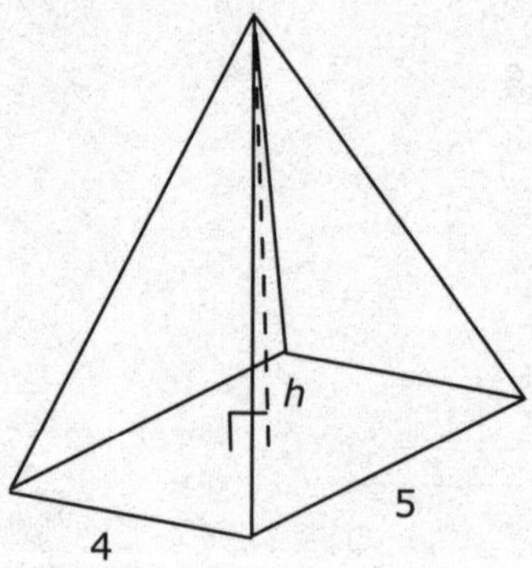

A. 9
B. 18
C. 27
D. 180

DO NOT USE A CALCULATOR FOR QUESTION 8.

8. Tony stands a 13-foot ladder up against the side of a building. The top of the ladder touches the building 12 feet above the ground. Assuming the building and the ground meet at a right angle, what is the distance, *d*, from the building to the bottom the ladder?

A. 5
B. 10
C. 25
D. 30

DO NOT USE A CALCULATOR FOR QUESTIONS 9-10.

9. Triangle *ABC* is isosceles, such that *AB* = *BC*. What are the angle measurements of the missing angles?

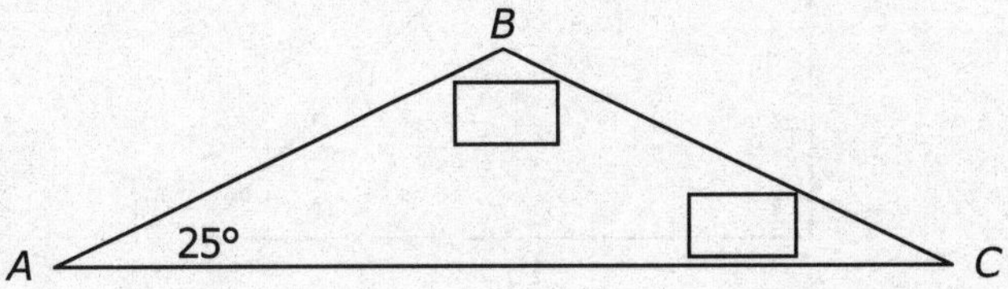

25	30	45	60
100	105	130	150

10. What is the measure of $x°$ in the figure below?

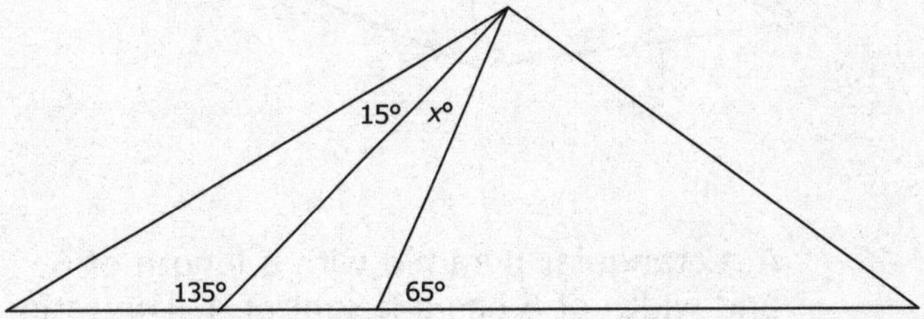

A. 20°
B. 25°
C. 65°
D. 160°

11. What is the area of the triangle with length 10 and hypotenuse 14?

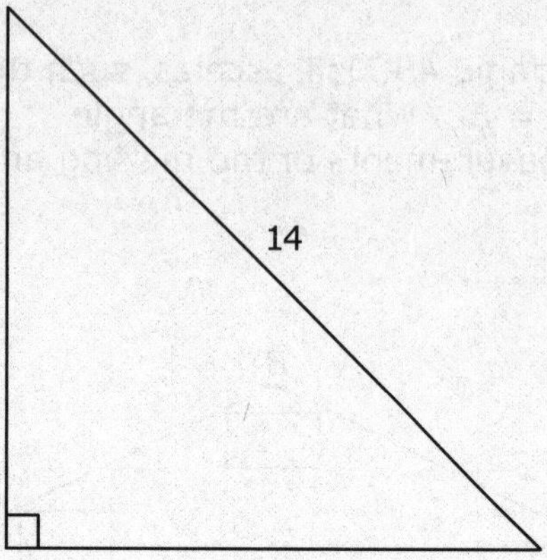

A. 20

B. $20\sqrt{6}$

C. $40\sqrt{6}$

D. 480

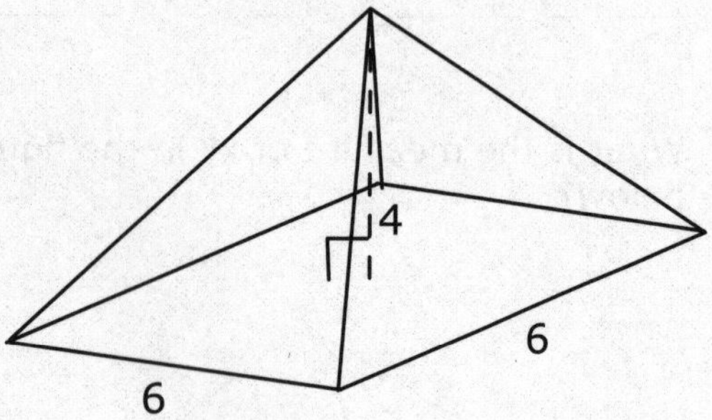

12. A rectangular pyramid with a length of 6 and width of 6 has a height of 4. The ratio of the volume to the surface area would

be [Select... ▼] : [Select... ▼] .

Select...	Select...
1	1
2	2
3	3
4	4

DO NOT USE A CALCULATOR FOR QUESTION 13.

13. An isosceles right triangle has an area of 16. What is the measure of one of its legs?

A. 4

B. $4\sqrt{2}$

C. 8

D. $8\sqrt{2}$

14. Anne is painting the front of her house. The front of the house is rectangular for the first two stories and has a 15 ft. vaulted ceiling on the third floor, as shown below. The house spans 20 feet wide and 20 feet tall for the first two stories. It also contains 4 medium sized 3 ft. by 4 ft. windows, one 2 ft. by 2 ft. window on the top floor, and an oak front door 3 ft. wide and 8 ft. tall that does not need to be painted. If one can of paint covers 40 square feet, how many cans will she need to paint the front of the house?

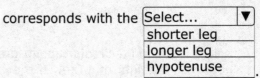

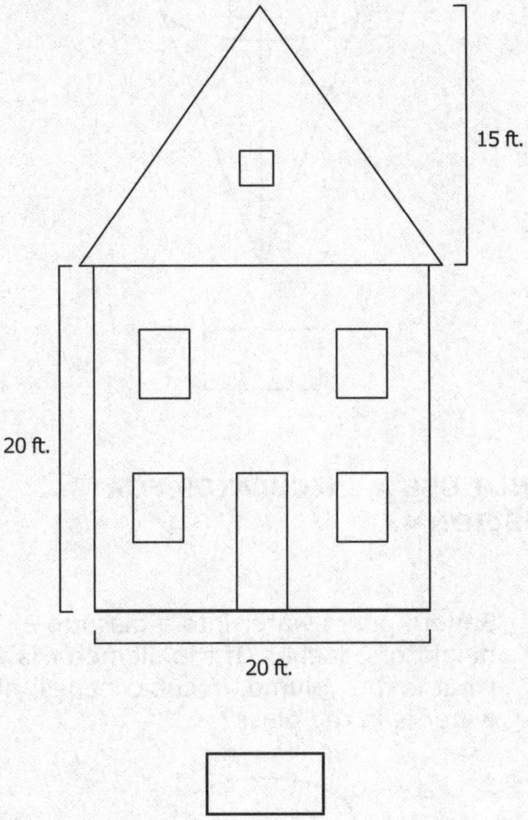

DO NOT USE A CALCULATOR FOR QUESTION 15.

15. In a 30°-60°-90° triangle, the 90° angle corresponds with the [Select... ▼ | shorter leg | longer leg | hypotenuse].

The 30° angle corresponds with the [Select... ▼ | shorter leg | longer leg | hypotenuse], and the 60° angle corresponds with the [Select... ▼ | shorter leg | longer leg | hypotenuse].

Circles, Spheres, Cylinders and Cones Drill

1. Ken is installing a circular above-ground pool with a height of 4 feet. If the diameter of the pool is 22 feet, what is the maximum volume it can hold?

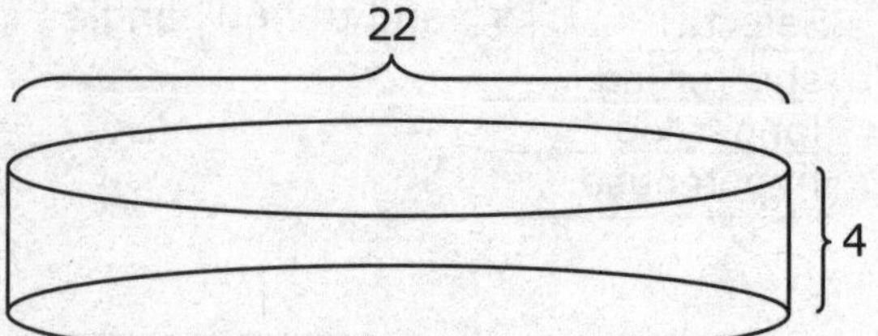

A. 44π
B. 88π
C. 484π
D. 1736π

2. A sphere has a diameter of 6.

The surface area is Select... ▼

- four times
- twice
- equal to
- half
- one fourth

the volume of the sphere.

3. A waffle cone has a height of 5 in. and a diameter of 4 in. What is the volume, to the nearest tenth of an inch, of the cone?

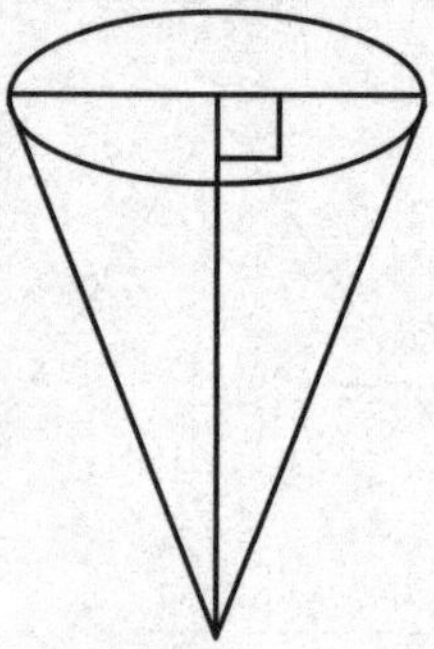

DO NOT USE A CALCULATOR FOR QUESTION 4.

4. Sandra pours water into a glass to a height of 2 inches. If the diameter is 7, what is the volume, in cubic inches, of the water is in the glass?

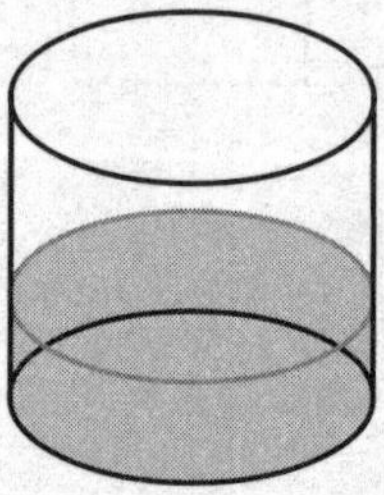

A. 7π

B. 14π

C. $\frac{49}{2}\pi$

D. 49π

DO NOT USE A CALCULATOR FOR QUESTION 5.

5. The circumference of a circle is 10π. What is the area of the circle?

   A. 5π
   B. 10π
   C. 25π
   D. 100π

6. David has a commemorative baseball with a radius of 1.25 in. What is the surface area of the ball to the nearest tenth of an inch?

   [ ]

DO NOT USE A CALCULATOR FOR QUESTIONS 7-8.

7. The circumference of the circle is equal to one half its area. What is the radius of the circle?

   [ ]

8. The diameter of a circle is 7. What is the circumference of the circle?

   A. 7
   B. 14
   C. 7π
   D. 14π

DO NOT USE A CALCULATOR FOR QUESTION 9.

9. The circumference of circle A is 25π. What is the radius of the circle?

   A. 2.5
   B. 5
   C. 12.5
   D. 25

10. A circular rotary has an area of $22{,}500\pi$ square meters. What is its radius?

    [ ]

11. The radius of a cylindrical coffee mug is 3 cm. The diameter is

    [Select... ▼] the radius.
    - four times
    - twice
    - equal to
    - half
    - one quarter of

    The area of the mug's base is

    [Select... ▼].
    - 36π
    - 9π
    - 6π
    - 3π

    The circumference of the mug's base

    is approximately [Select... ▼]
    - six times
    - three times
    - twice
    - equal to
    - half
    - one third
    - one sixth

    the length of the radius.

DO NOT USE A CALCULATOR FOR QUESTIONS 12–13.

12. The area of the circle is 36π. What is the diameter of the circle?

A. 6
B. $6\sqrt{2}$
C. 12
D. 18

13. The area of the circle is 100π. What is the circumference of the circle?

A. 10π
B. 20π
C. 50π
D. 100π

14. A donut has a diameter from its outer edges of 12 inches. Its center hole has a radius of 1 inch. To the nearest hundredth of a square inch, what is the area of the face of the donut?

A. 109.96
B. 113.10
C. 449.25
D. 452.39

15. The circumference of a circle is 16π. To the nearest hundredth, what is its area?

☐

Setup Geometry Drill

1. A solid, spherical ball of mozzarella, with diameter of 3 inches, is cut exactly in half. What is the surface area for one of these halves?

   A. $\frac{4\pi(1.5)^2}{2} + \pi(1.5)^2$

   B. $\pi(3)^2 + (3)^2$

   C. $\pi(1.5)^2 + (1.5)^2$

   D. $\frac{4\pi(3)^2}{2} + \pi(3)^2$

2. A closed cone has a height and radius of 6. A second smaller cone has dimensions of half the height and half the radius of the first. What is the surface area of the smaller cone?

   A. $\frac{1}{3}\pi(3)^2(3)$

   B. $\pi(3)(3\sqrt{2}) + \pi(3)$

   C. $\pi(3)(3) + \pi(3)^2$

   D. $\pi(3)(3\sqrt{2}) + \pi(3)^2$

3. Kevin is making a garden in his backyard. He wants to put in some fencing around the flowerbeds to keep the deer from eating the flowers. He has one freestanding vegetable garden that is 4 feet by 5 feet and two flowerbeds with long sides against the house that are 2 feet by 10 feet. If he does not need fencing against the house, how much fencing should he buy?

   A. (4)(5) + 2(2)(10)
   B. [2(4) + 2(5)] + 2[2(2) + 10]
   C. [2(4) + 2(5)] + [2(2) + 2(10)]
   D. [2(4) + 2(5)] + 2[2(2) + 2(10)]

4. Chandra is assembling a bureau. There are four drawers measuring 3 feet long by 10 inches deep with a height of 5 inches. At the top of the bureau, there are three sock drawers measuring 11 inches by 10 inches deep, with a height of 4 inches. What is the total volume, in cubic feet, that the dresser can hold?

   A. $(3)\left(\frac{10}{12}\right)\left(\frac{5}{12}\right)+\left(\frac{11}{12}\right)\left(\frac{10}{12}\right)\left(\frac{4}{12}\right)$

   B. $4(3)(10)(5) + 3(11)(10)(4)$

   C. $4(3)\left(\frac{10}{12}\right)\left(\frac{5}{12}\right)+3\left(\frac{11}{12}\right)\left(\frac{10}{12}\right)\left(\frac{4}{12}\right)$

   D. $\frac{4(3)(10)(5) + 3(11)(10)(4)}{12}$

5. Kemisa is figure skating and wants to complete half circles in a hockey rink. If the lines in the ice rink are 84 feet long, how many semicircles could she complete before hitting the boards if each half circle has a radius of 7 feet?

   A. $\frac{84}{2(7)}$

   B. $\frac{84}{7}$

   C. $\frac{84}{2\pi(7)}$

   D. 2(7)

Graphing Drill

DO NOT USE A CALCULATOR FOR QUESTION 1.

1. Place an x on the graph to show where the fourth vertex of the rectangle should be.

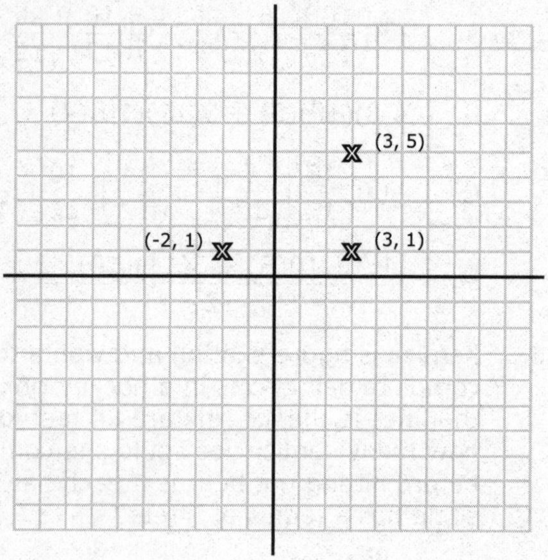

DO NOT USE A CALCULATOR FOR QUESTION 2.

2. Choose the graph that expresses the equation $4y - 3x = 16$ on the *xy*-coordinate plane:

A.

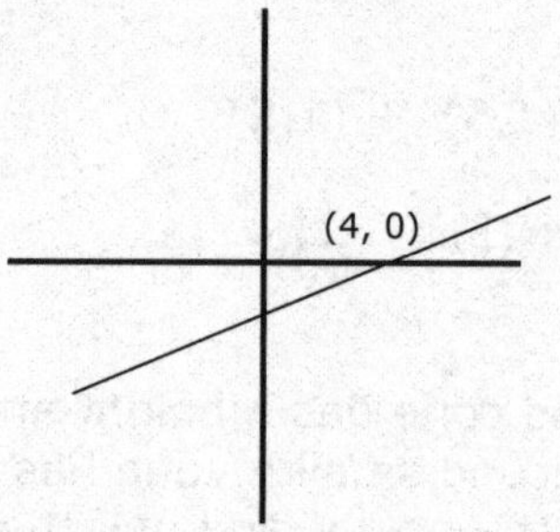

B.

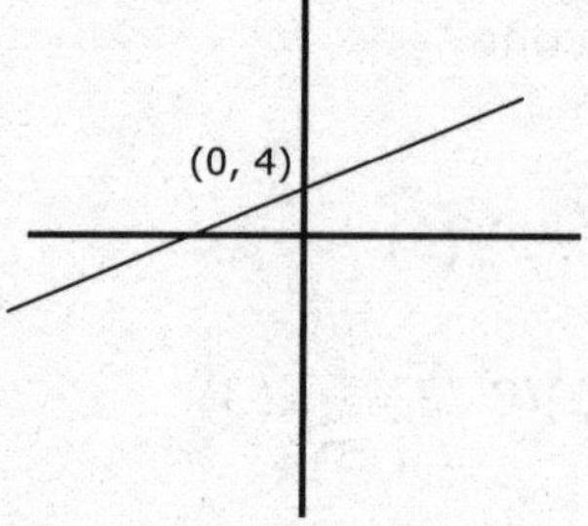

C.

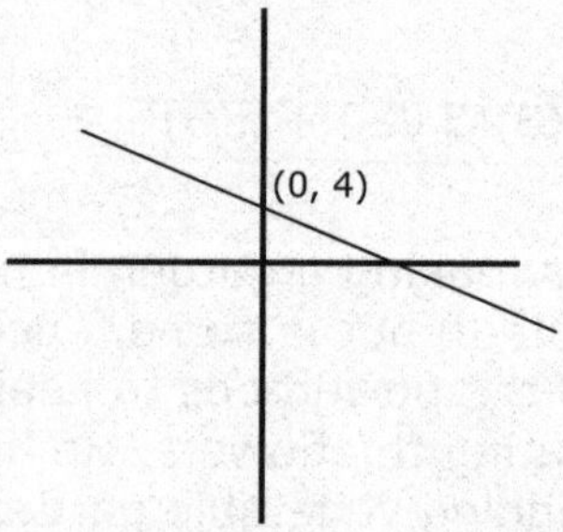

D.

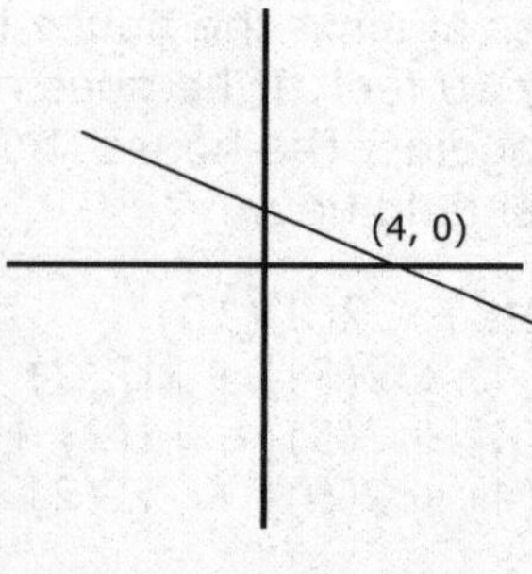

DO NOT USE A CALCULATOR FOR QUESTIONS 3–4.

3. Points (–4, –3) and (8, 2) lie on the *xy*-coordinate plane. What is the distance between the two points?

4. Select the curve from the graph below that represents the function $f(x) = -x^2 + 2$:

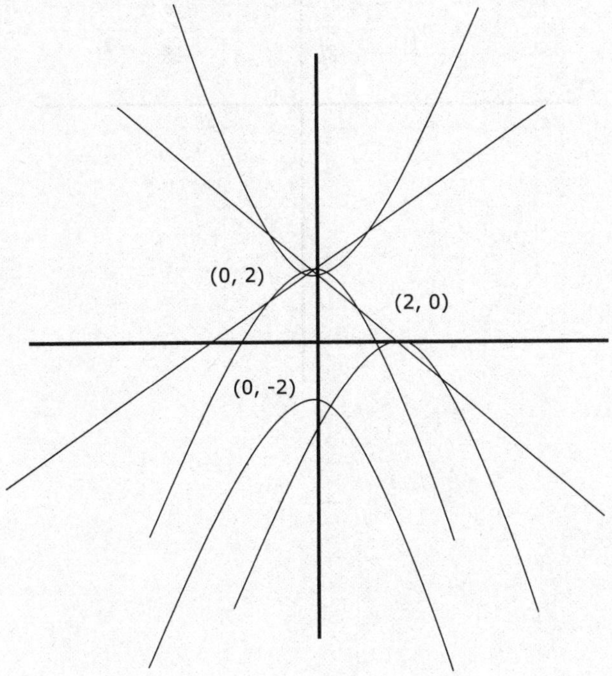

<u>Questions 5–6</u> refer to the following information:

A handicap on-ramp has a horizontal length of 44 feet and a rise of 2.5 feet.

5. Approximately what is the slope of the ramp?

A. .06
B. 5.6
C. 17.6
D. 41.5

6. Approximately how long is the ramp from start to finish?

A. 41.5
B. 44.1
C. 46.5
D. 1942.25

DO NOT USE A CALCULATOR FOR QUESTION 7.

7. Jamia drives 5 miles due north from her house to the grocery store. Then, she drives due east 4 miles to the pet grooming store to pick up her poodle, and continues another 5 miles east to take her poodle to the park. After she is done walking in the park, she drives another 3 miles east to meet a friend for coffee. How far is Jamia from home?

8. Put the following equations in order from least to greatest based on slope:

_____, _____, _____, _____

$y = 4x + 3$	$4 = 4x + 4y$
$3x = 2y + 4$	$15 = x - 3y$

DO NOT USE A CALCULATOR FOR QUESTION 9.

9. Give the coordinates for the center of the circle with a radius of 4 that is tangent to both the *x*- and *y*-axes and lies in Quadrant III.

A. (4, −4)
B. (−2. −2)
C. (−4, −4)
D. (2, −2)

DO NOT USE A CALCULATOR FOR QUESTION 10.

10. An isosceles triangle lies on the *xy*-coordinate plane, such that the given points are the vertices of the base and the height is parallel to the *y*-axis. Graph the vertex of the isosceles triangle with a height of 6 that lies in Quadrant IV in the graph below:

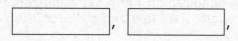

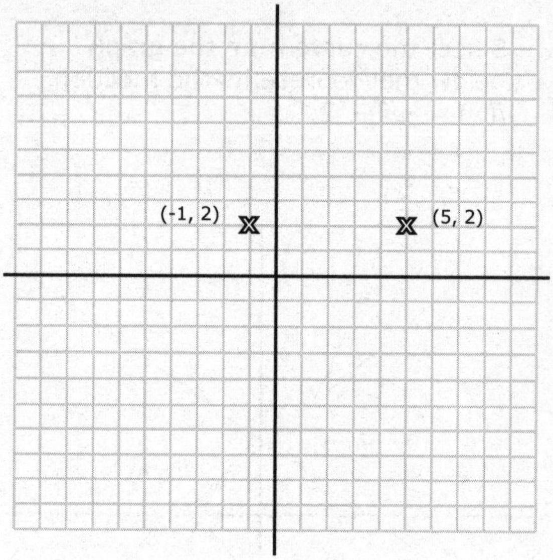

DO NOT USE A CALCULATOR FOR QUESTION 11.

11. Consider the following equations,

$h(x) = \frac{4}{5}x + 12$ and $f(x) = -\frac{1}{2}x + 9$.

The slope of $h(x)$ is

Select... ▼	that of $f(x)$.
less than	
equal to	
the negative reciprocal of	
greater than	

The y-intercept of $f(x)$ is

Select... ▼	that of $h(x)$.
twice	
four thirds	
equal to	
three fourths	
half	

12. On a playground, Alice is playing on a swing set that is 12 feet north of Billy, who is on the seesaw. Caitlin is across from Billy on the other side of the seesaw, 9 feet to the west. If Billy's end of the seesaw is in line with Alice and the seesaw creates a right angle with the swing set, how far apart are Alice and Caitlin?

A. 3 feet
B. 9 feet
C. 15 feet
D. 21 feet

Equation of a Line Drill

DO NOT USE A CALCULATOR FOR QUESTIONS 1–2.

1. Where, on the *xy*-coordinate plane, do the following lines intersect?

$$y = 4x - 4$$
$$y = 2x + 2$$

$x =$	$y =$

1	−1	3	−3
4	−4	6	−6
8	−8	9	−9

2. What is the formula of the line containing points (−1, 4) and (3, −2)?

A. $y = -\frac{3}{2}x - 5$

B. $y = -\frac{3}{2}x + \frac{5}{2}$

C. $y = -\frac{2}{3}x + \frac{5}{2}$

D. $y = \frac{2}{3}x - 5$

DO NOT USE A CALCULATOR FOR QUESTIONS 3–4.

3. What is the slope of the line perpendicular to $-3 = 3x + 2y$?

4. What is the slope of the line perpendicular to $y - 4x = -6$?

A. $2y + \frac{1}{2}x = -4$

B. $y + 4x = 4$

C. $2y - \frac{1}{2}x = -4$

D. $2y - 4x = -4$

5. Which of the following lines intersects the line $y = \frac{4}{3}x + 5$ at point (3, 9)?

A. $y = -\frac{9}{2}x - \frac{9}{2}$

B. $y = -\frac{9}{2}x + \frac{9}{2}$

C. $y = \frac{9}{2}x - \frac{9}{2}$

D. $y = \frac{9}{2}x + \frac{9}{2}$

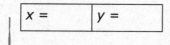

DO NOT USE A CALCULATOR FOR QUESTIONS 6–7.

6. Add one number to each of the columns so that it shows the function $y = 3x + 4$. Do not repeat an ordered pair.

Write the correct numbers in boxes.

x	y
0	4
2	10
3	13

5	6	10

19	22

7. What is the equation for the following points?

x	y
1	3
2	5
3	7
4	9
5	11
6	13

A. $y = 2x$

B. $y = 2x + 1$

C. $y = \frac{1}{2}x + 1$

D. $y = -2x + 1$

DO NOT USE A CALCULATOR FOR QUESTION 8.

8. Which of the following graphs represents the line $5y - x = 15$?

A.

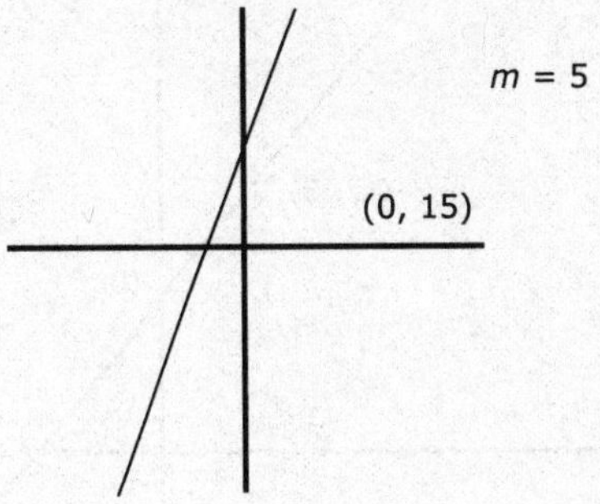

B.

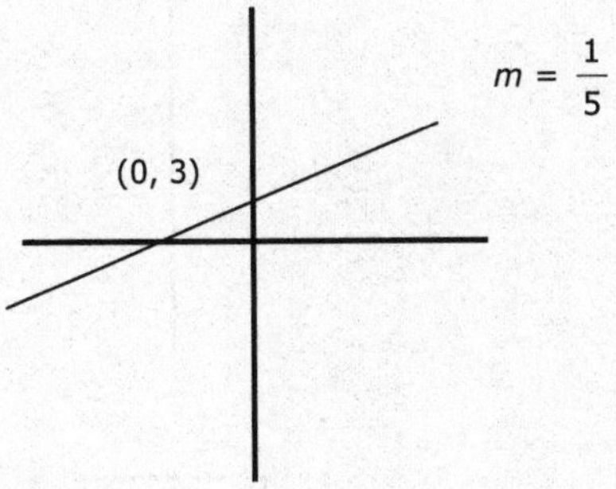

C.

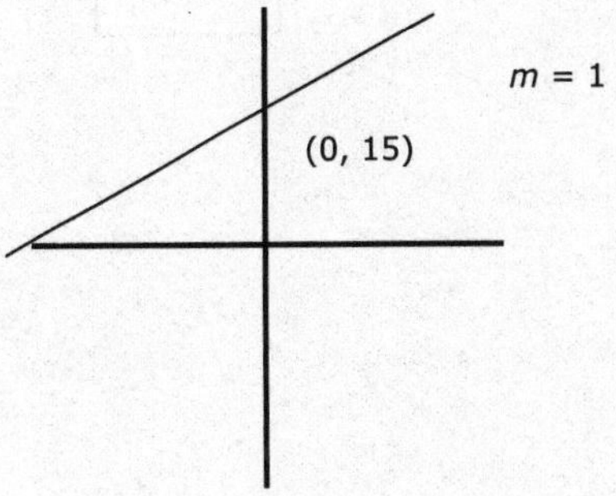

D.

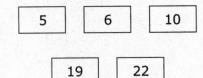

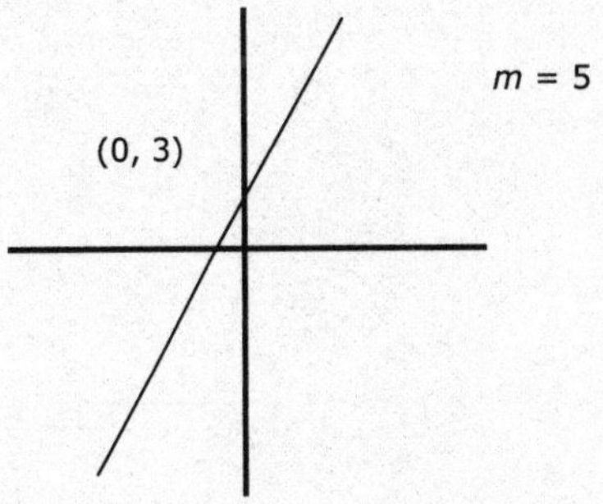

DO NOT USE A CALCULATOR FOR QUESTION 9.

9. What is the slope of the line?

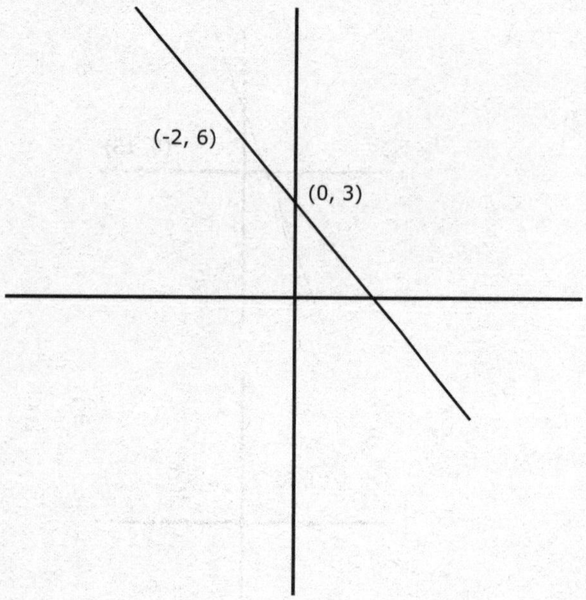

10. Mark on the *xy*-coordinate plane two points that lie on the line $-5x + 6y = 6$.

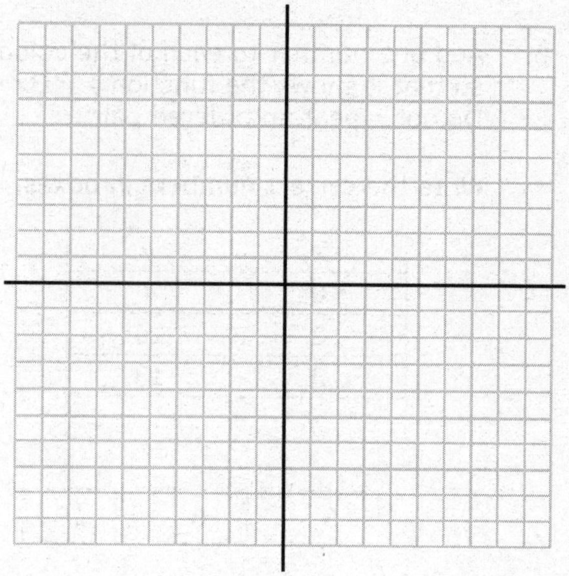

11. Where do the lines $4 = 2y - 4x$ and $-9x + 3y = 18$ intersect?

$x =$	$y =$

−8	−6	−4	−2
2	4	6	8

12. Which of the following equations is parallel to the line $5y - 4x = 10$?

A. $10y - 8x = 14$
B. $8y - 10x = 2$
C. $10y + 8x = 14$
D. $8y - 10x = 2$

Percents Drill

1. Approximately what percent of the circle is shaded?

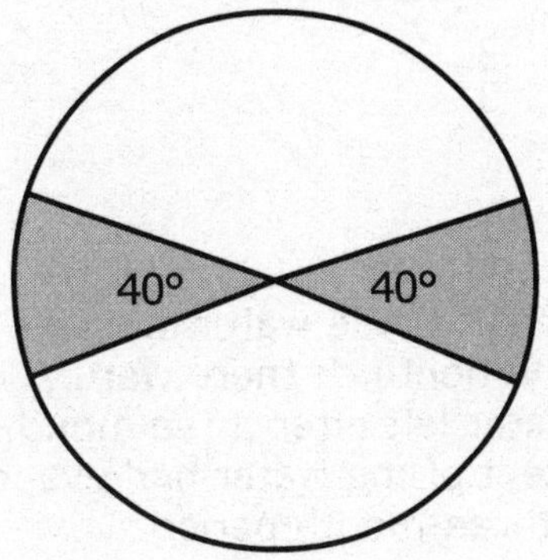

A. 11%
B. 20%
C. 22%
D. 40%

2. A circle is inscribed in a square. Approximately what percent of the square is the circle?

A. 21.5%
B. 25%
C. 75%
D. 78.5%

DO NOT USE A CALCULATOR FOR QUESTION 3.

3. Two circles share the same center, *O*. If *OB* = 4 and *OA* = *AB*, what is the ratio of the total area to the area of the smaller circle?

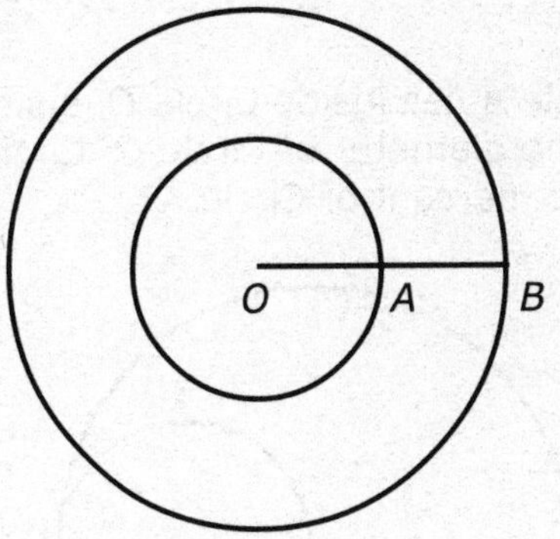

Select... ▼	:	Select... ▼
4		4
3		3
2		2
1		1

DO NOT USE A CALCULATOR FOR QUESTION 4.

4. A rectangle has a length of $x + 2$ and a width of x. If both sides were doubled, what ratio of the new area to the old area?

[ ] : [ ]

[1] [2] [3] [4]

[5] [6] [7]

5. Circle A lies inside Circle O, such that OB is the diameter of Circle O. Circle O is what percent of Circle A?

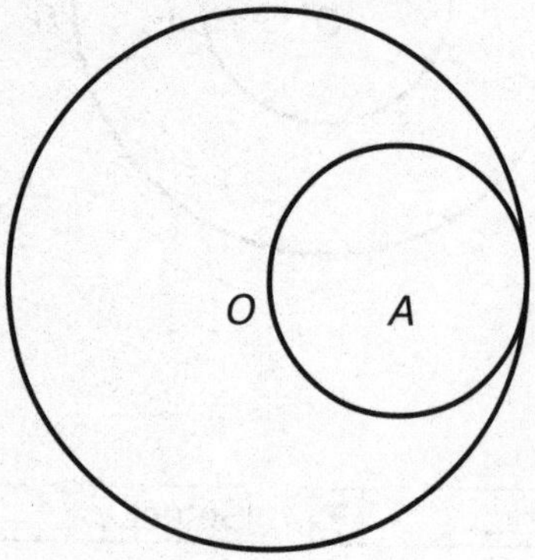

A. 25%
B. 40%
C. 200%
D. 400%

DO NOT USE A CALCULATOR FOR QUESTION 6.

6. A glass of milk with a diameter and height of 5 inches is filled to a height of 2 inches. What percent of the glass remains empty?

A. $\frac{2}{5}$
B. $\frac{3}{5}$
C. $\frac{5}{3}$
D. $\frac{5}{2}$

7. One half of the water in a lake evaporates every month. If there were 1000 gallons of water left after three months, what percent of the water had evaporated over the three-month period?

[ ]

Questions 8 and 9 refer to the graph below.

Shoe Company A is doing an end-of-year analysis to determine sales percentages per three-month quarter. The following graph represents the percentages of sales by quarter:

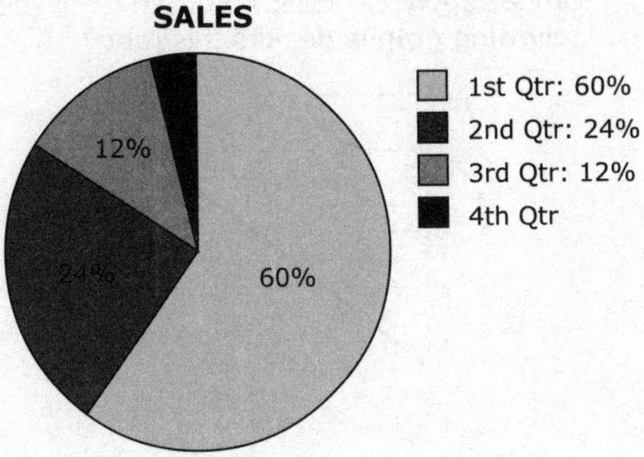

8. The percent of sales in the 4th quarter is

☐.

The angle measurement of the 1st quarter is

☐.

9. What is the sum of the degrees in the second and third quarters?

A. 36°
B. 43.2°
C. 86.4°
D. 129.6°

Questions 10 and 11 refer to the chart below.

A recent poll of an elementary school asked 400 students what kinds of pets they own. The results of the poll can be found in the following table:

Type of Pet	Percent owned
Dog(s) only	30%
Cat(s) only	28%
Other(s)	8%
Dog(s) and Cat(s)	13%
Dog(s) and Other(s)	4%
Cat(s) and Other(s)	7%
None	10%

10. If the students were to create a pie graph with this information, approximately what is the sum of the degrees of students who own dogs?

A. 14°
B. 47°
C. 108°
D. 194°

11. How many students only own cats?

☐

Proportions and Graphs Drill

1. Mariam is riding the train at a constant rate from New York to Boston. The trip takes four hours and thirty minutes in total. The graph below shows her mileage-to-distance ratio. At approximately what rate is she traveling?

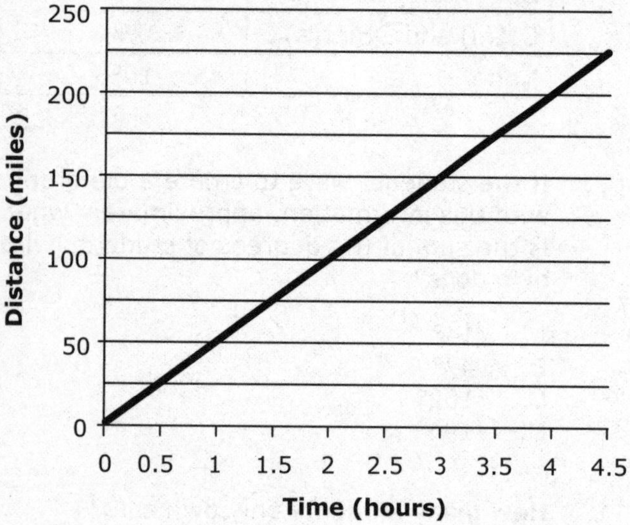

A. 45 mph
B. 50 mph
C. 55 mph
D. 60 mph

2. The ratio of staplers to paperclips in an office supply closet is 1:30. Which of the following graphs depicts this ratio?

A.

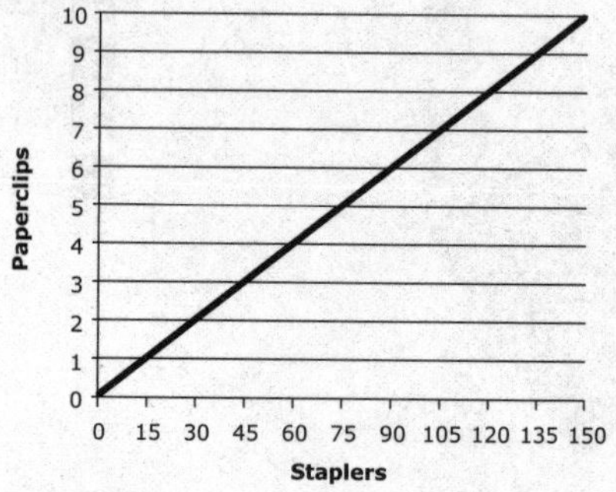

B.

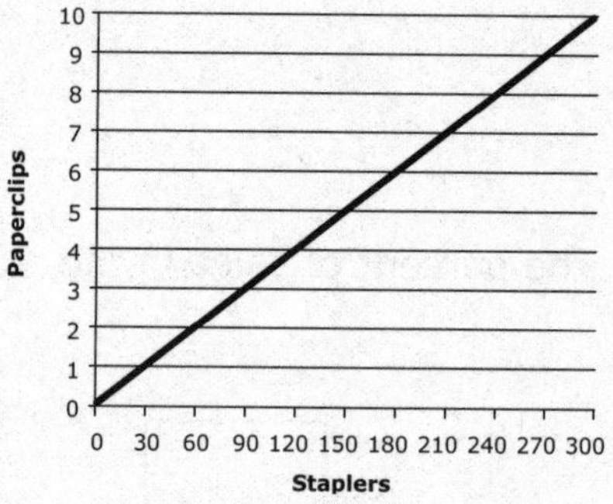

C.

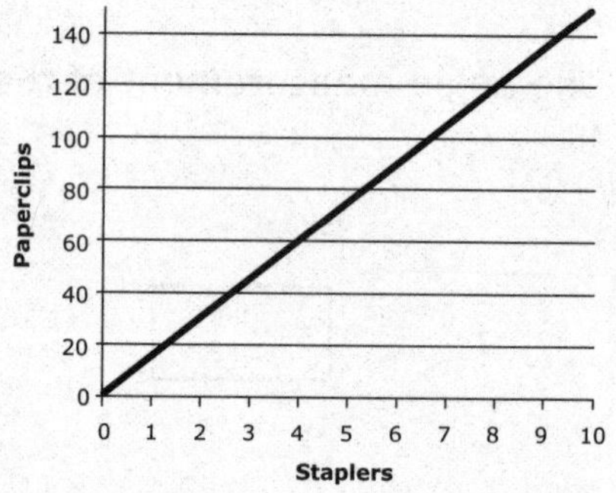

D.

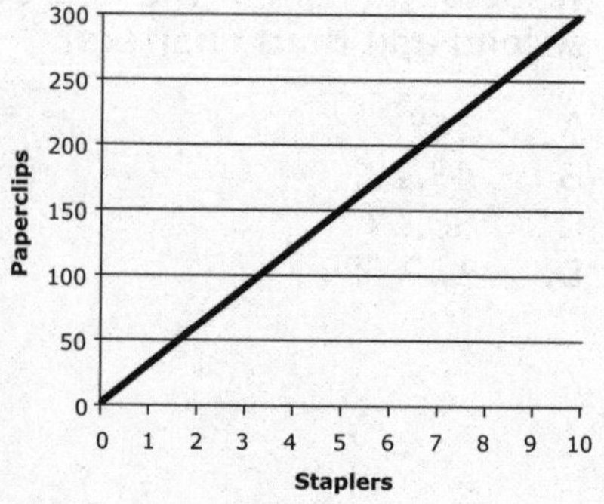

3. Lisa and Tim are taking a bike ride. They are riding at a rate of 6 miles per hour. Which of the following graphs represents their trip?

A.

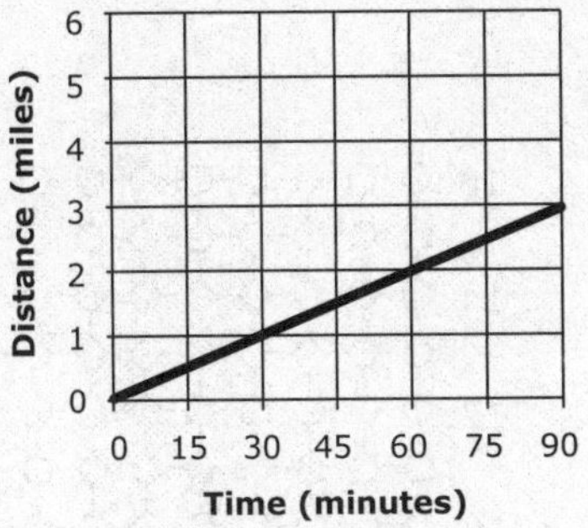

B.

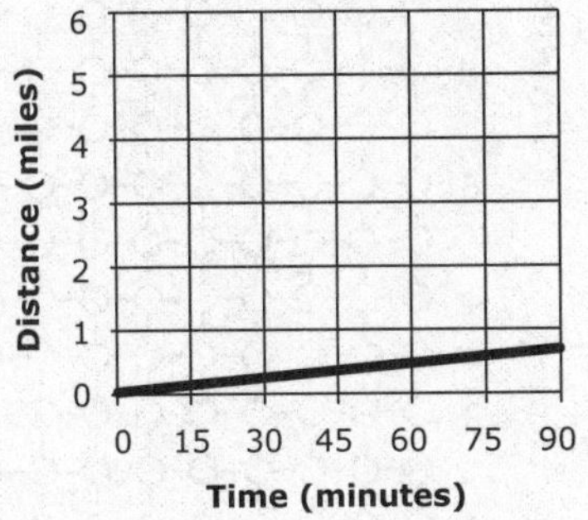

C.

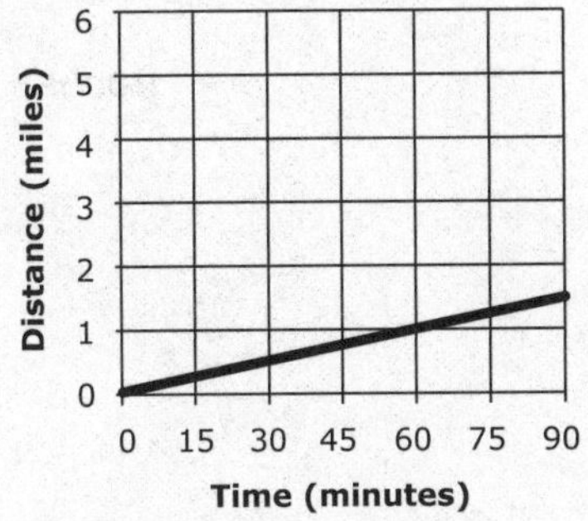

D.

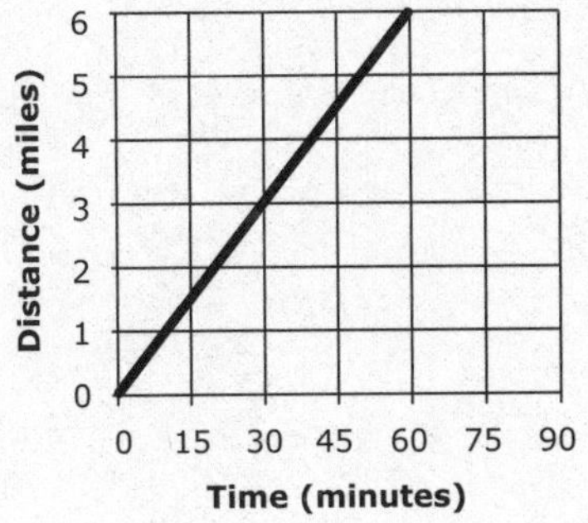

4. Cab Company A charges a $2.50 flat rate plus 25 cents for every tenth of a mile traveled. Cab Company B's prices are depicted in the graph below.

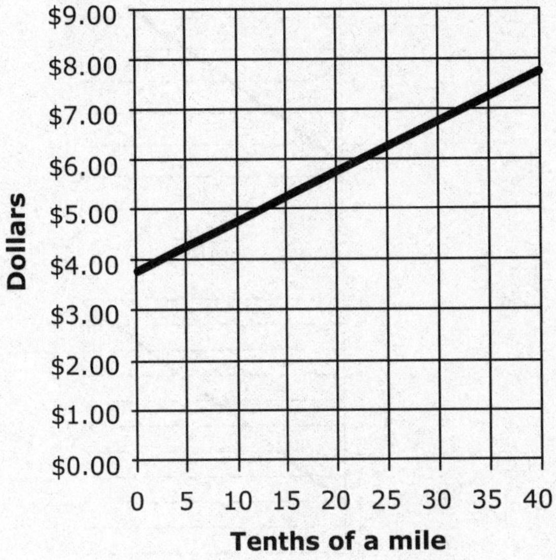

When traveling a distance of 5 miles, Cab

Company A [Select... ▼]
- costs more than
- costs the same as
- costs less than

Cab Company B.

5. Alesia owns 4 pairs of flats for every 6 pairs of heels. Which graph represents this proportion?

A.

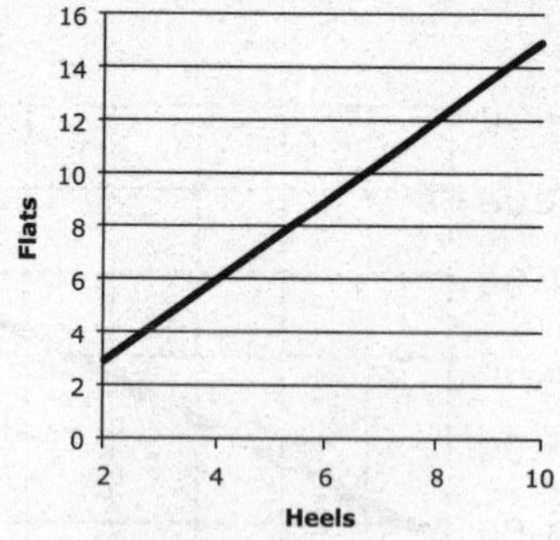

B.

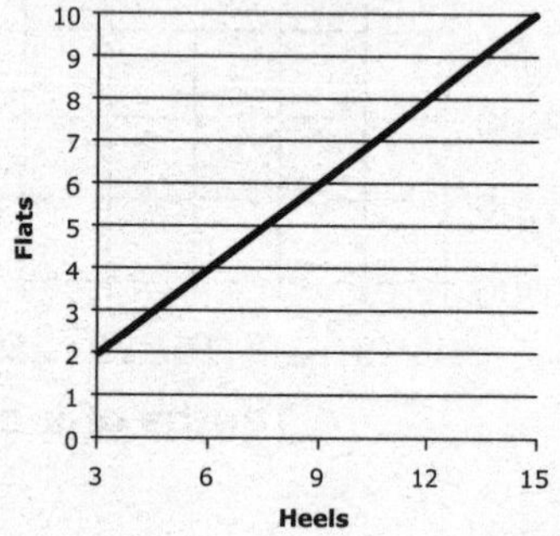

C.

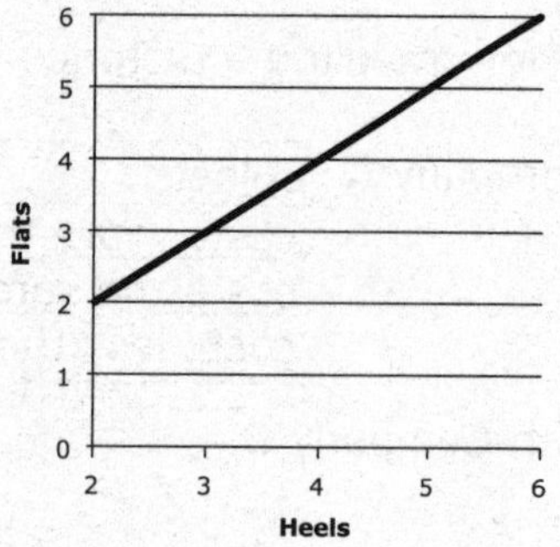

D.

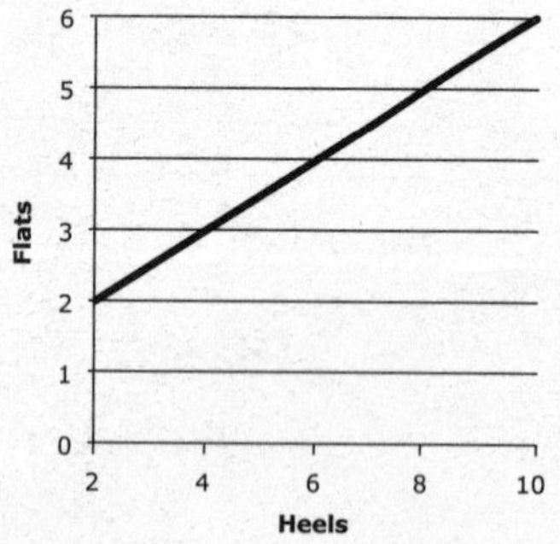

6. A store sells roses and carnations in a ratio of 3:4. Plot 4 distinct points on the following graph to show this relationship. Let the x-axis represent roses and the y-axis represent carnations.

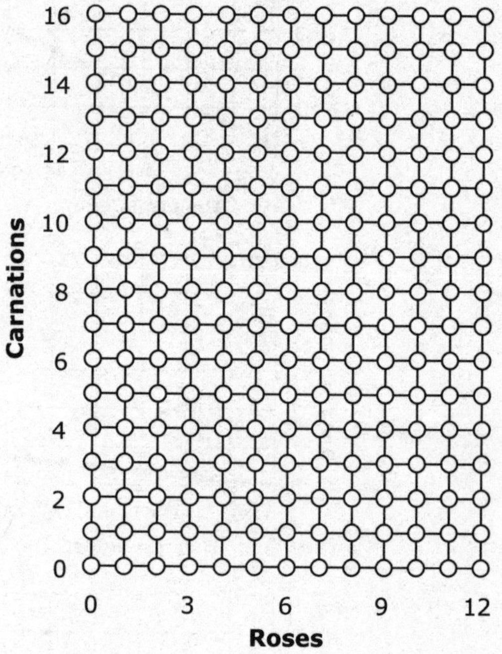

7. For every 40 miles James travels, Vivek travels 60 miles. James starts with a 20 mile head start and they drive in the same direction. Which of the following graphs represents their travels?

A.

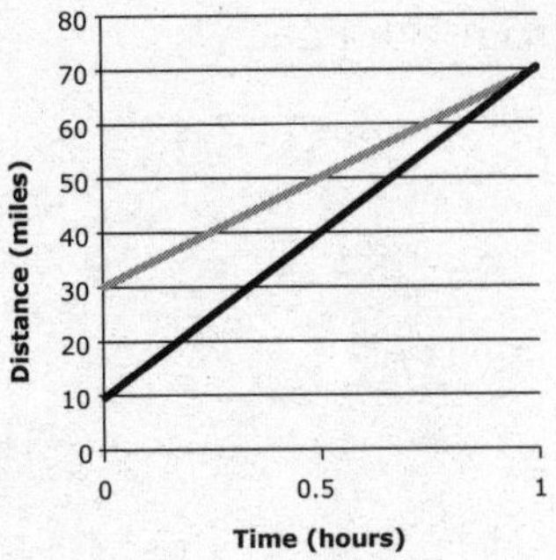

B.

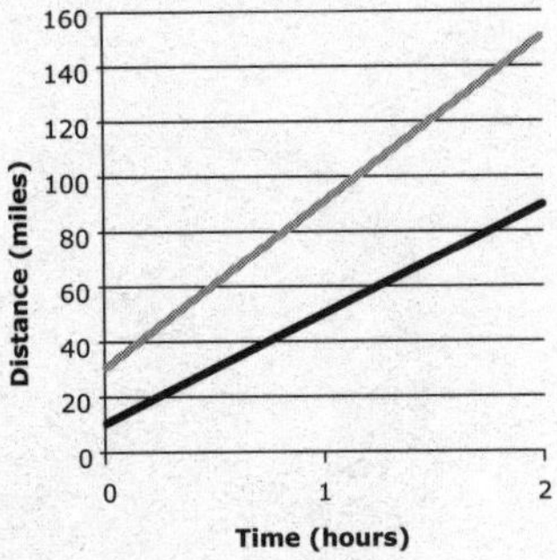

C.

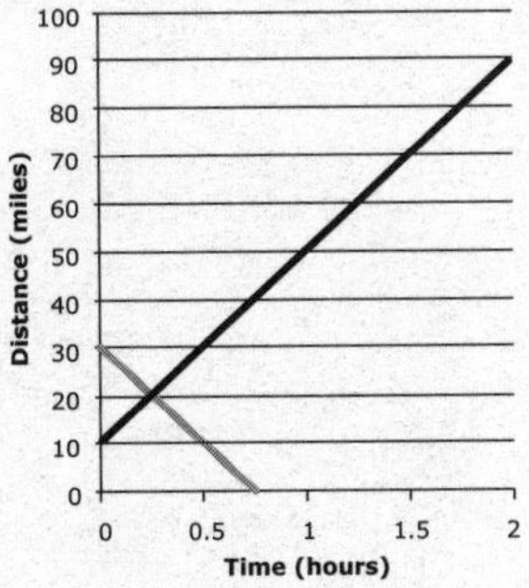

D.

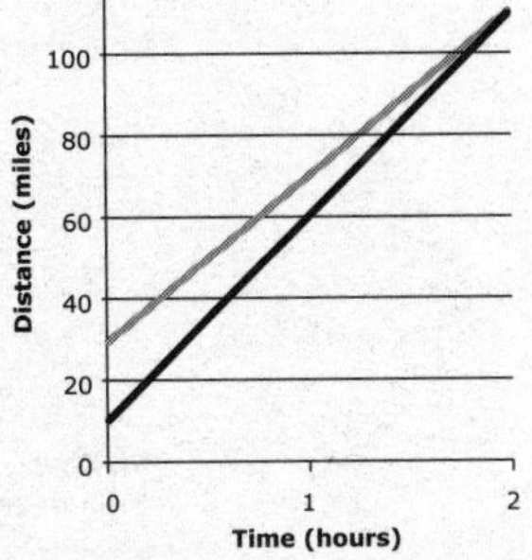

8. The population of Rehoboth, MA grows at a rate of 550 people every 5 years. If the population was 11,600 in 2010, plot 4 points on the graph of its population growth.

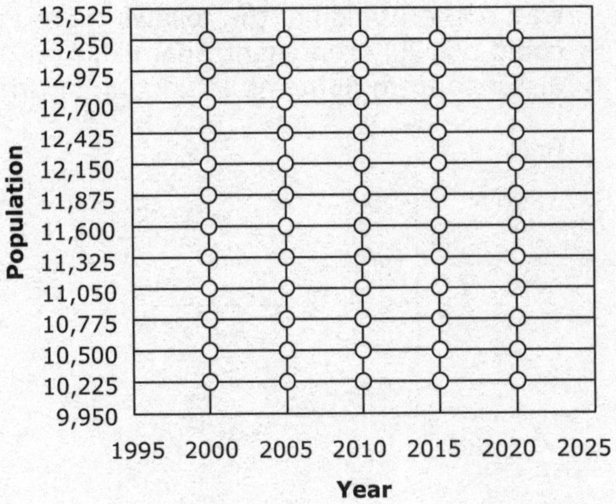

9. Shamika left work towards home. She stopped at the gym for her daily workout, and then continued on her way home. She got a mile from home when she realized she was almost out of gas, so she quickly retraced her steps to the nearest gas station. Once she finished filling her tank, she drove the rest of the way home. Which of the following graphs could possibly represent Shamika's distance from home as a function of time?

A.

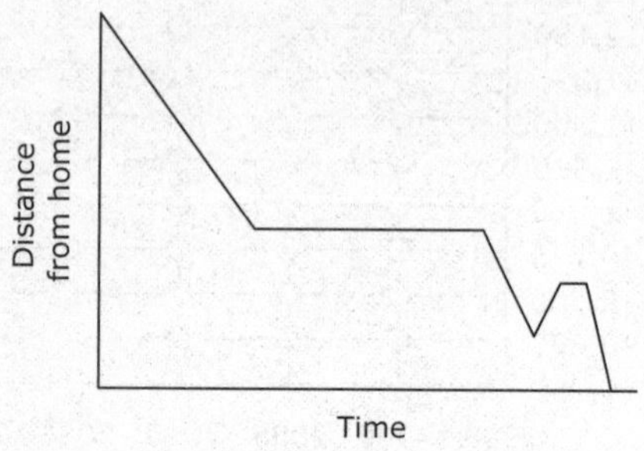

B.

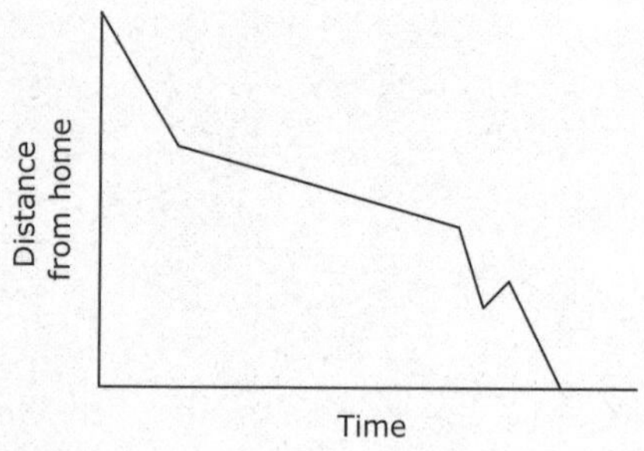

C.

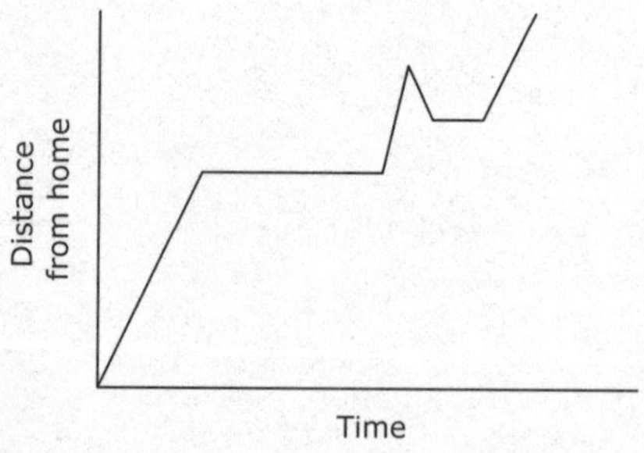

D.

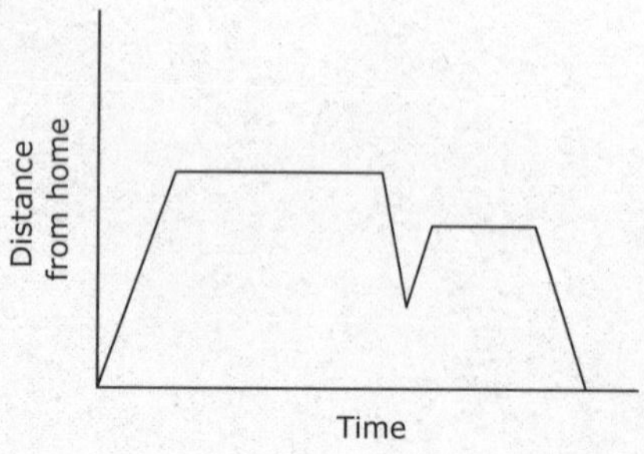

10. Rafael travels on his bike for 3 hours at a constant rate of 20 mph from his home to the beach. He returns home from the beach at a constant rate of 15 mph. Which of the following pie charts represents the amount of time spent to and from the beach?

A.

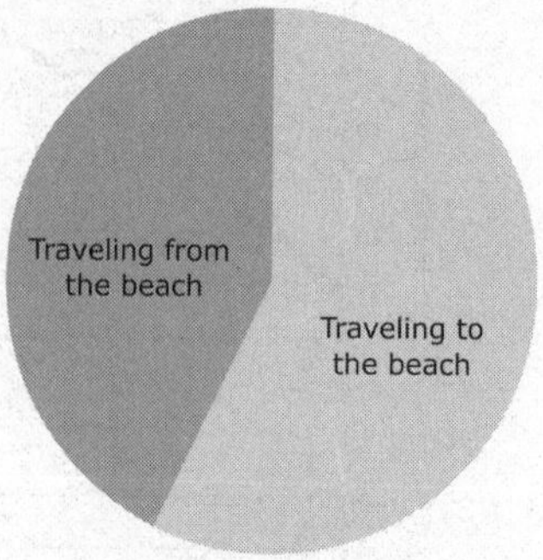

B.

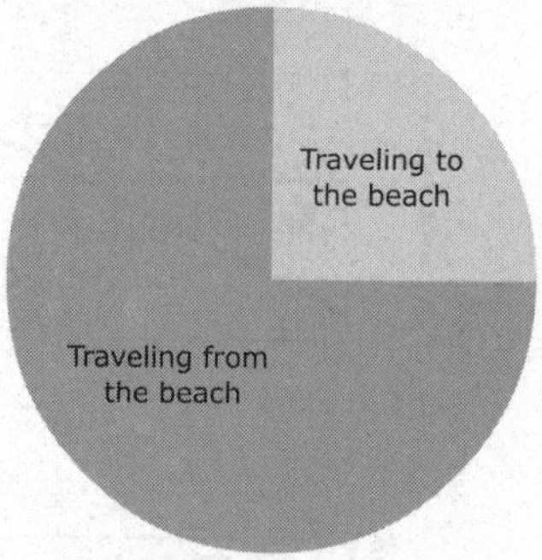

C.

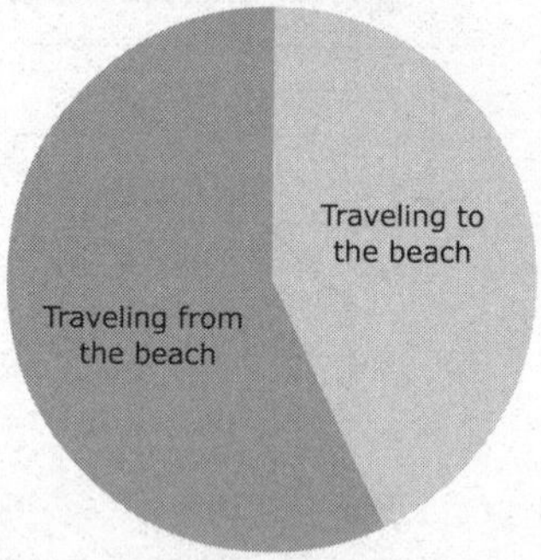

D.

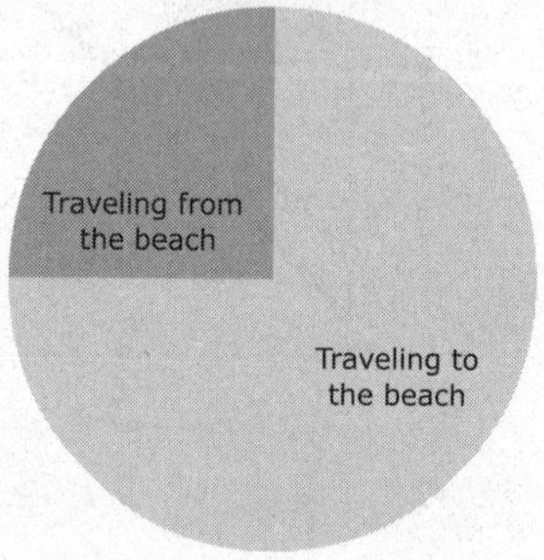

11. A line is defined by the equation $y = \frac{1}{4}x$.

The ratio of the x-values to the y-values is

[ ] : [ ]

1	2	3
4	6	8

12. A figure skater spins at a rate of 4 revolutions per second. Which of the following graphs represents his amount of revolutions in proportion to time in minutes?

A.

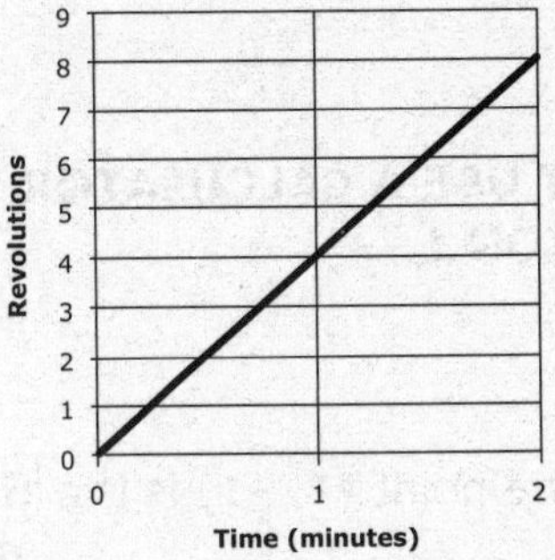

B.

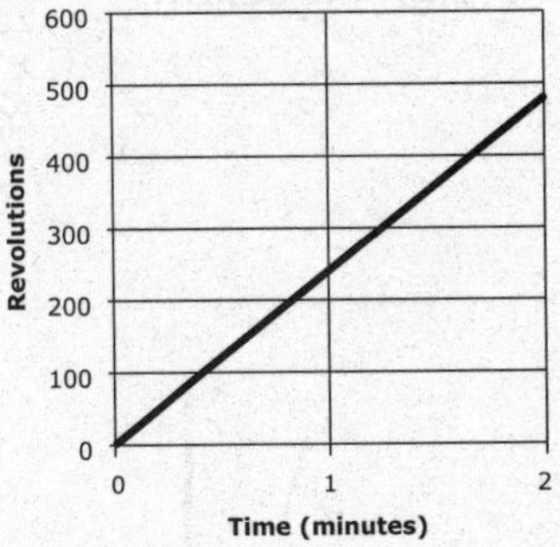

C.

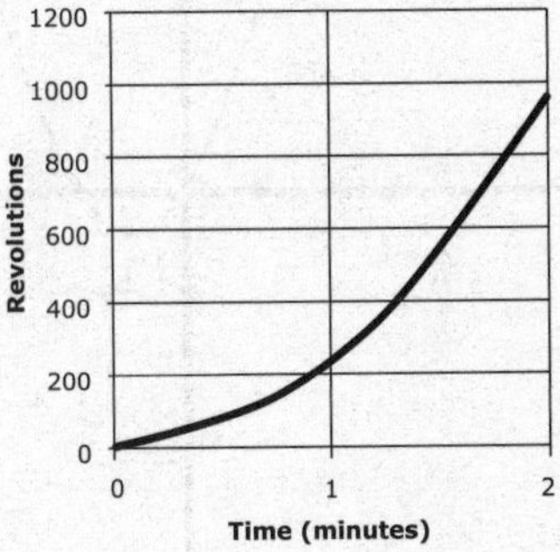

D.

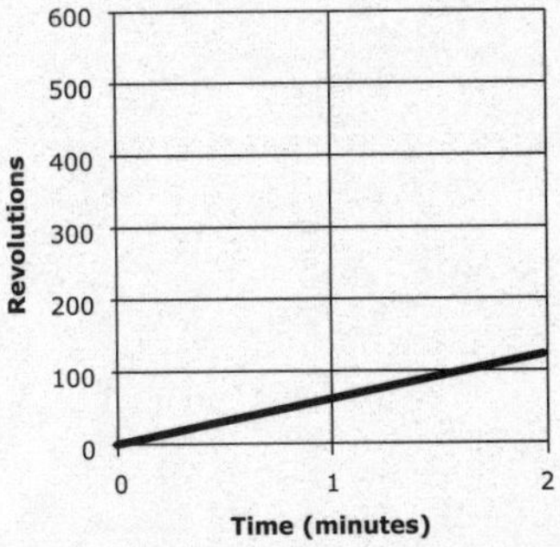

Interpreting Graphs Drill

DO NOT USE A CALCULATOR FOR QUESTION 1.

1. The point (1, −1) is the [Select... ▼] of the graph below.

Select... ▼
minimum
y-intercept
x-intercept
maximum

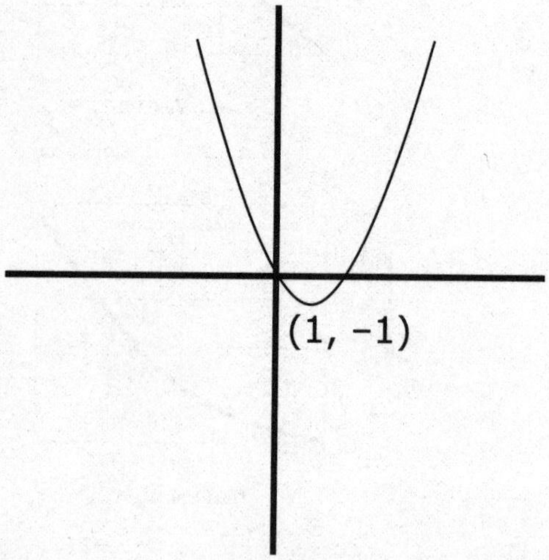

2. Which of the following graphs is symmetrical about the *y*-axis?

A.

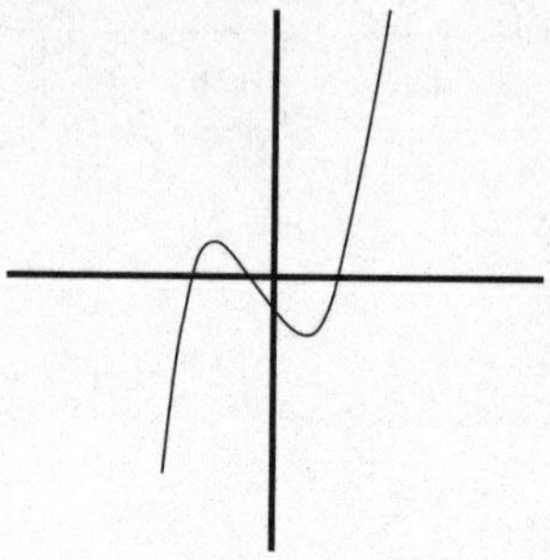

B.

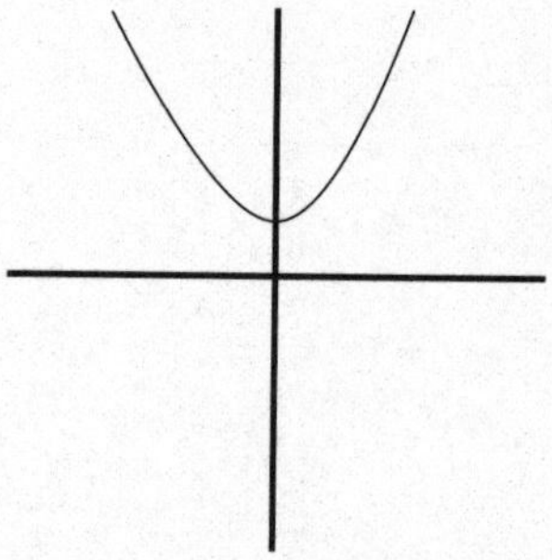

C.

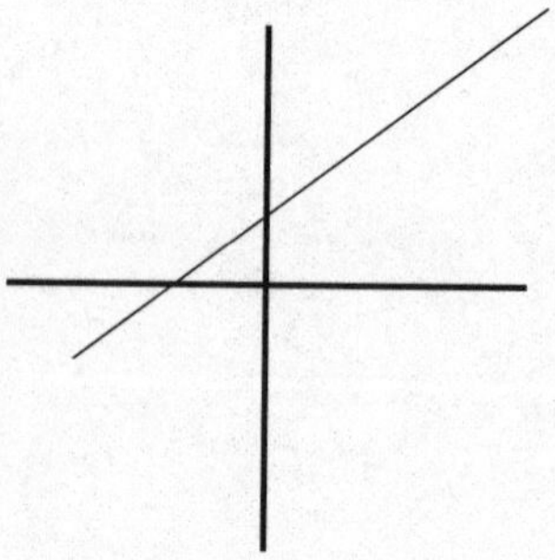

D.

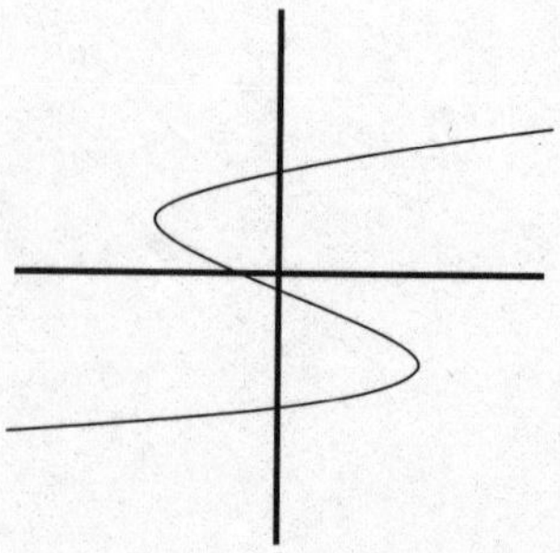

3. Which of the following graphs is symmetrical about the line $y = x$?

A.

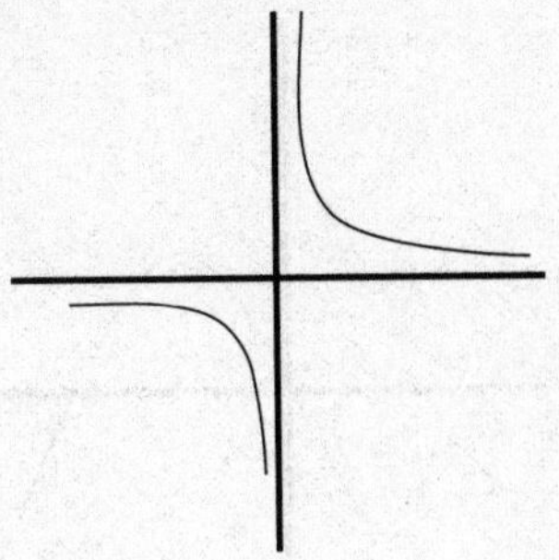

B.

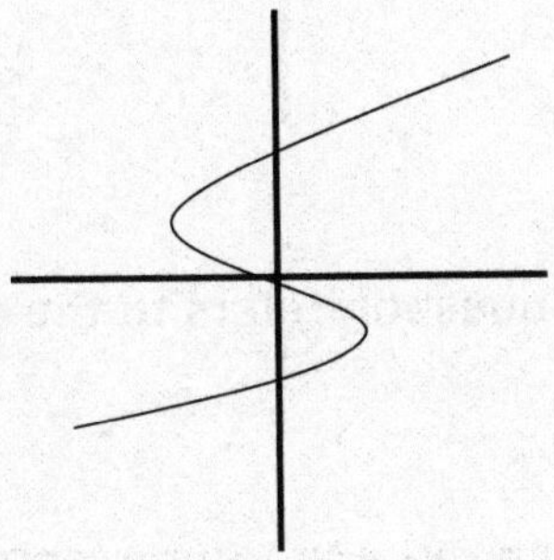

C.

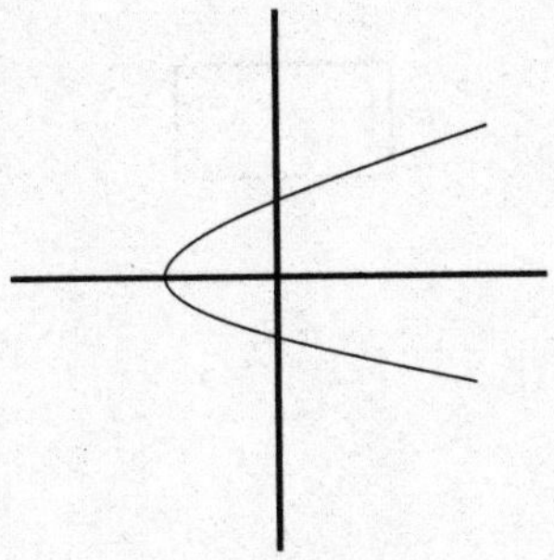

D.

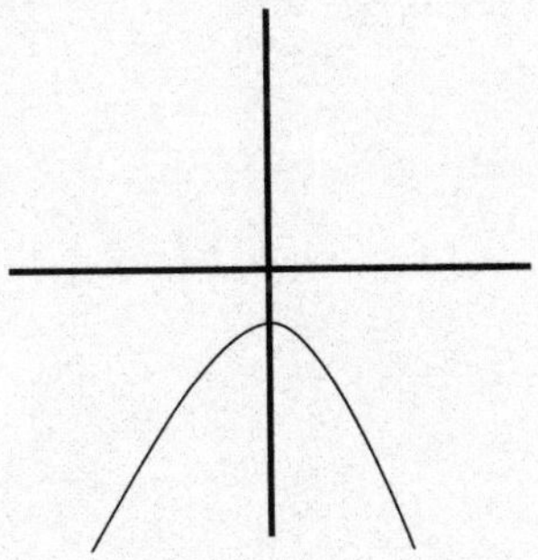

4. On which of the following graphs is the period the greatest?

A.

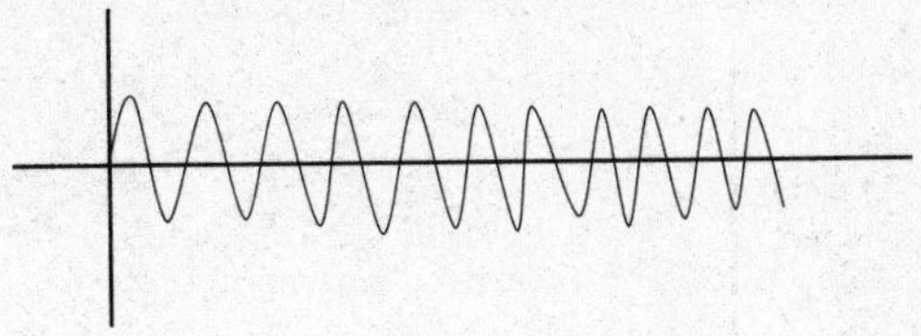

B.

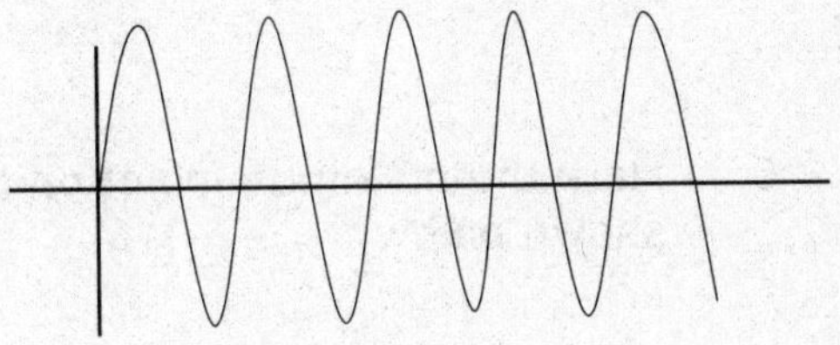

C.

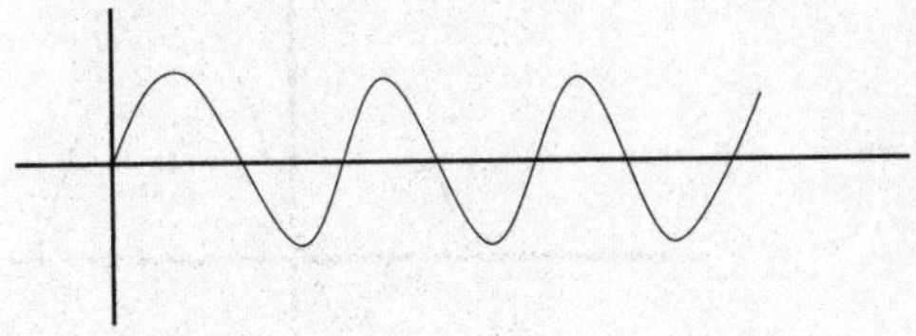

D.

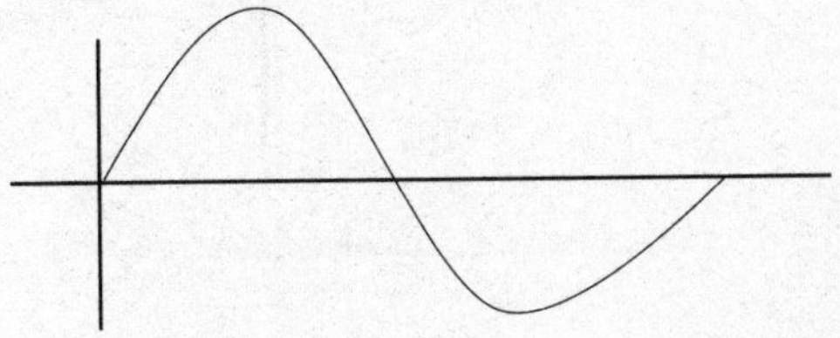

5. Tom threw a football down the field. Mark on the graph where the ball was released.

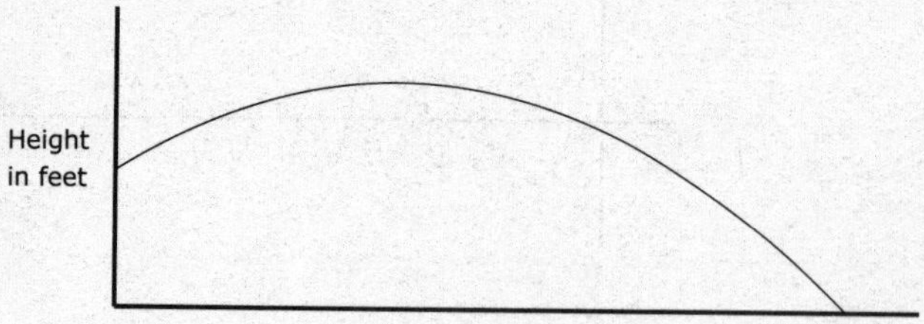

6. Mark the maximum point on the graph shown below:

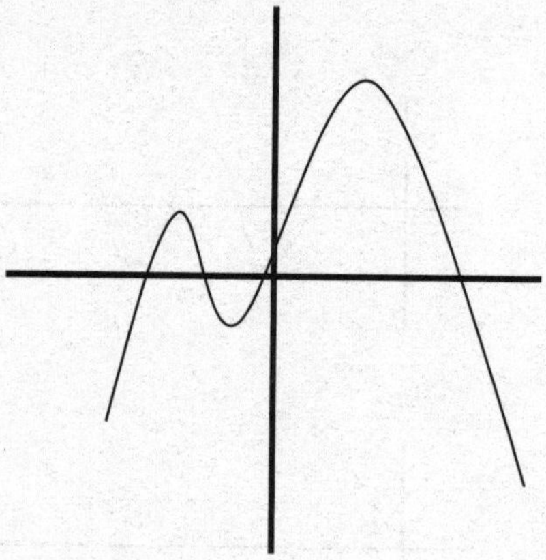

7. Mark the *x*-intercept(s) on the graph below:

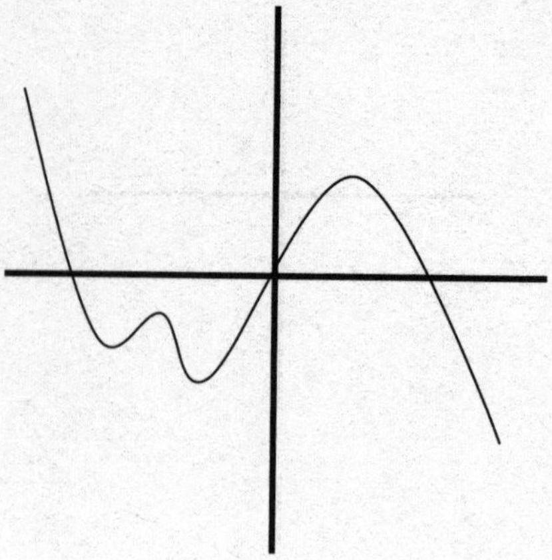

The following question refers to the graph in question 7:

8. How many *x*- and *y*-intercepts are present?

9. Which of the following graphs contains the shortest period?

A.

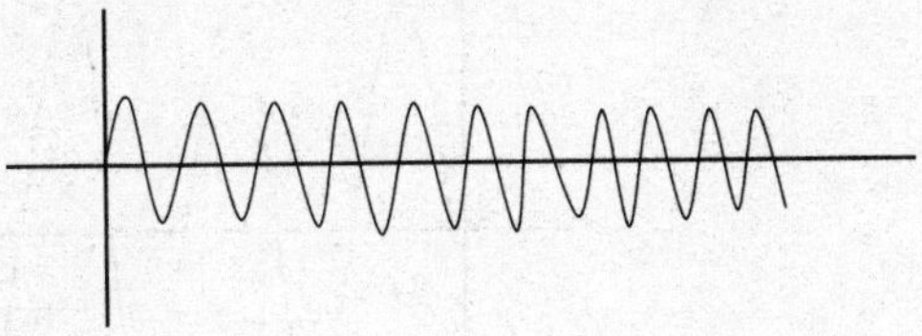

B.

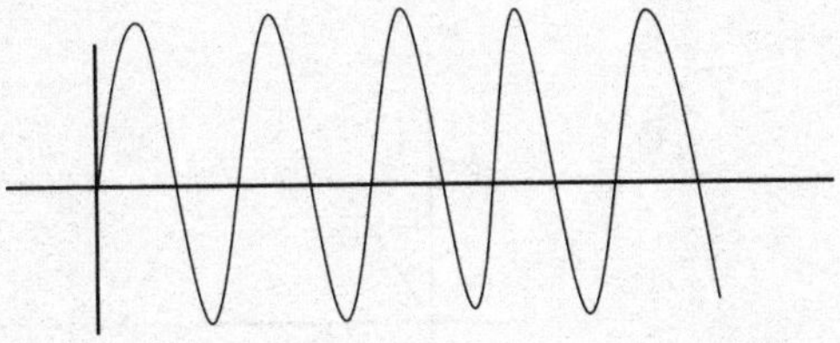

C.

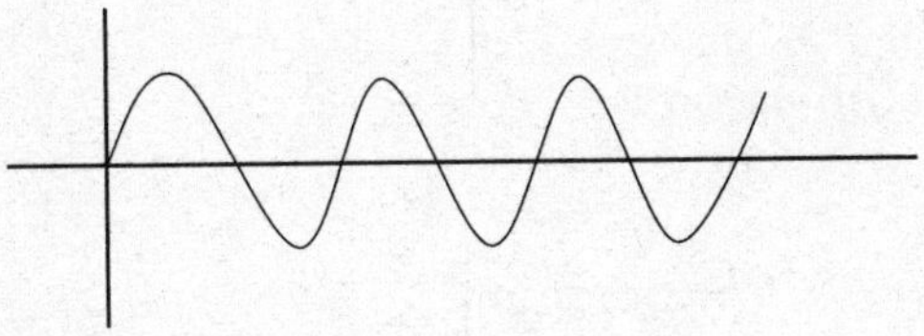

D.

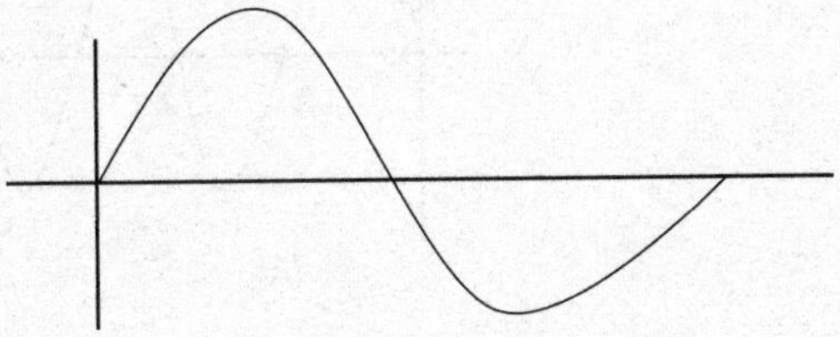

10. Mark the y-intercept on the graph:

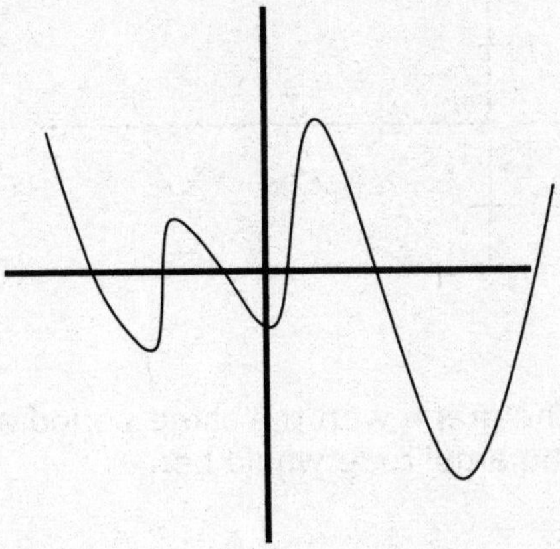

Questions 11 and 12 refer to the graph below.

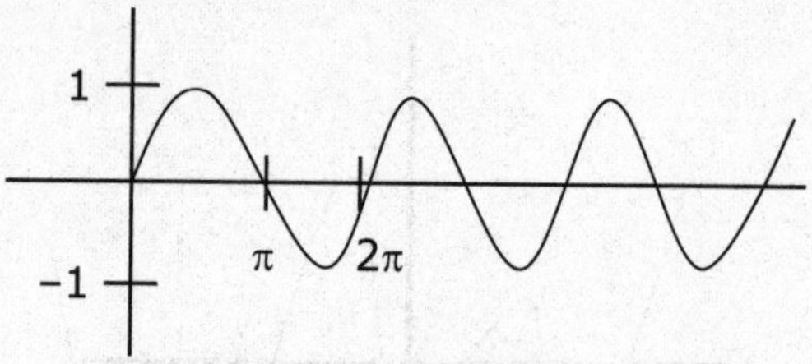

11. The graph with the same period and twice the amplitude would be:

A.

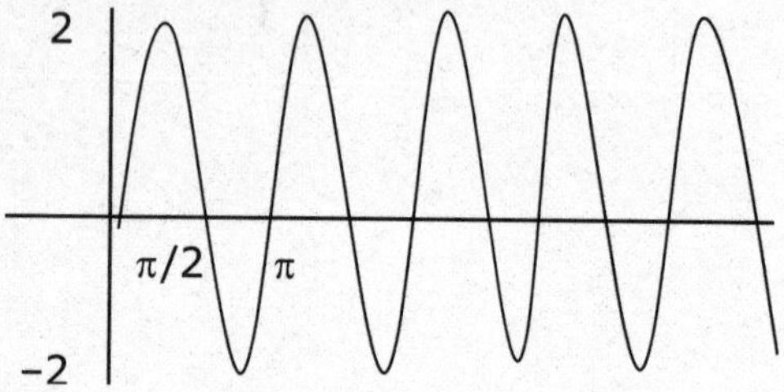

B.

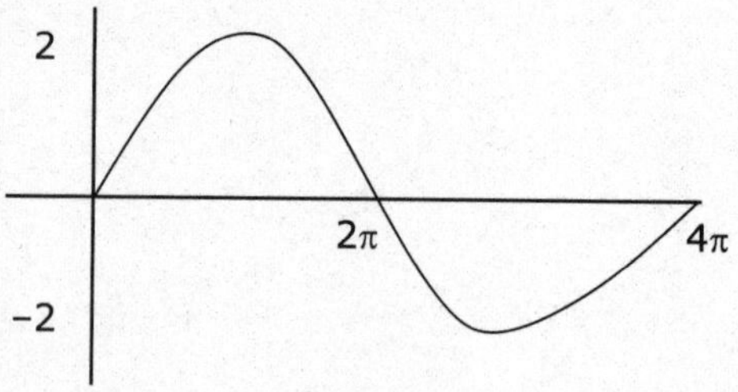

C.

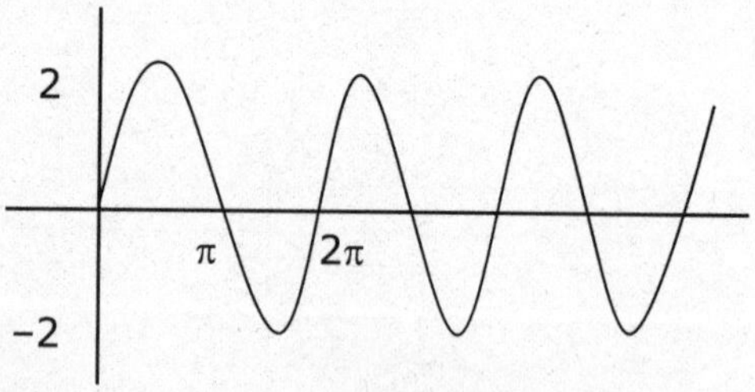

D.

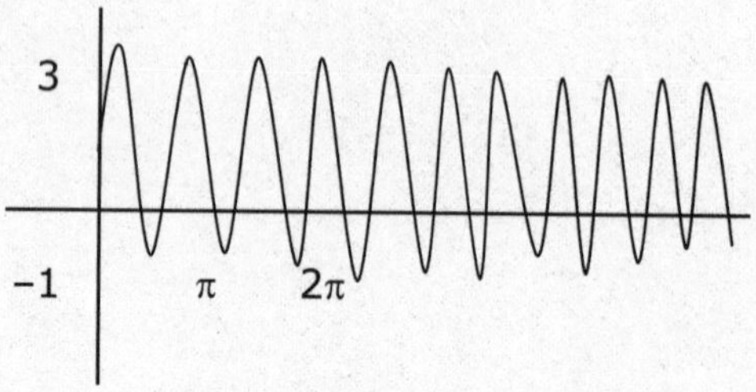

12. The graph with four times the amplitude and twice the period would be:

A.

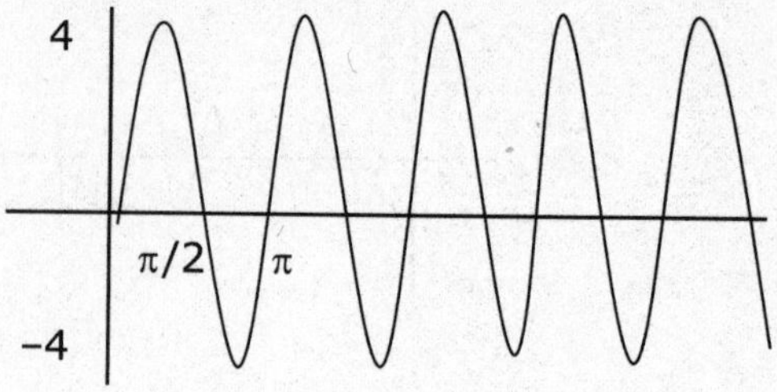

B.

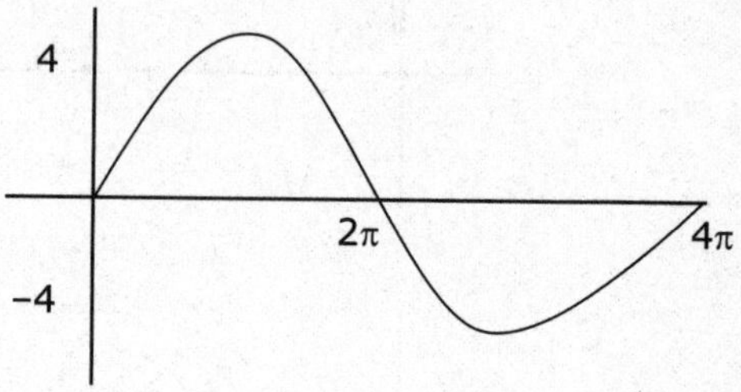

C.

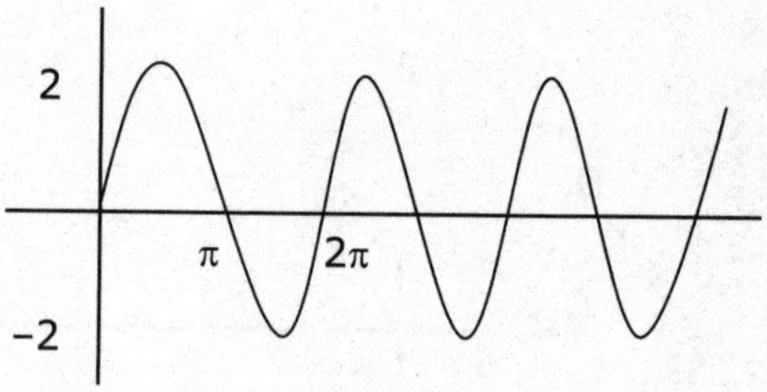

D.

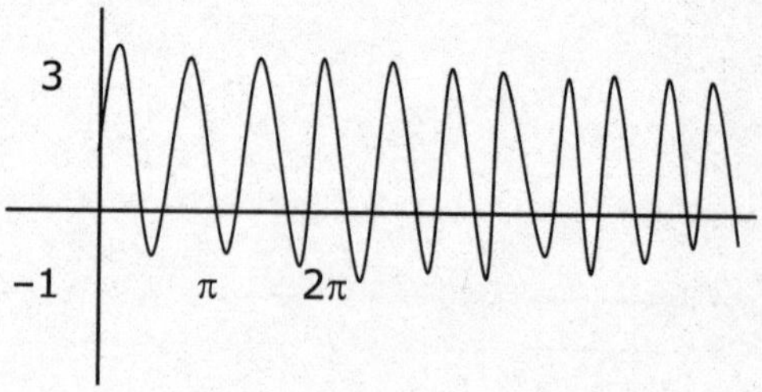

13. Which of the following is NOT a function?

A.

x	y
−3	−6
−2	1
−1	8
0	15
1	22

B.

x	y
−3	1
1	$\frac{5}{3}$
0	2
1	$\frac{7}{3}$
3	5

C.

x	y
−3	−22
−1	−14
0	−10
2	−2
5	10

D.

x	y
−1	−1
0	2
1	−1
2	2
3	7

14. Which of the following functions remains the same when the graph is reflected over the y-axis?

A.

B.

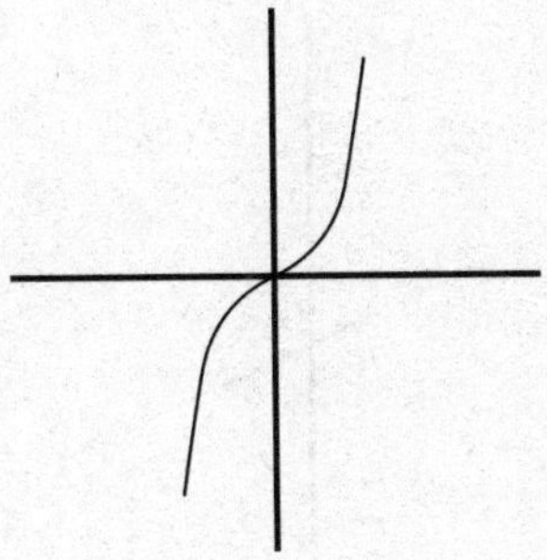

C.

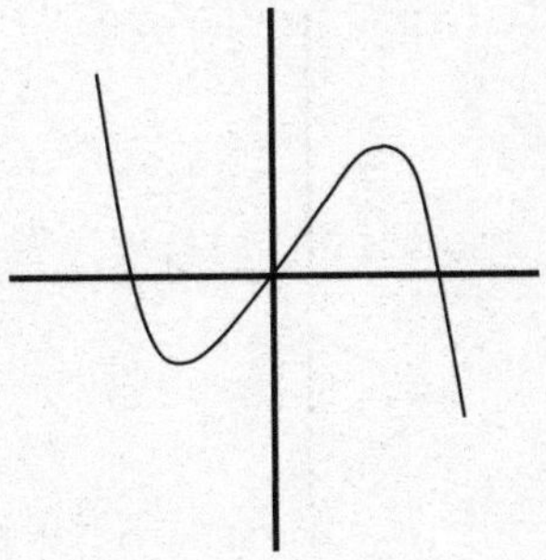

D.

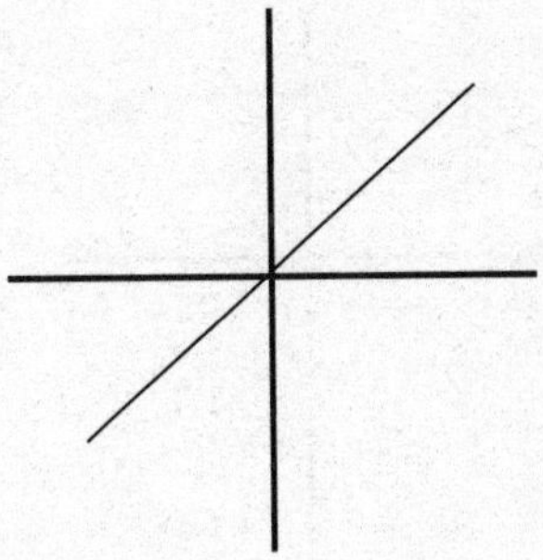

15. Which of the following is the graph of $y = -\frac{1}{3}x + 3$?

A.

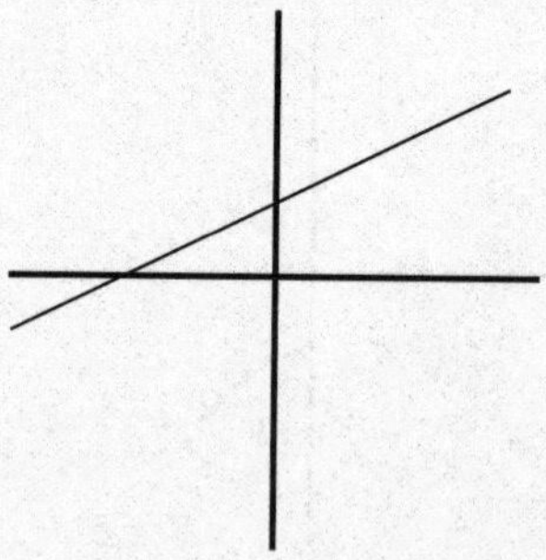

B.

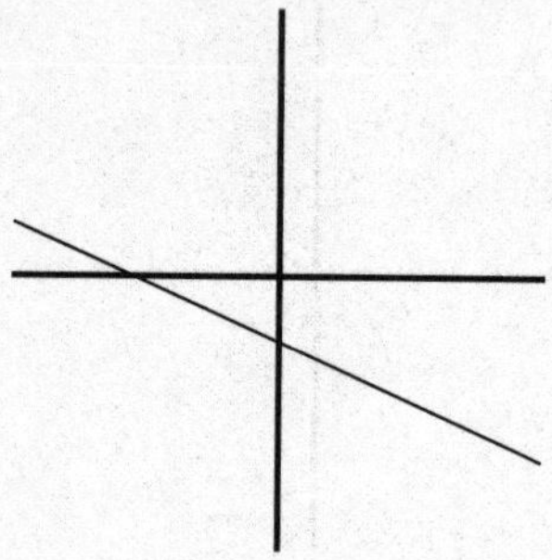

C.

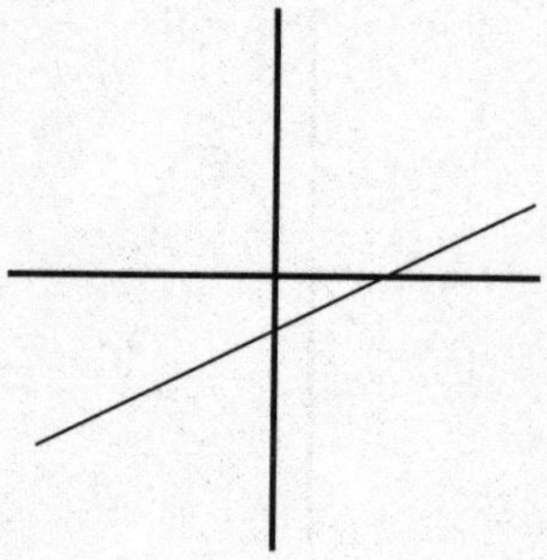

D.

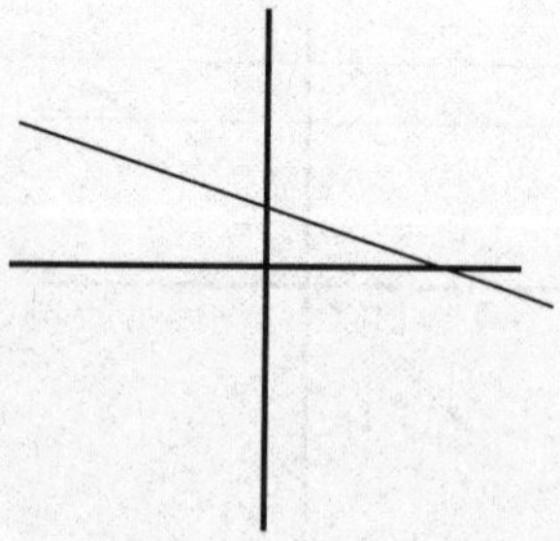

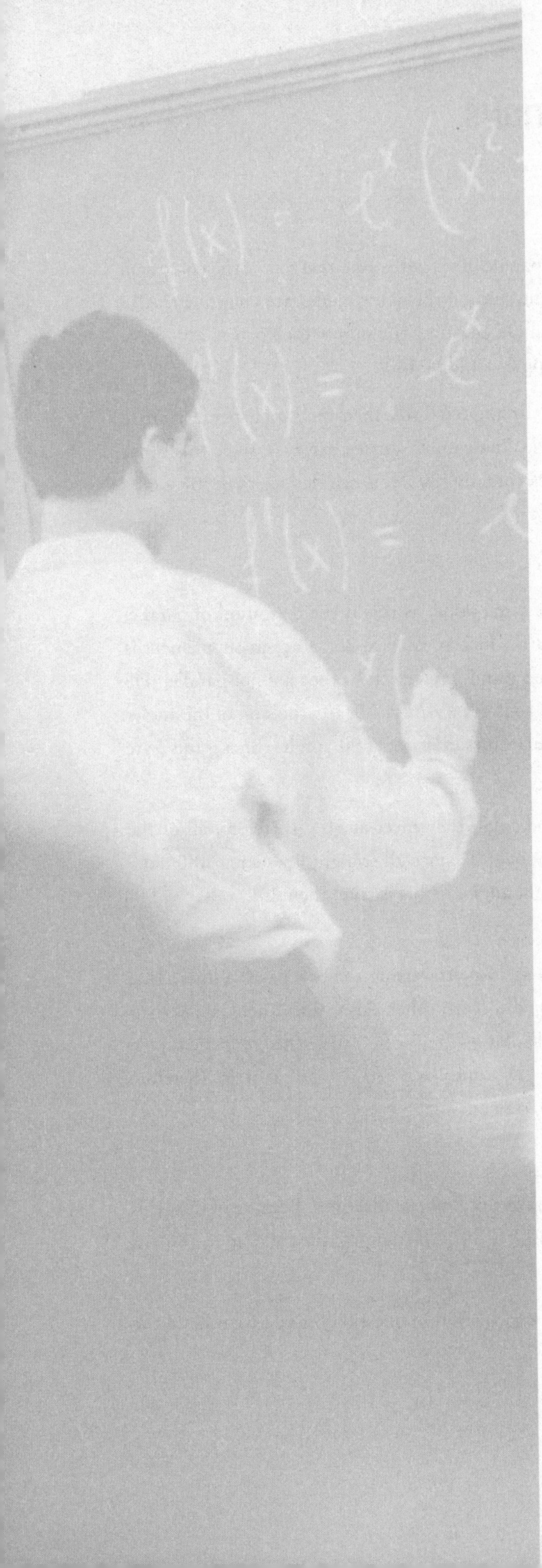

Geometry: Answers and Explanations

GEOMETRY: ANSWERS AND EXPLANATIONS

Lines and Angles Drill

1. **140** Since the lines are parallel, the line traversing the parallel lines will create two sets of the congruent vertical angles: all the obtuse angles are congruent, and all the acute angles are congruent. Also, each obtuse angle is supplementary to each acute angle, meaning the sum of each pair is 180. Since the acute angle below is 40°, the supplementary angle would be 140°.

2. **C** Starting at point C, if the angle outside the inner triangle is 130°, then the supplementary angle would have to be 50° on the interior of the triangle. You can eliminate answer A, since this is not the answer you are looking for. Since all triangles contain 180°, you can deduce that 50° + 60°+ $x°$ = 180, so the missing angle must be 70°.

3. **[the same] [greater than] [intersecting]**

   Since the lines are parallel, j and k must have the same slope, as this is the definition of parallel lines. $\angle CAB$ = 40°, so you can compare it to $\angle ABC$, which is equal to 30°, since its supplement is 150°. Therefore, $\angle CAB$ is greater than $\angle ABC$. Lines g and h intersect, so they are not parallel. Determine whether they are perpendicular. Since $\angle CAB$ is 40, $\angle ABC$ is 30, and the sum of the angles in a triangle is 180, $\angle ACB$ is 110. Since perpendicular lines intersect at 90° angles, lines g and h are not perpendicular but merely intersecting.

4. **35** Since the horizontal and vertical lines are perpendicular, they meet at 90°. Therefore, all of the angles other than the right angle must add up to equal 90°, since all straight lines equal 180°, and the right angle's complement would be another right angle. If this is true, then 20°+ $x°$ + $x°$ = 90°. After solving, you will find $x°$ = 35°.

5. **D** Since lines r and s are parallel, you can treat line t as a line traversing the two parallel lines. That means that the small angles $x°$ and $y°$ must be equal to each other. Also, since there is a perpendicular line next to the 40° angle, you can conclude that 40° + $x°$ = 90°, since they must be supplementary to the right angle created. Therefore, $x°$ = 50°, and $x°$ = $y°$, so $y°$ = 50° as well. Therefore, $x°$ + $y°$ = 100°. Choices (A), (B), and (C) are partial, trap answers.

6. **[less than | less than | greater than]**

   Since $AC \parallel DE$, you can treat DC and AE as lines traversing two parallel lines. Because of this, $y°$ is equal and opposite to 30°, and $z°$ is equal and opposite to 40°. All triangles must add up to 180°, so the third angle, $x°$, must equal 110°.

7. **100°** Be sure to subtract $\angle z$ instead of add! Refer to the explanation in question 6 to derive each of the angles measurements and get 30 + 110 – 40 = 100.

8. Bottom left **[120°]** top left **[60°]** top right **[50°]** bottom right **[130°]**. Use your knowledge of supplementary angles to find the supplement of 50° is 130°, and that opposite angles are congruent, so the bottom right corner of the trapezoid would be 120° as well. Transverse lines have equal sets of vertical angles, so the upper corners will correspond to the angles below.

9. **17** The figure looks more complicated than it is. All the question is asking is for corresponding angles from a transverse line. Since the bottom left angle is 17°, so too must be x°. All the other information in the figure is extraneous.

10. **B** Two angles that combine to form a straight line are supplementary. The supplement to the 140° angle would be 40°, trap answer A. However, you need the value of y such that the three angles of the triangle total 180°, so the answer must be 180° – 90° – 40° = 50°.

11. **B** Use the rule that angles opposite each other are equal. Since all straight lines total 180°, the missing angle must be 50°, since 25° + 50° + 105° = 180°.

12. **[parallel to][perpendicular to][cannot be determined from the information given].**

The figure gives parallel arrows in lines j and k, so you know that to be given from the figure. Similarly, lines g and h meet at a right angle (angle A), so therefore they are perpendicular to each other. There is no other information about the figure, though, so it is therefore impossible to know what the other angle measurements are. $\angle CBA$ may appear on the figure to be 40° or 45°, but there is no proof of this being true.

Rectangles, Squares, and Prisms Drill

1. **C** The perimeter is all of the sides added up, so in this problem, you must find possible side measurements in order to find possible perimeters. Since the area is 48, the possible factors of 48 are 1 and 48, 2 and 24, 3 and 16, 4 and 12, and 6 and 8, which could be multiplied together in the formula of a rectangle to find 48. With the following dimensions, you can find the corresponding perimeters (remember to double each side to account for all four sides of a rectangle), 96, 52, 38, 32, and 28, respectively. Since 35 is not one of these possible perimeters, the answer must be (C).

2. **5** The volume of a prism is $V = lwh$, where $l = 12$ and $w = 4$ in this case. If you plug these numbers into the equation, you can solve for h: $240 = (12)(4)h$, so $5 = h$.

3. **C** The key with this question is to be sure that you have everything in the same units before you start. First, convert the dimensions of the coffee table and the TV stand into feet, by dividing the length and width of each by 12. (Make sure to do this before computing area). Find the area of the entire room [choice (D)], and subtract the pieces of furniture, which are also rectangles, to get choice (C).

4. **3,456**

First, convert everything into either feet or inches. Using feet, one coaster would measure $\frac{1}{2}$ ft. by $\frac{1}{2}$ ft. by $\frac{1}{24}$ ft. to give a volume of $\frac{1}{96}$ cubic feet: $\frac{1}{2} \times \frac{1}{2} \times \frac{1}{24} = \frac{1}{96}$. Next, you can find the volume of one box by multiplying $2 \times 3 \times 1.5 = 9$ ft^3. To find how many coasters fit in one box divide 9 by $\frac{1}{96}$, and you will find that one box contains 864 coasters. Since the question is asking for 4 boxes, simply multiply 864 by 4.

5. **B** The volume of the cube is 64, so the equation would be $V = 64 = s^3$, and the sides of the cube are therefore 4 when you solve the formula. To find the surface area, find the area of one side (in this case 16, trap answer A) and multiply it by the number of sides there are, in this case 6. Therefore the surface area is 96. Make sure you cube rooted 64 instead of divided or square rooted to find the correct sides, which would lead to answers (C) and (D).

6. **[greater than]**

Since the side of the cube is 5, then the surface area must be $SA = 6(5 \times 5) = 150$ and the volume must be $V = s^3 = 5^3 = 125$, so the surface area is greater in this case.

7. **B** Break the trapezoid up into three easy-to-solve sections: two right triangles and a rectangle in the center. Since the height, 4, is known, you may either use the Pythagorean theorem to find the bases of each of the triangle or recognize that the triangle containing points A and B is an isosceles right triangle (so the base would be 4), and that the one containing points C and D is a 3-4-5 right triangle (so the base would be 3). Be careful not to fall into the trap of calling the base of the rectangle 14 (answer choice D). Since parts of the entire base *AD* belong to the triangles, you must subtract those portions of base to find *BC*, which is 7. Therefore, the area of the rectangle is 28, the left hand triangle has an area of 8, and the right hand triangle has an area of 6.

8. **D** The base, *DE*, is given, but there is not enough information to determine what the height is. *CD* is a side of the parallelogram, not the height (which would lead to answer choice C), because the height must meet the base at a right angle. Since there is no other information, we cannot solve the problem.

9. **12** Since *JKLM* is a parallelogram, the area would be equal to the base times the height. However, the question is asking for the triangle *JLM*. Therefore, the area must be one half the area of that of the parallelogram. Since the area of the parallelogram is 24, the area of the triangle must be 12.

10. **108** The length is decreased 25%, and 25% of 4 is 1. Therefore, you can subtract 1 from the old length to find the new length, 3. Similarly, 40% of 20 is 8, so the new length of the width would be 12, since $20 - 8 = 12$. Finally, 50% of the old height 2 is 1, so the new height would be 3. $lwh = 3 \times 12 \times 3 = 108$.

11. **Six times**

The area of the circle with a radius of 10 is 100π. Since the diagonal of the rectangle is 10 and the width is 6, you can either recognize the special right triangle or use the Pythagorean theorem to find that the length is 8. Therefore, the area of of the rectangle is $A = lw = (6)(8) = 48$. Note that the question refers to the *circle* first instead of the rectangle in the drop down list, which is the larger shape. A common mistake is to reverse this, and instead answer $\frac{1}{6}$.

12. **21** The area of the base is 3, so there is nothing further you need to do to find length and width because this step is already done for you. From this point, simply multiply by the height, 7, to find the volume of the prism.

13. **D** Since the maximum volume of a carry-on bag is 3307 in.^{3}, you can make the following formula to find the height: $V = 3307\text{ in}^3 = (20\text{ in})(18\text{ in})(h)$. When you solve this, you will find that the height is slightly over 9 inches. The question says that h must be an integer (you can eliminate (C) with this information), the largest integer would be 9. Choices (A) and (B) are possible heights that would be suitable carry-on bags, but the question is asking for the *maximum,* so only choice (D) is correct.

14. **C** The question states that the shape is a square, so the sides must be equal, and therefore $x + 1 = 2x - 3$. By solving this equation, you will find that $x = 4$, which happens to be answer choice (A). Do not be fooled! The question is asking for the *area*, which is $4^2 = 16$.

15. **840** Simply use the volume of a rectangular solid and multiply by $\frac{7}{8}$. By simplifying before multiplying, you will make your life a whole lot easier (i.e. 4 can cancel out and the 8 will become 2, then the 20 will cancel the remaining 2 and become 10). $\frac{7}{8}(20)(12)(4) = (7)(10)(12) = 840$.

Triangles and Pyramids Drill

1. **18.71** You have the height of the triangle, but not the base, so you need to use the Pythagorean theorem to find the base. You will find that the base is equal to $\sqrt{56}$, and from there, you can use the area formula of a triangle to calculate the area. Remember that the area of a triangle is $A = \frac{1}{2}bh$.

2. **C** Since it is an equilateral triangle, you know that all the sides are equal, so each side is 4, given the perimeter of 12. To find the area, you need to find a height, so draw a height from the peak to the base. You will have split the top angle in half, into two 30° angles. Therefore, you'll have a 30°-60°-

90° triangle, which has special side relationships of for the shortest leg, $2x$ for the hypotenuse (in this case 4, so $x = 2$), and $x\sqrt{3}$ for the longer leg. Therefore, the height of the triangle would be $2\sqrt{3}$, and you can use the area formula from here: $A = \frac{1}{2}bh = \frac{1}{2}(4)(2\sqrt{3}) = 4\sqrt{3}$.

3. **C** The third side of any triangle must be larger than the difference of the other two sides but less than their sum. In this case, the other two sides are 6 and 7. The difference between the two sides would be 1, so the third side must be greater than 1. The sum of 6 and 7 is 13, so the third side must be less than that (otherwise we would have to lay the other two sides out in a straight line, and then we wouldn't have a triangle anymore). 14 is greater than the sum of 6 and 7, so therefore it is not a possible length for the third side.

4. **30** If you can remember that a 5-12-13 triangle is a special Pythagorean triple, fantastic. Be sure to look for *perimeter,* not the *hypotenuse* or the *area.* For the perimeter, simply add the three sides, 5, 12, and 13 together.

5. **B**

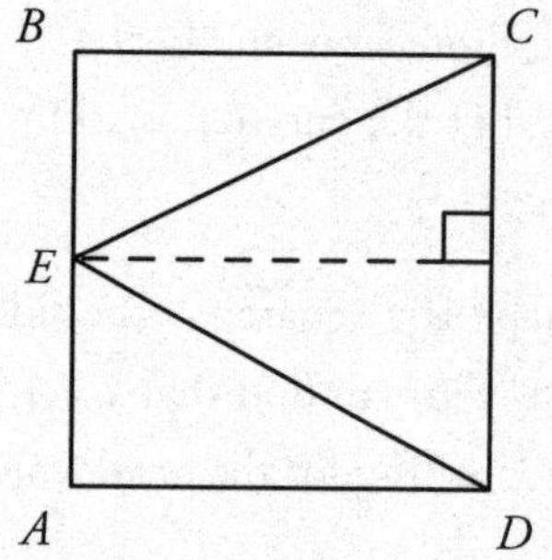

Since you know the area of the square is 16, you can find that the sides are all 4. Since this is not a right triangle, you will need to draw a height (or altitude) from the peak to the base, which in this case is *CD*. You know that the base of the triangle is the same as the side of the square, so the base is 4, and the height you drew is also 4, as it is equal and parallel to *BC* and *AD*. Therefore, our height is 4 as well. $A = \frac{1}{2}(4)(4) = 8$.

6. **B** The area, 32, is given, as is the base of the triangle, which is 8. It is not necessary to know the dimensions of the dotted lines, but rather to simply solve for the height using the area of the triangle formula. Be sure to include the $\frac{1}{2}$ in the formula, as you will get the trap answer, (D).

7. **C** Use the volume of a pyramid formula, $V = \frac{1}{3}(lw)h$ with the area of a rectangle for a base. Since the area of the base is 20 and the volume of the pyramid is 180, you know that $180 = \frac{1}{3}(20)h$, so you can solve algebraically to find that the height is 27. Don't forget the $\frac{1}{3}$ since you have a pyramid!

8. **A** Use the Pythagorean theorem to find the third side. 12, the building height, would be one of the legs, while the 13-foot ladder resting on the building is the hypotenuse. $a^2 + 12^2 = 13^2$, so $a = 5$. Make sure to find a instead of a^2, which is trap choice (C). Be careful to answer the question and find the length of the other leg, not the area, as in choice (D).

9. B:[**130**] C: [**25**].

Since $AB = BC$, the corresponding angles will be equal, so $\angle A = \angle C = 25°$. Then, since all angles of a triangle total 180°, the missing angle, $\angle B$, must be 130°.

10. **A** You can use Ballparking to eliminate choice (D), since it is much too big. To find the measurements of the smaller triangle containing $x°$, 135° is supplementary with 45° and 65° is supplementary to 115°. By adding 45° and 115°, you will find that the missing angle in the center triangle is 20°.

11. **B** To find the other leg of the triangle, use the Pythagorean Theorem, where 14 is c and 10 is a or b. Plug these into $a^2 + b^2 = c^2$ to get $10^2 + b^2 = 14^2$, so $b = \sqrt{96} = \sqrt{16}\sqrt{6} = 4\sqrt{6}$. Make sure to do the square root to avoid the trap answer (D). To get the area, do $A = \frac{1}{2}bh = \frac{1}{2}(10)(4\sqrt{6}) = 20\sqrt{6}$.

12. **1:2** The volume of the pyramid is found as $V = \frac{1}{3}lwh$, while the surface area is $SA = 4\left(\frac{1}{2}bh\right) + lw$, since there are four triangular faces and one base. To find the volume, simply plug the given numbers into the formula, so the volume is 48. The surface area is a bit trickier because the height of the triangles is unknown. If you create a right triangle out of the height of the pyramid and half the length (6) of the base, you will find that the hypotenuse of that triangle is the height of the faces. Plug this into the surface area formula to get $SA = 96$. Therefore, the ratio is 48:96, which reduces to 1:2.

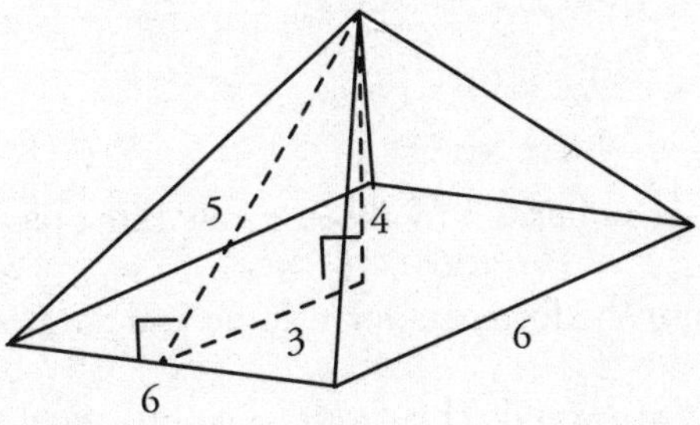

13. **B** It is easy to think that the answer might be 4, but you would have forgotten to factor in the $\frac{1}{2}$ for the area of a triangle. The formula should look like this: $16 = \frac{1}{2}(b^2)$, since 16 is the area and the sides must be the same, given that the triangle is an isosceles right triangle. Therefore, $32 = b^2$, so $\sqrt{32} = b = 4\sqrt{2}$.

14. **12** To find the dimensions of the house face, break it up into a triangle with a base of 20 and height of 15, and a square face 20 ft. by 20 ft. Together, those have an area of 550 sqft. From there, subtract the windows: four 3 ft. by 4 ft. windows, one 2 ft. by 2 ft. window, and one 3 ft. by 8 ft. door. All those smaller shapes add up to 76 sqft. To find the difference between them, subtract 76 from 550, and you will find that there are 474 square feet to paint. Since the question is asking for how many *cans of paint* are needed, divide 474 by 40, since one can will cover 40 sqft. You will find that 40 goes into 474 11 times with a remainder, so Anne will need 12 cans to be able to fully cover the house.

15. **[hypotenuse][shorter leg][longer leg]**

Note that the term *leg* refers to the two sides of a right triangle that are not the hypotenuse. The largest angle always corresponds to the longest side in any triangle and the shortest angle with the shortest side. Therefore, the 90° angle would correspond with the hypotenuse and the 30° angle would correspond with the shortest side, leaving the middle angle, 60°, to correspond with the longer leg.

Circles, Spheres, Cylinders, and Cones Drill

1. **C** Since the diameter of the pool is 22 ft., the radius must be 11 ft. From there, simply use the formula for a cylinder, since the pool would be a cylinder and filled to its maximum height of 4 ft. Remember to use the radius and not the diameter when making this calculation! $V = \pi r^2 h = \pi(11)^2\,(4) = 484\pi$.

2. **Equal to.**

Since the diameter is 6, the radius is 3 (make sure you didn't plug in diameter for the radius). From there, plug the radius into the formulas for volume and surface area of a sphere, $V = \frac{4}{3}\pi r^3$ and $SA = 4\pi r^2$ respectively. When you do this, both equations equal 36π.

$V = \frac{4}{3}\pi r^3$ $\qquad$ $SA = 4\pi r^2$

$V = \frac{4}{3}\pi(3)^3 = \frac{4}{3}\pi(27) = 36\pi$ $\qquad$ $SA = 4\pi(3)^2 = 4\pi(9) = 36\pi$

3. **20.9 cubic inches** (no need to write the units into the box).

Since the diameter is 4, the radius is 2. The height is 5, so this information can be plugged directly into the volume formula for a circular cone:

$V = \frac{1}{3}\pi r^2 h = \frac{1}{3}\pi(2)^2(5) = \frac{1}{3}\pi(20) \approx 20.9$ in.

4. **C** The height of the glass is irrelevant to the problem here because it is asking for the volume of the water, which has a height of 2 inches. Since the diameter of the glass is 7, the radius is 3.5 or $\frac{7}{2}$.

This information can then be inserted into the formula for volume of a cylinder:

$V = \pi r^2 h = \pi\left(\frac{7}{2}\right)^2(2) = \frac{49}{2}\pi$

5. **C** Since the circumference of the circle is 10π, the diameter is 10, and therefore the radius is 5. From there, you can plug 5 into the area formula of a circle, $A = \pi r^2$, and you will find that the area is 25π.

6. **19.6** Since you know the radius of the sphere, you can plug it into the surface area formula, which is $SA = 4\pi r^2$. Read the question carefully and be sure not to find the volume instead of surface area!

7. **4** The circumference is equal to one half the area, so you can translate this into math: $C = \frac{1}{2}A$. Since $C = 2\pi r$, $2\pi r = \frac{1}{2}\pi r^2$. You can divide both sides by an r and a π on either side, and you will be left with $2 = \frac{1}{2}r$, so $r = 4$.

8. **C** Since the diameter is 7, simply plug it into the formula for circumference. $C = \pi d = 7\pi$.

9. **C** The circumference is 25π, which means the diameter is 25. The radius is half the diameter, so the radius is 12.5. Be careful not to square root the diameter as you would from area to radius, as you will find answer choice B, and the diameter itself is choice (D).

10. **150** Simply use the area formula here. Since you already know the area, your formula will look like the following: $22{,}500\pi = \pi r^2$. You can cancel out π on either side, and from there you can square root each side to find that the radius is 150.

11. **[twice][9π][six times]**.

For the first sentence, the diameter is, by definition, two times the radius. For the second sentence, plug the radius into the area formula, and you will find that the area is 9π. Be careful not to put the diameter in for radius! Finally, the circumference is 6π, which is slightly over 18, which is six times the radius, 3.

12. **B** Since the area is 36π, you can find that the radius is 6 (A), and therefore the diameter is 12, twice the radius.

13. **B** Find the radius from the area, 100π, and you will find that the radius is equal to 10. From there, you can plug the radius into the circumference formula to find that the circumference is 20π: $C = 2\pi r = 2\pi(10) = 20\pi$.

14. **A** The area of the donut is the area of the large portion minus the hole in the center that is missing. Since you know the diameter is 12, the radius of the donut is 6, so you can plug this into the area formula: $A = \pi(6^2) = 36\pi$. The center hole has a radius of 1, so the area of the center you will need to subtract is simply π, since $1^2 = 1$. Therefore, $36\pi - \pi = 35\pi \approx 109.96$. If you forget to subtract π, you will end up with choice (B), and choices (C) and (D) are the result of using 12 as the radius with and without subtracting π, respectively.

15. **201.06**

Since the circumference is 16π, the radius is 8. Therefore, the area is: $A = \pi r^2 = \pi(8^2) = 64\pi \approx 201.06$.

Setup Geometry Drill

1. **A** The surface area of the mozzarella ball would be half the surface area plus the flat side. The surface area is $4\pi r^2$, so half is $\frac{4\pi r^2}{2}$. The flat side is a circle with radius, so its area is πr^2. Therefore, the total surface area is $\frac{4\pi r^2}{2} + \pi r^2$. The diameter is 3, so the radius is 1.5. Plug this into the surface area to get $\frac{4\pi(1.5)^2}{2} + \pi(1.5)^2$.

2. **D** Make sure you are solving for surface area and not for volume. Choice (A) contains the volume of the smaller cone, and (B) and (C) are common mistakes of not squaring the results correctly. To find the slant height, use the base and height of the cone as a right triangle. Since the base and height of the smaller triangle are both 3, it is an isosceles right triangle. If you recognized this, great! If not, no worries. Just use the Pythagorean theorem to find the hypotenuse, which in this case is $3\sqrt{2}$. From there, just follow the surface area formula: $SA = \pi rs + \pi r^2$.

3. **46** The freestanding garden measures 4 ft. by 5 ft., so the perimeter would be $2(4) + 2(5)$. The two flowerbeds against the house have only one long side of 10 ft., and 2 sides of 2 ft., so each of their perimeters would be $2(2) + 10$. The total perimeter for all three flowerbeds would be $[2(4) + 2(5)] + 2[2(2) + 10]$.

4. **C** The four large drawers have dimensions 3 ft. by 10 in. by 5 in., so make sure the units are consistent. The question asks for the volume in cubic feet, so convert the inches into feet by dividing by 12. Therefore the volume of each of the large drawers is $(3)\left(\frac{10}{12}\right)\left(\frac{5}{12}\right)$, making the total volume of all four $4(3)\left(\frac{10}{12}\right)\left(\frac{5}{12}\right)$. Do the same for the sock drawers, which have the dimensions 11 inches by 10 inches by 4 inches. Convert all three to feet to get a volume of $\left(\frac{11}{12}\right)\left(\frac{10}{12}\right)\left(\frac{4}{12}\right)$, making the total volume of all three $3\left(\frac{11}{12}\right)\left(\frac{10}{12}\right)\left(\frac{4}{12}\right)$. Thus, the total is $4(3)\left(\frac{10}{12}\right)\left(\frac{5}{12}\right)+3\left(\frac{11}{12}\right)\left(\frac{10}{12}\right)\left(\frac{4}{12}\right)$, which is choice (C).

5. **A** Each semicircle will take up a length on the rink equal to the circle's diameter. Therefore, to determine the number of semi-circles she can form, divide the length of the rink, 84, by the diameter of each semi-circle to get $\frac{84}{d}$. Since the diameter is twice the radius and the radius is 7, $d = 2(7)$. Therefore, the answer is choice (A).

Graphing Drill

1.

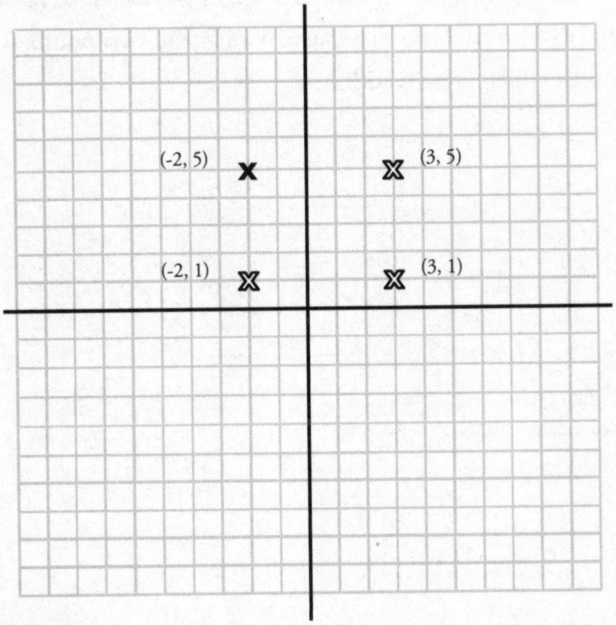

(–2, 5)

Use the coordinates to ballpark where the fourth vertex ought to be to get a rough sense for where the point should be (quadrant II). Then, use the *x*-coordinate from the bottom left hand point to find the x-coordinate of the missing point, and the top right hand point to find the *y*-coordinate. Because the lines of the rectangle are completely horizontal and vertical, these points will share the same *x*- and *y*-coordinates.

2. **B** First, manipulate the equation $4y - 3x = 16$ into $y = mx + b$ form: $4y = 3x + 16$ and divide by 4: $y = \frac{3}{4}x + 4$. Since the slope, $\frac{3}{4}$, is positive, eliminate (C) and (D). Since the y-intercept, b, is 4, the coordinate for where the line crosses the y-axis must by (0, 4), so eliminate (A).

3. **13** Graph the points on an xy-coordinate plane and draw a right triangle:

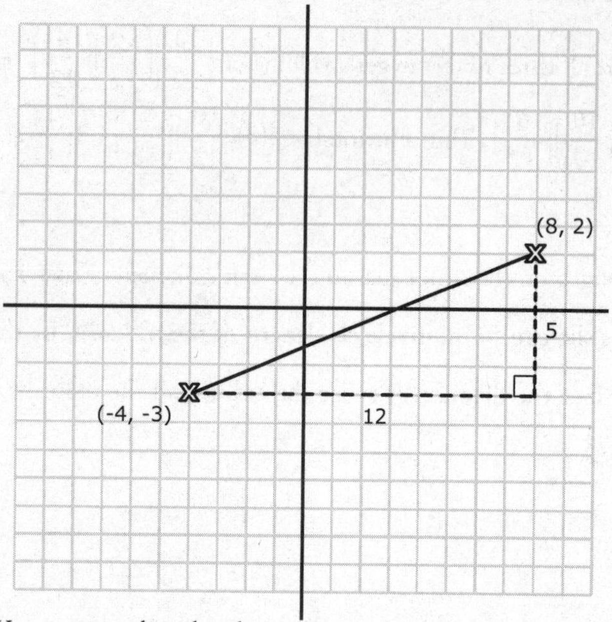

You can see that the change in x-values is 12, and that the change in y-values is 5. From here, you can use the Pythagorean theorem to find that the distance between the two points is 13. If you recognized that this is a Pythagorean triple, great work!

4.

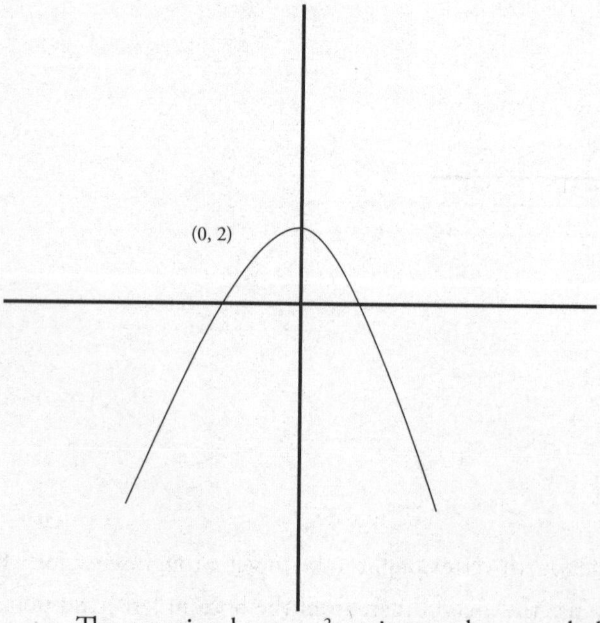

The equation has an x^2, so it must be a parabola. The coefficient on the x^2 term is negative, so it must open down. Furthermore, when $x = 0$, $y = 2$. The only curve with these properties is the one above.

5. **A** The rise of the ramp is 2.5 feet and the run is 44 feet. Therefore, $\frac{rise}{run} = \frac{2.5}{44} \approx .06$

6. **B** To find the length of the ramp, simply use the Pythagorean theorem: $(2.5)^2 + (44)^2 = 1942.25$. Remember to square root your answer (or else you will be tempted to choose D), and you will find the length to be approximately 44.1.

7. **13** Make an *xy*-coordinate plane for yourself and graph Jamia's progress. First, she travels north along the *y*-axis 5 miles to the grocery store. Then she travels east along the *x*-axis 4 miles, 5 miles, and 3 miles respectively, a total of 12 miles. Since she has traveled with a right angle between the north and east directions, you can use the Pythagorean theorem to find the third side.

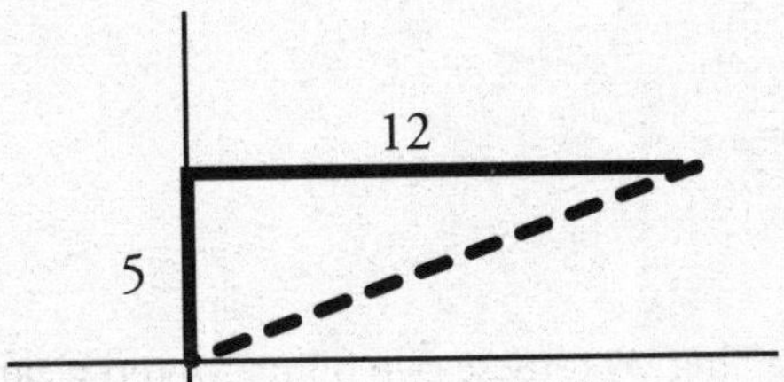

8. **[4 = 4x + 4y][15 = x – 3y][3x = 2y + 4][y = 4x + 3]**

Find the slopes for each of the equations in $y = mx + b$ form, and you will find the slopes to be -1, $\frac{1}{3}$, $\frac{3}{2}$, and 4, respectively. Be sure to treat your negatives and fractions carefully.

9. **C** Since the circle is in the third quadrant, both coordinates must be negative, eliminating (A) and (D). Since the circle is tangent to both the *x*-axis and the *y*-axis, the radius is equal to the absolute value of the *x* and *y* coordinates. Since the radius is 4, not the diameter or the area, you can eliminate (B) as well.

10.

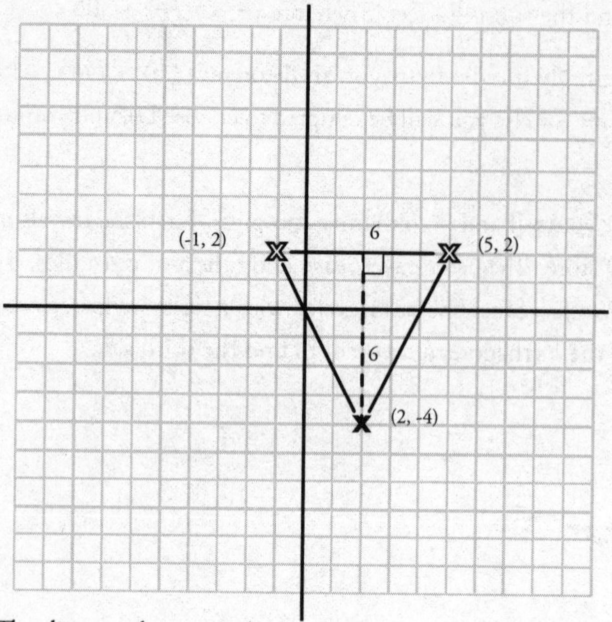

The distance between the x-values is 6, so halfway between these two points would yield an x-value of 2. This must be halfway because the triangle is isosceles, so you may use the symmetry. Since the height is 6, the triangle must either go straight up or straight down from the line $y = 2$, but the question says that the point lies in the fourth quadrant, meaning that the height must descend. Descending 6, the y-value must be –4.

11. **[greater than][three fourths]**.

Compare the m values of each of the equations. $\frac{4}{5}$ is greater than $-\frac{1}{2}$, so the first sentence would be greater than. The y-intercept for $f(x)$ is 9, while the y-intercept for $h(x)$ is 12, so 9 : 12 is 3 : 4, or $\frac{3}{4}$.

12. **C** This is a Pythagorean triple, but if you are not sure or want to double check, graph these on the *xy*-coordinate plane.

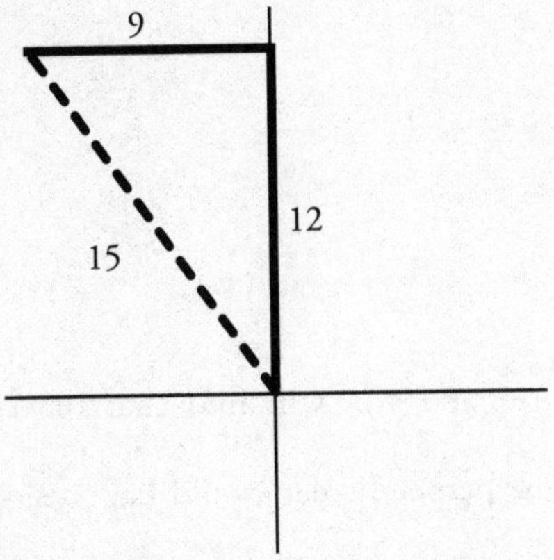

12 north would be 12 up on the *y*-axis and 9 west would be 9 to the left on the *x*-axis. Using the Pythagorean theorem, you will find the hypotenuse to be 15, which is the distance between the points.

Equation of a Line Drill

1. **[3],[8]**

Set the equations equal to each other and you will find the following:

$$4x - 4 = 2x + 2$$
$$2x = 6$$
$$x = 3$$

From here, plug 3 into one of the equations to find the *y*-value:

$$y = 2(3) + 2$$
$$y = 6 + 2 = 8$$

2. **B** First, find the slope by finding $m = \frac{y_2 - y_1}{x_2 - x_1}$ In this case, the slope will be

$$m = \frac{(-2) - 4}{3 - (-1)} = -\frac{6}{4} = -\frac{3}{2}$$

By finding the slope, you can automatically eliminate (C) and (D). Once this is done, you can find the intercept by plugging one of the points into your equation, $y = -\frac{3}{2}x + b$.

Using (–1, 4) as an example:

$$4 = -\frac{3}{2}(-1) + b$$

$$4 = \frac{3}{2} + b$$

$$\frac{5}{2} = b$$

3. $\frac{2}{3}$ Manipulate the formula to be in $y = mx + b$ form and you will find that the equation is $y = -\frac{3}{2}x - \frac{3}{2}$. The slope is therefore $-\frac{3}{2}$, so the line perpendicular would have a slope of $+\frac{2}{3}$, the negative reciprocal of the current slope.

4. **A** The formula is not in $y = mx + b$ form, so first manipulate the equation to be in this form. If you do so, you will find $y = 4x - 6$. Since the question asks for the slope of the line *perpendicular* to this one, the slope will need to be the *negative reciprocal,* so $m = \frac{-1}{4}$ and A is the only one to have this slope. Be careful to make sure it is the negative, as positive $\frac{1}{4}$ will be incorrect, as in (C). Choices (B) and (D) either have the same slope or the negative, not the negative reciprocal.

5. **C** Plug the point into the following equations and see which equation is true for the point (3, 9). The only one that works is (C):

$$y = \frac{9}{2}(3) - \frac{9}{2}$$

$$y = \frac{27}{3} - \frac{9}{2}$$

$$y = \frac{18}{2} = 9$$

6. **(5, 19) or (6, 22).**

You can use the other points in the chart to find the equation of the line, which is $y = 3x + 4$. From here, you can plug in the potential values into the x-coordinate to see if the y value is another one of the choices (you could do the opposite as well, though plugging in for x might be easier in this case). If you plug 5 in for x, y comes out to 19, so that pair of numbers works. If you plug 6 in for x, y comes out to 22, so that pair works as well. Any other number plugged in for x will get a y value greater than all of the answer choices, only these two are correct.

7. **B** If you look at the values in general, the *x*-coordinates are increasing as the *y*-coordinates are also increasing, so you automatically know that the slope must be positive, eliminating (D). Then, use any two points to find the slope. Using points (1, 3) and (2, 5):

$$m = \frac{5-3}{2-1} = \frac{2}{1} = 2$$

Since the slope is 2, you can also eliminate (C). To find the *y*-intercept, you can plug a point in to find *b*:

$$3 = 2(1) + b$$
$$1 = b$$

8. **B** First, put the formula into the form, $y = mx + b$. You will find that the formula is $y = \frac{1}{5}x + 3$, which eliminates all but (B). If you left the function in its original form, you might be tempted to think that the y-intercept were 15, as in (A) or (C).

9. $-\frac{3}{2}$ The slope is found by finding the rise over the run, or the change in *y* over the change in *x*. The formula, thus, is the following: $\frac{6-3}{-2-0} = \frac{3}{-2} = m$. Be careful to keep the first and second points separate from one another, and to keep the *y*-values in the numerator and the *x*-values in the denominator.

10. First, put the equation into the form, $y = mx + b$. You will find that the formula is $y = \frac{5}{6}x + 1$, so you know your y-intercept will be (0, 1) and your slope will be $\frac{5}{6}$. Be careful to count your rise and run accurately, and your graph will look like the following:

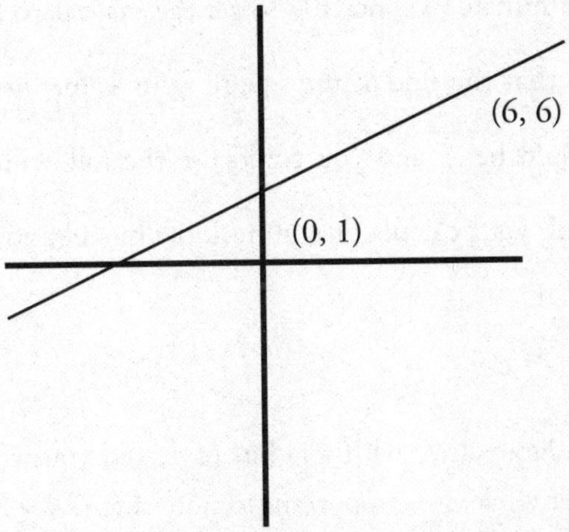

However, note that any two points that satisfy the equation are correct.

11. [–4], [–6]

First, put the lines in $y = mx + b$ form, such the two lines to be $y = 2x + 2$ and $y = 3x + 6$. Then, set the equations equal to each other and solve for x:

$$2x + 2 = 3x + 6$$

x is equal to –4. Once at this point, plug –4 into one of the equations and solve for y.

12. **A** First, put the lines in $y = mx + b$ form, and you will find the following equation, $y = \frac{4}{5}x + 2$. When you do the same to the answer choices, the only answer choice to have a slope of $\frac{4}{5}$ is (A). Be careful with your positive and negative signs, as you can get your answers backwards if one of these is reversed.

Percents Drill

1. **C** First add the two 40° sections together. If you do so, you will find that the part you are looking for is 80° out of 360° total degrees. Therefore, $\frac{80°}{360°} \times 100 = \frac{2}{9} \times 100 = 22\%$. Choice (A) is a trap that only includes one of the shaded regions, and 40% is a distraction and does not correlate to the 40° in the center.

2. **D** First, draw the figure. You will notice that the circle is a large portion of the square, your "whole" in this problem, so you could immediately eliminate (A) and (B). To get the exact percentage, find the part over the whole. If you were to say that the side of the square were 4, for instance, you would find that the radius of the circle would be 2, and you could use the following formula: $\frac{circle}{square} = \frac{\pi r^2}{s^2} = \frac{4\pi}{16}$. If you simplify this with your calculator and multiply by 100, you will find the percentage to be approximately 78.5%.

3. [4] : [1]

Using the area formula, find the area of the large circle with a radius of 4, and you will get 16π. Repeating the same procedure for the smaller circle, it is important to note that $OA = AB$, so the radius of the smaller circle is 2. Plugging 2 into the area formula, you will find that the area of the smaller circle is 4π. The question asks for the ratio of the *total area* to the *area of the smaller circle*, so the ratio must go in that specific order, 16π : 4π. If you simplify, you can cancel out π and divide 4 from each side. Your simplified ratio will be 4:1.

4. **[4] : [1]**

Let's say that $x = 4$. If this were the case, the sides would be 4 and 6. If you were to double both sides, you would have sides of 8 and 12. The area of the new rectangle would be 96, and the area of the old rectangle would be 24. Since the question asks for the new to the old, the ratio would be 96 : 24, which reduces to 4 : 1.

5. **D** The diameter of Circle *A* is *OB*, which is also the radius of Circle *O*. If we were to assign a value of 4 to *OB*, then the area of Circle *O* would be 16π. The radius of circle *A* is 2, half that of diameter *OB*. Therefore, the area of Circle *A* is 4π. The question asks for the percent of Circle *O* (the part) out of Circle *A* (the whole), so the equation would be $\frac{16\pi}{4\pi} \times 100 = 400\%$. Do not waiver if the "part" you are looking for is larger than the whole.

6. **B** While it's tempting to do the opposite, the part that you are looking for is the part that remains *unfilled*, not the part that remains filled. To do so, find the height of the unfilled portion (3), which is the difference between the entire glass (5) and the filled part (2). The whole glass would be the denominator of the equation:

$$\frac{\textit{unfilled portion}}{\textit{whole glass}} \times 100 = \frac{75\pi}{125\pi} \times 100 = 60\%$$

7. **87.5%**

After three months, the lake had 1000 gallons of water. Working backwards, the lake had 2000 gallons after two months, 4000 gallons after one month, and 8000 gallons initially. The part that has evaporated is 7000 out of the original whole of 8000, so the percent is $\frac{7}{8}$, or 87.5%.

8. **[4%] [216°]**

For the first part of the question, add up the first three quarters to find that the first three quarters comprise 96% of the pie. Therefore, the 4th quarter must be the difference, 4%.

For the second part, create a proportion between the first quarter's percent and degrees:

$$\frac{60\%}{100\%} = \frac{x^\circ}{360^\circ}$$

and you will find that $x^\circ = 216^\circ$.

9. Since you are looking for a degree measurement, first add the percents, and you will find that the two quarters add up to 36%. Eliminate A, as this is a trap. Then, you can make a proportion, as you did in question 8 to find the angle measurement:

$$\frac{36\%}{100\%} = \frac{x°}{360°}$$

Therefore, $x° \approx 129.6°$

10. **D** The amount of students who own dogs is 47% because it is the combined percentage of all those who own dogs, as well as dogs and other animals. From there, you can create a proportion:

$$\frac{47}{100} = \frac{x°}{360°}$$

so $x° = 169.2$.

11. **112** Since there are 28% of students who only own cats and there are 400 students, 28% of 400 is 112. Translating these words into math, the equation would be $\frac{28}{100}(400) = 112$.

Proportions and Graphs Drill

1. **B** The question asks for the rate, which is another way of asking for the slope of the line. The line passes through the origin since she starts from 0 miles and at time = 0 minutes, so you know one point. You also are given the point at the end time, which is 4.5 hours and 225 miles. Therefore, use the slope formula, $\frac{y_2 - y_1}{x_2 - x_1} = m$. Therefore, $\frac{225 - 0}{4.5 - 0} = \frac{225}{4.5} = 50$ mph. Misreading the graph will result in the other answer choices.

2. **D** The question gives the ratio of staplers to paper clips as 1:30, meaning that for every one stapler, there are 30 paperclips. Choices (A) and (B) are incorrect because the paperclips increase in increments of 1, while the staplers increase in increments of 15 and 30 respectively. Choice (C) is closer because the staplers increase in increments of 1, though the paperclips increase in increments of 15 instead of 30. Choice (D) is correct because the staplers increase in increments of 1 and paperclips in increments of 30.

3. **D** The question says that the rate is 6 miles per hour, so the rates of the answer choices can be calculated by finding the slopes. Be careful to check units, as the graphs are all in minutes. Since this is the case, choose points that will make the conversion easy; the point at 60 minutes would be a great choice (since 60 minutes = 1 hour), and you can always use the origin, since all the graphs start at the origin. In choice (A), the point at 60 min (1 hr.) corresponds to 2 miles. The slope

would therefore be $\frac{2 \text{ mi}}{1 \text{ hr}} = 2 \text{ mph}$, so eliminate (A). In graph (B), which increases in increments of .1 miles every 15 minutes, the coordinate at 60 minutes is (60 min., .4 miles). Substituting 1 hour for 60 minutes, the rate (slope) would be $\frac{.4 \text{ mi}}{1 \text{ hr}} = .4 \text{ mph}$, which is also incorrect. In choice (C), 60 minutes corresponds with 1 mile traveled. Repeating the same procedure for this, $\frac{1 \text{ mi}}{1 \text{ hr}} = 1 \text{ mph}$, which is also incorrect. Finally, choice (D) corresponds to 6 miles at 6 minutes, so $\frac{6 \text{ mi}}{1 \text{ hr}} = 6 \text{ mph}$, so (D) is correct.

4. **[Costs more than]**

The question is comparing the cab companies at a distance of 5 miles. The graph depicting Cab Company B shows that at 0 miles, the cost is \$3.75, meaning that it has a flat rate of \$3.75, and the graph increases 10 cents every .1 miles. Therefore, the equation for Cab Company B is $y = 3.75 + .1x$, where x represents .1 miles. Since the question asks for a distance of 5 miles, convert the 5 miles into tenths of miles, so $5 \text{ mi} \times \frac{10 \text{ tenths}}{\text{mile}} = 50 \text{ tenths}$. Plug 50 into both equations for x, and you will find that Cab Company A costs \$15.00: $y = 2.50 + .25(50) = 2.50 + 12.50 = 15.00$. Cab Company A costs more than Cab Company B, since Cab Company B costs \$8.75: $y = 3.75 + .10(50) = 3.75 + 5 = 8.75$.

5. **B** For every 4 pairs of flats, Alesia has 6 heels. Since heels are represented by the x-axis and flats by the y-axis, the point should be (6, 4). Eliminate (A), the trap answer, and (C) with this information. If you doubled these numbers, she would have 8 flats and 12 heels. Only (B) contains this point as well, so eliminate (D).

6. **Choose 4.**

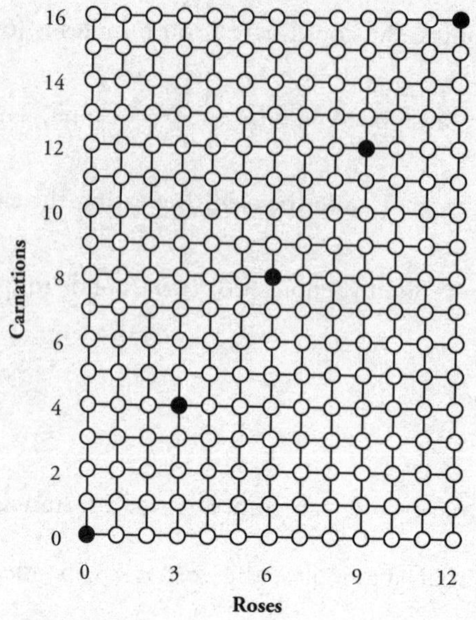

Select the points with the ratio of 3 to 4. Take each value in the ratio and multiply it by an integer. Multiply by 0 to get (0, 0). Multiply by 1 to get (3, 4). Multiply by 2 to get (6, 8). Multiply by 3 to get (9, 12). Multiply by 4 to get (12, 16). Fill in these points.

7. **A** Both drivers are traveling in the same direction, so eliminate (C) right away, since one driver is traveling in the opposite direction (the mileage is going down as a function of time). From here, decide who should be starting with a head start. Since James starts with the 20 mile head start and is traveling at a slower rate than Vivek, eliminate (B) since the line starting ahead has a steeper slope. Find the slopes of the lines on the remaining graphs (A) and (D) by choosing convenient points. Both graphs contain (0, 10) and (0, 30). In (D), one of the points on the line with (0, 10) is (1, 60). Using the slope formula, $\frac{y_2 - y_1}{x_2 - x_1} = m$, $\frac{60 - 10}{1 - 0} = \frac{50}{1}$. Neither of the drivers is traveling at this rate, which eliminates (D). Therefore, (A) is the correct answer.

8. **Choose 4.**

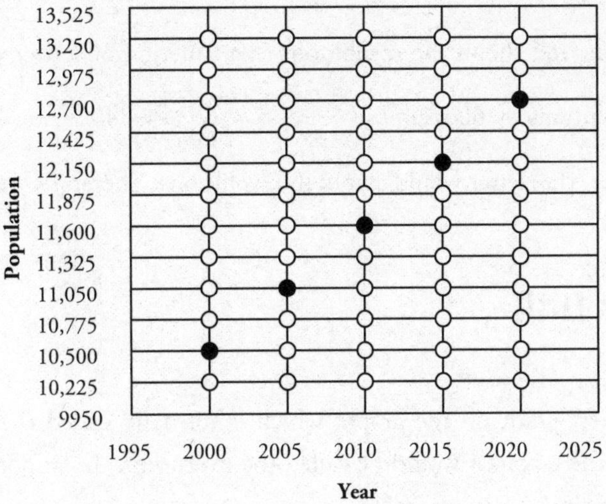

From the point (2010, 11,600), add and subtract 550 to find the populations for 2015 and 2005, respectively. Repeat this procedure to find another point in either direction to find a fourth point to plot on the graph.

9. **A** Shamika is traveling towards home from her office, so she cannot start from zero. Eliminate (C) and (D). In (B), she continues to travel, just at a reduced rate, whereas she stops and stays in places for various lengths of time at (A). She is not still traveling if she has stopped at the gym and at the gas station, so the graph must contain horizontal lines as in (A), so eliminate (B). Choice (A) is the correct answer.

10. **C** Since the rate going to the beach is faster than traveling from the beach, Rafael must have gotten there quicker and in less time. Therefore, eliminate (A) and (D). Since he traveled 3 hours at a rate of 20 miles per hour, find the distance by multiplying these numbers together. $3 \times 20 = 60$, so he traveled 60 miles. Divide this distance by the return rate, 15 mph: $\frac{60}{15} = 4$, so he traveled for 4 hours on the way back. The total time he spent traveling was 7 hours, so the charts must be divided into 7 parts, three-sevenths of the total time spent traveling to the beach and four-sevenths spent on the return. Eliminate (B), leaving (C) as the correct answer.

11. **4:1 or 8:2**

Plug values into the equation. When $x = 1$, $y = \left(\frac{1}{4}\right)(1) = 1$. When $x = 4$, $y = \left(\frac{1}{4}\right)(4) = 1$. From these points, it is clear that $x : y$ is 4:1. 8:2 is correct as well, as it is the same proportion and can be simplified to 4:1 by dividing each side by 2.

12. **B** The figure skater spins at a constant rate, which means the answer must be a linear equation. Therefore, eliminate (C), which is a quadratic equation. Choice (A) does not account for the second-to-minute conversion, and shows the revolutions as a function of seconds. To make this conversion, multiply the revolutions by 60 seconds: $\frac{4 \text{ revs}}{\text{sec}} \times \frac{(60 \text{ sec})}{1 \text{ min}} = 240\frac{\text{revs}}{1 \text{ min}}$. This conversion shows that for every 1 minute, the skater would spin 240 revolutions. Therefore, (B) is the correct answer.

Interpreting Graphs Drill

1. **[minimum]**

(1, –1) is the lowest point on the graph, which is formally called the minimum. If it were the highest point on the graph, it would be called the maximum. It cannot be either of the intercepts because neither of the coordinates is 0.

2. **B** Think of the graphs as being made of wet ink. When you fold the graphs along the *y*-axis, which of them would leave an imprint on the graph? This kind of symmetry is only true for the parabola, as all the other graphs would leave an imprint if the wet ink that is not on the already present graph.

3. **A** Similar to the explanation in question 2, if the graphs were made of wet ink and you folded the paper along the graph $y = x$, you would see that (A) is the only graph that would not leave a mark outside of the graph that already exists.

4. **D** The period is the time it takes to complete one full cycle (peak to peak or valley to valley, which also is every other time it crosses the *x*-axis). The one that takes the longest to complete a cycle is (D), even if it is not the largest amplitude.

5.

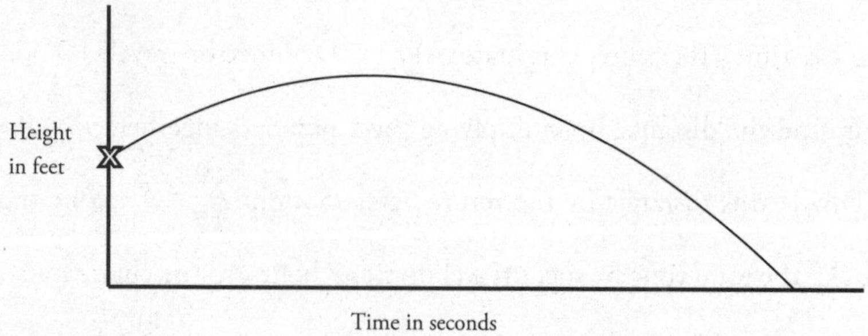

When the ball is released, we can assume that it is at 0 seconds, so it is to the left, at the start of the graph. The ball is released from a height where the curve intersects the *y*-axis, which represents height in feet.

6. The maximum is the highest point on the graph:

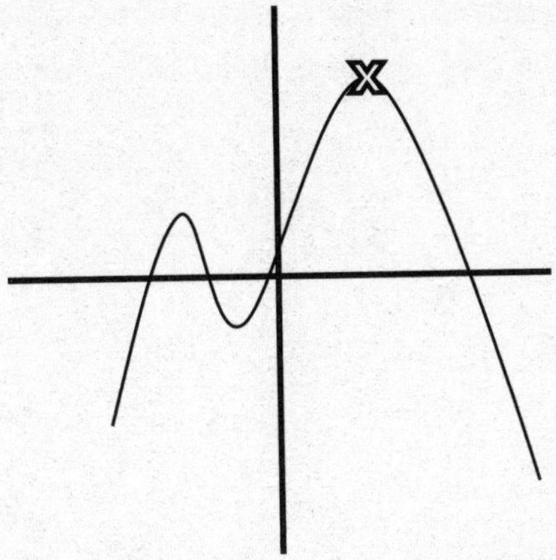

7. The x-intercepts on the graph are where the graph crosses the x-axis:

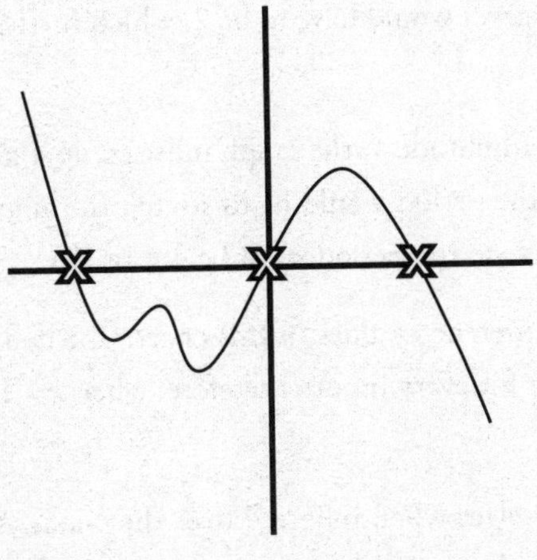

8. **3** Because the graph passes through the origin, the points are actually the same as in the previous question because the y-intercept is the same as the second x-intercept in this particular case.

9. **A** The shortest period is the one that takes the shortest distance to complete one full cycle. In this case, the graph with the shortest period is (A).

10.

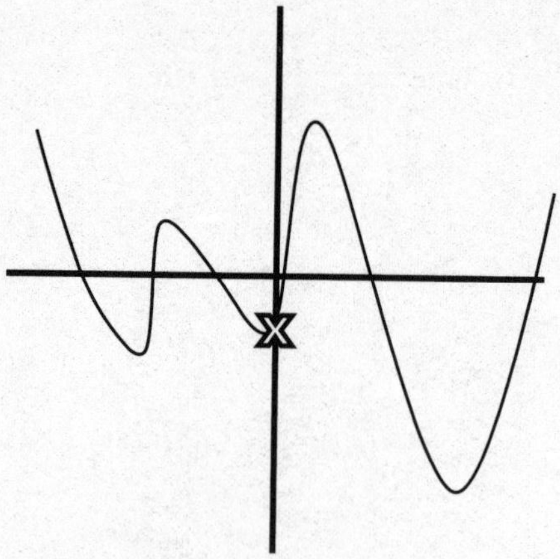

11. **C** The period in this graph is 2π for a complete cycle. Since the question is asking for the same period, you can eliminate (A), (B), and (D). The question is also asking for twice the amplitude, which is 1 in the original graph (the distance from the center to either a peak or a valley; in this case, the amplitude is 1), so the amplitude in the correct answer would have to be 2, which further confirms (C).

12. **B** To have four times the amplitude of the original amplitude 1, the graph must go up 4 and down 4 from the center, eliminating (C) and (D). Twice the period would be to stretch the graph to make one cycle twice as long as the original period of 2π, so the period must be 4π, or (B).

13. **B** There are two identical x-coordinates that have different y-values in this chart. The definition of a function states that there must be only one output for every input. Therefore, when $x = 1$, it cannot have two y-values and still be a function.

14. **A** All of the graphs will be mirror versions of themselves when reflected over the y-axis. When this happens, only the coordinates in graph A remain the same because it is symmetrical about the y-axis.

15. **D** Since the slope of the equation is $-\frac{1}{3}$, the line must be descending, which means you can eliminate (A) and (C). The y-intercept is positive 3, so you may eliminate (B) and choose (D).

Mathematics Formula Sheet

Area of a:		
square	$A = s^2$	
rectangle	$A = lw$	
parallelogram	$A = bh$	
triangle	$A = \frac{1}{2}bh$	
trapezoid	$A = \frac{1}{2}h(b_1 + b_2)$	
circle	$A = \pi r^2$	
Perimeter of a:		
square	$P = 4s$	
rectangle	$P = 2l + 2w$	
triangle	$P = s_1 + s_2 + s_3$	
circumference of a circle	$C = 2\pi r$ OR $C = \pi d$; $\pi \approx 3.14$	
Surface Area and Volume of a:		
rectangular prism	$SA = 2lw + 2lh + 2wh$	$V = lwh$
right prism	$SA = ph + 2B$	$V = Bh$
cylinder	$SA = 2\pi rh + 2\pi r^2$	$V = \pi r^2 h$
pyramid	$SA = \frac{1}{2}ps + B$	$V = \frac{1}{3}Bh$
cone	$SA = \pi rs + \pi r^2$	$V = \frac{1}{3}\pi r^2 h$
sphere	$SA = 4\pi r^2$	$V = \frac{4}{3}\pi r^3$
	(p = perimeter of base B; $\pi \approx 3.14$)	
Data		
mean	mean is equal to the total of the values of a data set, divided by the number of elements in the data set	
median	median is the middle value in an odd number of ordered values of a data set, or the mean of the two middle values in an even number of ordered values in a data set	
Algebra		
slope of a line	$m = \frac{y_2 - y_1}{x_2 - x_1}$	
slope-intercept form of the equation of a line	$y = mx + b$	
point-slope form of the equation of a line	$y - y_1 = m(x - x_1)$	
standard form of a quadratic equation	$y = ax^2 + bx + c$	
quadratic formula	$x = \frac{-b \pm \sqrt{b^2 - 4ac}}{2a}$	
Pythagorean Theorem	$a^2 + b^2 = c^2$	
simple interest	$I = prt$	
	(I = interest, p = principal, r = rate, t = time)	
distance formula	$d = rt$	
total cost	total cost = (number of units) × (price per unit)	

The Princeton Review®

International Offices Listing

China (Beijing)
1501 Building A,
Disanji Creative Zone,
No.66 West Section of North 4th Ring Road Beijing
Tel: +86-10-62684481/2/3
Email: tprkor01@chol.com
Website: www.tprbeijing.com

China (Shanghai)
1010 Kaixuan Road
Building B, 5/F
Changning District, Shanghai, China 200052
Sara Beattie, Owner: Email: sbeattie@sarabeattie.com
Tel: +86-21-5108-2798
Fax: +86-21-6386-1039
Website: www.princetonreviewshanghai.com

Hong Kong
5th Floor, Yardley Commercial Building
1-6 Connaught Road West, Sheung Wan, Hong Kong
(MTR Exit C)
Sara Beattie, Owner: Email: sbeattie@sarabeattie.com
Tel: +852-2507-9380
Fax: +852-2827-4630
Website: www.princetonreviewhk.com

India (Mumbai)
Score Plus Academy
Office No.15, Fifth Floor
Manek Mahal 90
Veer Nariman Road
Next to Hotel Ambassador
Churchgate, Mumbai 400020
Maharashtra, India
Ritu Kalwani: Email: director@score-plus.com
Tel: + 91 22 22846801 / 39 / 41
Website: www.score-plus.com

India (New Delhi)
South Extension
K-16, Upper Ground Floor
South Extension Part–1,
New Delhi-110049
Aradhana Mahna: aradhana@manyagroup.com
Monisha Banerjee: monisha@manyagroup.com
Ruchi Tomar: ruchi.tomar@manyagroup.com
Rishi Josan: Rishi.josan@manyagroup.com
Vishal Goswamy: vishal.goswamy@manyagroup.com
Tel: +91-11-64501603/ 4, +91-11-65028379
Website: www.manyagroup.com

Lebanon
463 Bliss Street
AlFarra Building - 2nd floor
Ras Beirut
Beirut, Lebanon
Hassan Coudsi: Email: hassan.coudsi@review.com
Tel: +961-1-367-688
Website: www.princetonreviewlebanon.com

Korea
945-25 Young Shin Building
25 Daechi-Dong, Kangnam-gu
Seoul, Korea 135-280
Yong-Hoon Lee: Email: TPRKor01@chollian.net
In-Woo Kim: Email: iwkim@tpr.co.kr
Tel: + 82-2-554-7762
Fax: +82-2-453-9466
Website: www.tpr.co.kr

Kuwait
ScorePlus Learning Center
Salmiyah Block 3, Street 2 Building 14
Post Box: 559, Zip 1306, Safat, Kuwait
Email: infokuwait@score-plus.com
Tel: +965-25-75-48-02 / 8
Fax: +965-25-75-46-02
Website: www.scorepluseducation.com

Malaysia
Sara Beattie MDC Sdn Bhd
Suites 18E & 18F
18th Floor
Gurney Tower, Persiaran Gurney
Penang, Malaysia
Email: tprkl.my@sarabeattie.com
Sara Beattie, Owner: Email: sbeattie@sarabeattie.com
Tel: +604-2104 333
Fax: +604-2104 330
Website: www.princetonreviewKL.com

Mexico
TPR México
Guanajuato No. 242 Piso 1 Interior 1
Col. Roma Norte
México D.F., C.P.06700
registro@princetonreviewmexico.com
Tel: +52-55-5255-4495
+52-55-5255-4440
+52-55-5255-4442
Website: www.princetonreviewmexico.com

Qatar
Score Plus
Office No: 1A, Al Kuwari (Damas)
Building near Merweb Hotel, Al Saad
Post Box: 2408, Doha, Qatar
Email: infoqatar@score-plus.com
Tel: +974 44 36 8580, +974 526 5032
Fax: +974 44 13 1995
Website: www.scorepluseducation.com

Taiwan
The Princeton Review Taiwan
2F, 169 Zhong Xiao East Road, Section 4
Taipei, Taiwan 10690
Lisa Bartle (Owner): lbartle@princetonreview.com.tw
Tel: +886-2-2751-1293
Fax: +886-2-2776-3201
Website: www.PrincetonReview.com.tw

Thailand
The Princeton Review Thailand
Sathorn Nakorn Tower, 28th floor
100 North Sathorn Road
Bangkok, Thailand 10500
Thavida Bijayendrayodhin (Chairman)
Email: thavida@princetonreviewthailand.com
Mitsara Bijayendrayodhin (Managing Director)
Email: mitsara@princetonreviewthailand.com
Tel: +662-636-6770
Fax: +662-636-6776
Website: www.princetonreviewthailand.com

Turkey
Yeni Sülün Sokak No. 28
Levent, Istanbul, 34330, Turkey
Nuri Ozgur: nuri@tprturkey.com
Rona Ozgur: rona@tprturkey.com
Iren Ozgur: iren@tprturkey.com
Tel: +90-212-324-4747
Fax: +90-212-324-3347
Website: www.tprturkey.com

UAE
Emirates Score Plus
Office No: 506, Fifth Floor
Sultan Business Center
Near Lamcy Plaza, 21 Oud Metha Road
Post Box: 44098, Dubai
United Arab Emirates
Hukumat Kalwani: skoreplus@gmail.com
Ritu Kalwani: director@score-plus.com
Email: info@score-plus.com
Tel: +971-4-334-0004
Fax: +971-4-334-0222
Website: www.princetonreviewuae.com

Our International Partners

The Princeton Review also runs courses with a variety of partners in Africa, Asia, Europe, and South America.

Georgia
LEAF American-Georgian Education Center
www.leaf.ge

Mongolia
English Academy of Mongolia
www.nyescm.org

Nigeria
The Know Place
www.knowplace.com.ng

Panama
Academia Interamericana de Panama
http://aip.edu.pa/

Switzerland
Institut Le Rosey
http://www.rosey.ch/

All other inquiries, please email us at
internationalsupport@review.com